Self-Harm in New Woman Writing

Edinburgh Critical Studies in Victorian Culture
Series Editor: Julian Wolfreys
Volumes available in the series

Visit the Edinburgh Critical Studies in Victorian Culture web page at www.edinburghuniversitypress.com/series/ecvc

Also Available
Victoriographies – A Journal of Nineteenth-Century Writing, 1790–1914, edited by Julian Wolfreys
ISSN: 2044-2416
www.eupjournals.com/vic

Self-Harm in New Woman Writing

Alexandra Gray

EDINBURGH
University Press

Edinburgh University Press is one of the leading university presses in the UK. We publish academic books and journals in our selected subject areas across the humanities and social sciences, combining cutting-edge scholarship with high editorial and production values to produce academic works of lasting importance. For more information visit our website: edinburghuniversitypress.com

Edinburgh University Press Ltd
The Tun – Holyrood Road,
12(2f) Jackson's Entry,
Edinburgh EH8 8PJ

Typeset in 11/13 Adobe Sabon by
IDSUK (DataConnection) Ltd, and
printed and bound in Great Britain by
CPI Group (UK) Ltd, Croydon CR0 4YY

A CIP record for this book is available from the British Library

ISBN 978 1 4744 1768 6 (hardback)
ISBN 978 1 4744 1769 3 (webready PDF)
ISBN 978 1 4744 1770 9 (epub)

Contents

Acknowledgements

This book has been possible due to the support of the Centre for Studies in Literature at the University of Portsmouth, which funded the postgraduate research project that served as my starting point. Not only was the funding essential to the development of the project, but the generosity of CSL members has shaped the direction of this study. I am indebted to Patricia Pulham, who supervised both my PhD and MA research, and whose careful reading and kind encouragement have been vital at every stage of my studies. I thank Patricia for her diligence, patience and judicious editorial input, particularly during the final stages of the publication process. I thank Charlotte Boyce at Portsmouth, whose advice on parts of this book has been invaluable, and other members of the English department whose input during the early stages of my doctoral studies helped determine the trajectory of the manuscript. Finally, I am grateful to the students I have taught at Portsmouth, who challenged me to think in unusual ways about some of the material contained herein.

I am thankful for the editorial support of Julian Wolfreys, especially for his deft reading and for supporting the development of *Self-Harm in New Woman Writing* from its infancy. I would also like to thank Jackie Jones and Michelle Houston at Edinburgh University Press, for believing in the project and championing its commission. Thanks are also due to the staff at London Metropolitan Archives and the Wellcome Collection, who kindly answered questions and located long-forgotten materials efficiently and with good grace.

I am grateful for the support of my husband Niall, whose patience has been unwavering, and whose technical skills have been (almost) as impressive. One of the kindest and cleverest people I know, he has been my touchstone since day one. Most importantly, special thanks are owed to my mother Catherine, an extraordinarily gifted critic, without whose love and belief in me this book could not have been completed.

Series Editor's Preface

'Victorian' is a term at once indicative of a strongly determined concept and an often notoriously vague notion, emptied of all meaningful content by the many journalistic misconceptions that persist about the inhabitants and cultures of the British Isles and Victoria's Empire in the nineteenth century. As such, it has become a byword for the assumption of various, often contradictory habits of thought, belief, behaviour and perceptions. Victorian studies and studies in nineteenth-century literature and culture have, from their institutional inception, questioned narrowness of presumption, pushed at the limits of the nominal definition, and have sought to question the very grounds on which the unreflective perception of the so-called Victorian has been built, and so they continue to do. Victorian and nineteenth-century studies of literature and culture maintain a breadth and diversity of interest, of focus and inquiry, in an interrogative and intellectually open-minded and challenging manner, which are equal to the exploration and inquisitiveness of its subjects. Many of the questions asked by scholars and researchers of the innumerable productions of nineteenth-century society actively put into suspension the clichés and stereotypes of 'Victorianism', whether the approach has been sustained by historical, scientific, philosophical, empirical, ideological or theoretical concerns; indeed, it would be incorrect to assume that each of these approaches to the idea of the Victorian has been, or has remained, in the main exclusive, sealed off from the interests and engagements of other approaches. A vital interdisciplinarity has been pursued and embraced, for the most part, even as there has been contest and debate amongst Victorianists, pursued with as much fervour as the affirmative exploration between different disciplines and differing epistemologies put to work in the service of reading the nineteenth century.

Edinburgh Critical Studies in Victorian Culture aims to take up both the debates and the inventive approaches and departures from convention that studies in the nineteenth century have witnessed for the last half-century at least. Aiming to maintain a 'Victorian' (in the most positive sense of that motif) spirit of inquiry, the series's purpose is to continue and augment the cross-fertilisation of inter-disciplinary approaches, and to offer, in addition, a number of timely and untimely revisions of Victorian literature, culture, history and identity. At the same time, the series will ask questions concerning what has been missed or improperly received, misread, or not read at all, in order to present a multifaceted and heterogeneous kaleido-scope of representations. Drawing on the most provocative, thought-ful and original research, the series will seek to prod at the notion of the 'Victorian', and in so doing, principally through theoretically and epistemologically sophisticated close readings of the historicity of literature and culture in the nineteenth century, to offer the reader provocative insights into a world that is at once overly familiar, and irreducibly different, other and strange. Working from original sources, primary documents and recent interdisciplinary theoretical models, Edinburgh Critical Studies in Victorian Culture seeks not simply to push at the boundaries of research in the nineteenth cen-tury, but also to inaugurate the persistent erasure and provisional, strategic redrawing of those borders.

Julian Wolfreys

Introduction

The designation 'New Woman' is a problematic one. It was variously applied to a plethora of late-Victorian female types who campaigned for gender equality, yet who rarely shared political viewpoints or agreed on key issues. The name was coined by the novelist Sarah Grand, during a published exchange with the British anti-feminist novelist Ouida in 1894.[1] Although the moniker came into popular usage in the mid-1890s, New Woman scholarship has broadened the terms of women's inclusion in the New Woman oeuvre, challenging narrow understandings of the term and arguing for the emergence of this 'feminist' fiction as early as 1880.[2] The British New Woman was not, as Sally Ledger has shown, a stable identity or easily definable stock character, but a composite of conflicting, contradictory and discursively constructed ideas about women, at a time of social and political upheaval (1997: 1–2). Those accused of best exemplifying this persona were often 'the most hesitant about, and critical of, the term, considering it a reductive – and potentially controlling – homogenization of their different views' (Richardson 2016: 151). As a number of literary critics have already established, supposedly 'new' women failed to agree on almost all aspects of the nineteenth-century campaign for women's rights and freedoms.[3] For example, Grand was scathing of gender double standards and regarded women's education as paramount, yet held very traditional views on the sanctity of marriage and motherhood.[4] Her fiction and political writings reveal her to be a staunch social purist, and – as Angelique Richardson has demonstrated – a proponent of eugenic science (2008: 95–155). Her faith in the potential for good in marriage remained unwavering despite her critique of ill-advised or genetically unsuitable unions (Forward and Heilmann 2000b: 44).

Conversely, Grand's contemporary Mona Caird viewed marital and maternal obligations as forms of bondage from which women needed to free themselves before they could gain equality with men.[5] Despite this, Caird's fiction often represented female sexual liberation as morally questionable, and her heroines are usually punished severely for desiring men to whom they are not married, regardless of the unhappiness of their marital circumstances.[6] The writings of George Egerton and Victoria Cross campaigned for women's maternal freedoms, representing the horrible consequences of enforced marriage and motherhood. While both writers dramatise relationships in which marriage is secondary to maternity and sexual fulfilment, they are usually neither healthy nor successful. In the last decade, scholarship in the field has focused on the diverse nature and at times shifting boundaries of New Woman writing, on the often less-than-subtle differences in the methods and aims of the women who contributed to this corpus of work. This study sets out to do the opposite; it engages with a variety of texts by women writers who appear to have very little in common, but whose shared recourse to the trope of self-harm reveals one of the mutual threads linking New Woman writers, despite their otherwise divergent agendas. In *Self-Harm in New Woman Writing* I argue that self-harm functions as a way of understanding and emphasising the parallels between works usually considered emblematic of the diversity of New Woman thought.

Self-Harm in New Woman Writing examines fictional acts of self-harm by women in novels, poems and short stories by and about the New Woman of the late nineteenth century. At times, it references men's writing about the New Woman, which enriched the literary landscape of the *fin de siècle* and dealt with self-harm in ways that were different to those exhibited in the work of female writers. Although infrequently, female self-harm did appear in men's writing, providing a gendered counterpoint that, while relatively limited in scope, suggests a clear cultural association between self-harm and the instability of gender boundaries in the period.[7] I situate fictional acts of self-harm as a response to the particular cultural conditions of the *fin de siècle*, in which women writers were experimenting with new modes of literary expression; they were also deploying increasingly violent images of self-damage in the face of patriarchal pressures underpinned by bourgeois religion and morality. In the texts I examine, self-harm operates as a means by which to read these bodies of work alongside the bodies of the fictional women contained within them, as part of a formal continuum beginning with the unwieldy triple-decker novel, and reaching its zenith in the short-story format.

While depictions of violence enacted on the female body were not new, New Woman writers engaged with such images in a way that had not been seen since the emergence of eighteenth-century Gothic fiction.[8] While there is little documentary evidence to suggest that Victorian women (particularly those outside the working classes) resorted to self-harm in any other than the most extreme circumstances, I suggest that a history of self-harm as a resistive (literary) strategy can be traced in New Woman writing.[9] I place critical emphasis on the work of Mark Seltzer, whose conceptualisation of a Victorian 'wound culture' underscores my argument that the New Woman exploited *fin-de-siècle* concerns about the female body as an object of display and desire, opening a rhetorical space for the damaged body as a crucial juncture between notions of the public and the private. Furthermore, I argue that in adopting newer and more experimental forms of writing, the New Woman was progressively at liberty to express the inexpressible, the unwomanly and disruptive acts of violence enacted upon the body that challenged both Victorian notions of femininity and the supremacy of masculine corporeal control. I show how these acts can be schematised on a spectrum, beginning with passive-aggressive bodily protest in the traditional, three-volume novel, and ending with violent fantasies and spectacles of self-damage in the New Woman short story.

Anna Maria Jones has surmised that New Woman novels were 'predicated on an *a priori* failed narrative project [. . .] play[ing] off the structures of feeling that govern the world from which they emerge' (2007: 221) to challenge their readership. In examining self-harm in novels and other literary forms, *Self-Harm in New Woman Writing* demonstrates the ways in which New Woman authorship both disrupted and manifested the failed narrative project of women's inclusion in the literary canon. The trajectory of self-harm in New Woman writing was largely chronological; as New Women increasingly adopted shorter forms through which to dramatise self-destructive acts, these behaviours became gradually more overtly violent. Beginning with the novel, I posit that the movement away from Realism, through the transitional space of experimental poetry, and into the avant-garde of the short story, constituted a roughly consecutive arc of progression in terms of the violence with which self-harm could be expressed. Furthermore, *Self-Harm in New Woman Writing* demonstrates how New Woman fiction both adheres to and rejects Christian notions of the body's subordination to the soul, and how this dichotomy can be imagined in relation to the spatial dynamics of the texts into which self-harming female bodies were written by late-nineteenth-century women.

While the expression of taboo and unwomanly subject matter such as self-harm was, I argue, spatially and formally driven, it was also inextricably connected to the sense of outsiderism and marginality experienced by almost all the female authors whose work I examine. Sarah Grand, perhaps the most well-known New Woman author today, grew up in Ireland, was educated in England, but lived much of her life abroad as a military wife. In 1888 she moved to England to begin her career as a writer after leaving her husband, discarding her married name (Frances Elizabeth Bellenden McFall) and adopting a new persona as the Grand Dame of the New Woman movement (Mangum 2001: 3). Grand's focus on hunger throughout her body of fiction and criticism engages with Irish nationalist concerns on many complex levels, and evidences an ambivalent – although not entirely dissatisfied – perspective on Anglo-Irish relations. The novelist Mona Caird (Alice Mona Alison) was born in England to a Scottish father; she married a Scottish landowner and divided her time between Scotland, England and international travel (Heilmann 1999: 76–7).[10] Caird often metaphorically figured her cruel husband characters as an invading English force, and many of her heroines are imagined as colonised territories through textual affinities with ancient kingdoms, landscapes and cultures.

Victoria Cross (Anna Sophie Corey) was born and raised in British India, and although she finished her education in England, she largely lived on the Continent (Mitchell 2002: 1–3). Cross's nom de plume reflects her concerns with British military and colonial history, and her fiction both challenged gender norms and addressed issues of racial miscegenation. George Egerton was born in Australia to a Welsh Protestant mother and Irish Catholic father, and lived variously in Australia, New Zealand, Chile, Germany, America, Norway and Ireland, before settling in England in later life (De Vere White 1958: 12). According to Lisa Hager, Egerton challenges white, middle-class, heteronormative models of identity by 'showing the limits it places on women's ability to participate in reciprocal encounters and exploring the possibilities once women begin to resist such a fixed role' (2006). Egerton's own national and religious identity was unfixed. Her cultural hybridity, as well as her intense literary engagement with – and criticism of – her father's religion, signals her interest in unconventional social identities, and her own sense of liminality.

Amy Levy was an Anglo-Jewish poet, essayist, novelist and short-story writer, who was born and raised in London, but who felt alienated both from aspects of British culture and from Judaism. Levy's satirical depictions of Anglo-Jewish life made her, at times, unpopular with her own community; her association with prominent figures in London's artistic and political circles meant she was often caught between the traditions of one group and the radical values of the other (Pullen 2010: 132–7). Mary Angela Dickens was the granddaughter of Charles Dickens, one of the most famous and successful English novelists, yet very little is known about her. Her divergence from the structural and thematic formulae of her grandfather, and her resistance to assimilation by or into his literary legacy, suggest both a sense of rebellion and a taste for (at least literary) nonconformity.[11] All these women responded to the core of the English literary canon from positions of marginality in which most were twice removed from normative discourse.

As Tina O'Toole has convincingly argued, Irish national identity was deployed by New Woman writers as 'a disruptive sign, a means to express a dissident stance in relation to the dominant social and political formations of the late nineteenth century' (2013: 5). Arguably, it was not only Irish-ness but a general sense of non-English, non-heteronormative or non-mainstream identity that afforded the women with which this book is concerned a position both within and apart from late-Victorian society. They were women who wrote professionally, and thus were marginalised by their gender, a gender that, to a certain extent, accounts for their place outside of the canon and the fact that much of their work remains out of print. However, they were also largely non-English, racially or nationally other, and in writing about self-harm – a highly improper trope associated with deviance and degeneration – they wrote back to an imperial centre that saw them as doubly outside the margins and dangerously liminal.[12]

Late-Victorian culture was 'saturated with masochistic phenomena', and 'self-destructive New Woman heroines' (Kucich 2002: 79) were part of a wider cultural-philosophical nihilism and anarchism at play in the closing years of the century. As John Kucich explains, the New Woman operated a 'rigid code of sexual self-denial, [. . .] a programmatic defeatism, which transformed disappointment with women's social prospects into gestures of saintly martyrdom; and an idealization of self-sacrifice' (2002: 80). This study explores the specific practices through which women writers dramatised the *fin-de-siècle* preoccupation with such images, and through which the paradox of protest through self-defeatism can be understood as a major site of confluence for writers who have historically been deemed oppositional to, unaligned with, and even antagonistic in relation to, each other's ideas.

Victorian Wound Culture

The British New Woman appeared as both a fictional and a public figure at a time when notions of the body as a private and divinely ordained vessel were in a state of collapse, and – as Sarah Chaney's research demonstrates – asylum psychiatrists began to categorise certain behaviours as 'self-harm' (2017: 51–66). Late-century advances in medical knowledge 'breached Christian certitudes as they undermined the naturalness of pain and put in its place a bodily function that could be removed' (Bending 2000: 52). Whereas the early-nineteenth-century body (particularly the female body) had been largely designated personal and kept behind closed doors, as the century progressed, the body, its pains and its pleasures became the focus of debates both scientific and social. Set against the backdrop of industrialisation and an ever-expanding demographic, discourses on the suffering body were indissoluble from the conditions of modernity within which the New Woman writer emerged, and that she, however reluctantly, came to represent. Thus, self-harm operated within a broader political context, in which the body and the body politic became rhetorically elided.

By the late nineteenth century, many working-class women were established in industrial and manufacturing jobs, and their bodies were assimilated into a capitalist model of labour, production and commodity culture. As the urban space expanded, utterly dwarfing the agrarian, so too did the Victorians' reliance on new technologies, resulting in an increasingly mechanised state (Williams 1975: 2). New forms of mass transport not only made travel from and into the cities possible, mobilising a growing workforce, but also expanded the reach of women's participation in projects outside of their homes. Working-class women had traditionally been required to defend the domestic space, and had been denied access to the public domains of work and education. However, they undertook a pivotal role in the new machine culture, working in the factories and retail premises built to manufacture and distribute commodities (Sussman 2009: 3). Although this represented a change in the way in which the female body was perceived and experienced – from a domestic and maternal body to a labouring and public body – this change was not particularly radical. It represented a transactional analogue of women's status as commodities before the advent of industrialisation, as objects to be admired, owned and ultimately consumed.

In *Serial Killers: Death and Life in America's Wound Culture* (1998), Mark Seltzer identifies late-nineteenth-century machine culture as the turning point at which notions of the body began to change in response to technological advancement and mass production, when,

> paradoxically enough, public corporeal violence has come to provide one of the most powerful ways of keeping visible the possibility of the shared social spaces of the public sphere itself [. . .] public violence has come to provide one of the most powerful registers of the generalized intimacies with technology (technologies of reproduction, information, and mediation) in machine culture [. . .] These are, at the least, some ways in which mass spectacle and mass violence have come to indicate each other in machine culture: the private and natural body has, in unprecedented ways, become publicly relevant [. . .] as spectacle or representation – and, most insistently, as spectacle or representation of crisis, disaster, or atrocity [. . .] The commutability of word counts and body counts provides one register of the way in which the life process and the technological process have come to indicate each other in machine culture. (Seltzer 1998: 35–40)

For Seltzer, Victorian modernity bespeaks a moment of crisis during which notions of the private body and the public space as separate are brought into direct conflict and ultimately begin to break down. The site of this breakdown is what Seltzer calls a 'wound culture' (1998: 21), a social system in which desirable, desiring and damaged bodies, their pleasures and pains, are displayed, critiqued and consumed in public and en masse.[13] The public's visual consumption of bodies was significantly advanced by the advent of photography in the early nineteenth century, and its increasing use in print media at the *fin de siècle*. These pathologised bodies, mechanically produced and visually devoured, are citizens of Seltzer's wound culture, 'living dead subject[s]' (1998: 90) occupying a 'pathological public sphere' (1998: 31). They operated as a destabilising force for modernity that challenged class and gender hierarchies, yet were simultaneously exploited by hegemonic organising structures.

At the dawn of the twentieth century, and the birth of both New Journalism and the pathological public sphere, body counts and word counts represent the 'logic of simulation – conflating bodies with writing, [. . .] an excessive literalization [. . .] in the materialization of writing itself' (Seltzer 1998: 46). If the very act of writing during the late nineteenth century is inextricable from the increasingly violent public sphere, then the New Woman writer enters *fin-de-siècle* culture at an opportune moment when the rupture and display of the female body might be deployed as a subversive textual stratagem. If the atrocity exhibition 'indicate[s] something more than a taste for senseless violence' and functions as 'a way of imagining the relations of private bodies and private persons to public spaces' (Seltzer 1998: 21) then New Woman fiction can be read as an artefact of wound culture that attempts to rewrite separate sphere ideology altogether. New Woman writing is both symptomatic of late-nineteenth-century wound culture and critical of the exploitation of women's bodies that it employs. It is both indebted to and limited by the pathological public sphere, a paradox that can be traced in the self-destructive tendencies of female characters whose bodily pains are displayed in fictional exhibitions of internalised reproach, violence and despair.

Modernity, technology and mass production signalled the possibility of exchange between human and machine – made manifest at the *fin de siècle* by the modern railway system.[14] As well as the interaction between private bodies in a public space, the railway also heralded the birth of the traumatic mass spectacle in Victorian machine culture. Some of the earliest accounts of what twenty-first-century medicine and psychiatry now recognise as post-traumatic stress disorder originate from the several major railway accidents reported after the Railways Regulation Act of 1871 (Harrington 1999).[15] Train wrecks were also implicitly connected to capitalism and industrial greed, leading the columnist of an 1860 edition of the *Morning Post* to claim about the railway that 'we must prepare, I say, to bear the frightful mutilation or sudden death of our friends, and all owing to that great British "mistake" [. . .] the excessive love of money-making' (R.W. 1860: 3). The image of the train wreck became an important traumatic signifier in the Victorian literary and cultural consciousness, particularly after Charles Dickens was famously involved in a collision at Staplehurst in 1865.[16]

Train wrecks had been transformed into entertainment by both the melodrama of the Victorian stage and its literary counterpart, the sensation novel (Daly 2004: 10–19). It is by boarding a train that the eponymous anti-heroine deceives her husband in Mary Elizabeth Braddon's *Lady Audley's Secret* (1862); Émile Zola's *La Bête Humaine* (1890) features the deliberate wrecking of a train by a woman scorned; and in Richard Marsh's *The Beetle* (1897), the villain of the story disappears amongst railway wreckage. 'Feminist' writers also found inspiration in the potential collisions of the modern transport system, as the widely read American authors Kate Chopin and George Fleming respectively demonstrate in 'The Story of an Hour' (1894) and 'By Accident' (1898). Chopin's Mrs Mallard enjoys an hour of freedom after hearing the news that her husband has died in a rail accident, only to later discover that he has survived.[17] Similarly, Fleming depicts a woman who reveals her love for another man to her husband, as she lies dying after a collision in her carriage. Both texts reveal a preoccupation with the potential for dramatic change heralded by the conveniences of a modern world in which, as mechanisation increased, women's position and opportunities were altered, yet remained limited.

During the late nineteenth century, the major debates surrounding the compensation of victims of industrial accidents concerned the importance of bodily rather than psychological wounds. The Victorian legal system failed to recognise symptoms since 'any psychological impact [. . .] had to be proven to have been stamped on the body to reach the legal threshold' (Luckhurst 2008: 28). Trauma had become synonymous with new technologies, as industrial accidents provided evidence of the dangers faced by an expanding and poorly paid workforce, and the evolving machinery of war left behind an increasing number of casualties.[18] The development of a theoretical framework for understanding psychological trauma was under way in the nineteenth century, but was not fully developed until Freud's later work with shell-shocked soldiers following the Second World War.[19] In his 1919 paper on war neuroses, Freud claimed that 'the conflict is between the soldier's old peaceful ego and his new warlike one, and it becomes acute as soon as the peace-ego realizes what danger it runs of losing its life owing to the rashness of its newly formed, parasitic double' (2001b: 209). Freud recognised the importance of repression as a feature of the disorder: a constant aversion to, and relentless return of, the traumatic experience in the form of dreams, hallucinations and memories (2001b: 202).[20] In her twentieth-century work on trauma, Cathy Caruth defines the effect of traumatic experience as

> a response, sometimes delayed, to an overwhelming event or events, which takes the form of repeated, intrusive hallucinations, dreams, thoughts or behaviours stemming from the event, along with a numbing that may have begun during or after the experience, and possibly also increased arousal to (and avoidance of) stimuli recalling the event. (Caruth 1995: 4)

Arguing that any overwhelming experience might produce a traumatised response, Caruth establishes a theoretical structure within which gender inequality might be perceived as traumatic. As Laura Brown argues, the experience of being a woman – in a world in which fear of sexual harassment, rape, discrimination and unequal pay reflect masculine ideologies – operates as a form of psychic trauma (1995: 105). The authoritative power structures of twenty-first-century white, middle-class, male dominance arguably operated more forcefully during the period in which the New Woman emerged as a cultural phenomenon. Like Caruth and Brown, I conceptualise trauma using a much wider framework than that of nineteenth-century (or even some twenty-first-century) definitions, reading self-harming behaviour in New Woman fiction as a response to overwhelming patriarchal pressures. I contend that the wound culture of late-nineteenth-century industrial society and its proliferation in print media produced a space in which the traumatised female psyche could be expressed through images of, and stories about, the self-damaged female body.

Bodies which had been controlled, isolated and kept private, and which were now made sensationally public, came to symbolise damaged female subjectivity in the wound culture of *fin-de-siècle* fiction by women. These bodies are configured in New Woman writing through tropes such as self-starvation, excessive drinking and self-mutilation; they are figured both as inescapably subject to male oppression and, concurrently, as the authors of their own doom. While the forms of self-harm I examine are not exhaustive (New Woman writing also features drug addiction, trichotillomania, excoriation and self-performed abortion), I consider acts of self-harm that are most often fictionalised in New Woman writing, and those that constitute a strategy for female survival through frequent repetition over a sustained temporal or narrative space. While self-harm was a particular concern in New Woman writing, it was neither the first nor the most sensational or violent representation of trauma, wounding or female bodily display at the *fin de siècle*, but developed out of cultural responses to a far more explosive and public set of crimes.

The entrance of the traumatised or wounded body into the Victorian consciousness was compounded by highly publicised cases of bodily mutilation, many of which originated from the lurid reporting of colonial conflicts abroad. The *Pall Mall Gazette*, for example, reports of the British Army's presence in Afghanistan in 1880 that '[no] Englishman can be taken prisoner [. . .]; he is lucky if he escapes torture before death or mutilation after it' ('Imputations against the British Army in Cabul', p. 145). The huge losses of British life in conflicts across the world were reported in regional and national newspapers, which listed the dead and wounded and gave descriptions of the battles in which they had given lives or limbs.[21] Reports of horrific violence lined the columns of Victorian news publications in a way that had been impossible before New Journalism, or the invention of photography. Accounts of self-harm as a means by which to avoid military service were common, and began to be reported with increasing frequency. For example, on 28 February 1887 *The Huddersfield Daily Chronicle* reported that a man had cut off his own hand to avoid being conscripted.[22] Just as common were descriptions of domestic disputes and crimes of passion, in which bodily traumas were described with gruesome precision.

On 25 August 1888, just days before the first Whitechapel murder victim would be found, London's *Penny Illustrated Paper* reported a 'shocking case of murder and attempted suicide'.[23] In an East End slum, a sixty-year-old man had murdered his wife with a hammer while she slept, before attempting to slit his own throat. News reports such as this were reflected in *fin-de-siècle* literary Naturalism, and details of the violent working-class struggle for existence found expression in the work of, among others, French novelist Émile Zola. Zola's *Les Rougon-Macquart* series traced the social, sexual and criminal degeneration of one family across several generations. Similarly, George Gissing's *The Unclassed* (1884) and *The Nether-world* (1889), and Arthur Morrison's *Tales of Mean Streets* (1894) and *A Child of the Jago* (1896), depicted the poverty and violence of London's slums. In both fiction and Victorian media, the working-class body became the topic of middle-class debate, through a recasting of colonial discourses of savagery on to the bodies of the English poor, who inhabited what William Booth famously termed 'Darkest England' (2000: 45).

The most sensational – and perhaps culturally significant – of the accounts of wounded bodies that inundated the *fin-de-siècle* print market was that of the 1888 Whitechapel murders. As Casey Cothran notes, the popularity of the New Woman novel was framed and secured by both the Ripper murders in the late 1880s and the forced feeding of suffragettes in the early 1900s (2009: 80–2). While Chapter 2 examines self-starvation in the New Woman novel, the fictionalisation of which preceded the tactics of the suffragette movement by at least a decade, the Ripper murders were contemporary with many of the texts examined hereafter. During the autumn of 1888, at least five prostitutes were murdered and mutilated in London by a single serial killer dubbed 'Jack the Ripper' by the press (Warwick and Willis 2007: xiv). Their mutilated corpses constituted an increasingly violent spectacle of private female (sexual) bodies in the public space, a display that set off, as Seltzer argues, a 'public fascination with torn and open bodies and torn and open persons, a collective gathering around shock, trauma and the wound' (1998: 1).

The public staging of the Whitechapel victims solidified the fascination with the wounded body as a crucial site of intersection between the abundant scientific and cultural discourses of the *fin de siècle*. The popularity of the Newgate novels and gallows confessions of the early nineteenth century demonstrated the extent to which the narratives of violence that accompanied the rapid expansion of Victorian cities were bound up with the convergence of public bodies and private readership. In the case of many eighteenth- and early-nineteenth-century confessions, the skin of the criminal was removed following his or her execution and used to bind the finished literary product, in an act of 'graphical ventriloquism' (Connors 2004: 43). As with the media's dissection of the Ripper victims, whose ruined bodies emblematised a sexual threat to Victorian morality, the bodies of executed criminals were authenticated, made to bear witness to the violence they had once enacted on the wider social body. Violence, narrative and the damaged body came to constitute a reticular relationship that guaranteed publishing success and betokened the shift from understanding desire as (sexual) action to criminal identity in Victorian wound culture.

In the case of the Ripper victims, female corpses were made to speak; they formed tableaux that engaged Victorian fears about bodily corruption, female sexuality and seriality. They were photographed, and autopsy images were published in medical texts during the 1890s. While police photographs did not make it into the press at the time of the murders, drawings depicting the scenes of the crimes did appear (Odell 2006). Serial violence was intrinsic to the success of serial publication, and never had the wounded body been more integral to mass-market periodicals than in 1888. Consequently, the figure of the serial killer 'is invented [. . .] in the century that could be described as having invented seriality itself' (Warwick 2007: 71). In her work on nineteenth-century sexual transgression, Judith Walkowitz posits that the eviscerated Ripper victims

> triggered off a set of psycho-sexual and political fears that resounded, in different ways, across the social spectrum. Body fragments testified to the monstrous nature of the crime, of the criminal, and of the social environment. If, traditionally, the 'classical' body has signified the 'health' of the larger social body – of a classed, homogenous, regulated social order – then the mounting array of 'grotesque', mutilated corpses in this case

represented the exact inverse: a visceral analogue to the epistemological incoherence and political disorientation threatening the body politic. (Walkowitz 1992: 198)

Although the identity of the Ripper became the focus of wide-ranging and multitudinous discourses (social, political, medical, legal and journalistic), the mutilated bodies of the five confirmed victims were obscured by their very visibility within these diegetic strands. While the female body was a central concern in the journalistic reporting of the Whitechapel murders, it was also occluded by the focus on Gothic masculinity that informed the hunt for 'Jack' (Smith 2004: 69).

The post-Ripper cultural climate formed the locus of a host of new anxieties surrounding the Victorian body. Public murder became a privileged act through which 'our most basic sense of the body and society, identity and desire, violence and intimacy, are secured, or brought to crisis' (Seltzer 1998: 2).[24] This process was not simply a consequence of class and gender miscegenation, nor did it reflect purely political disorientation, but the threat to the human body of mechanisation: the shock of contact between human and machine. The repetitive machinations of mass production, the processes by which machines endlessly produced commodities for consumption, are reflected in the repetitions of both serial publication and serial killing. Late-Victorian technological advances facilitated increasingly mechanised mass printing, with most presses using little human labour by the end of the century.[25] Serial publications were produced using techniques that relegated the body to a subordinate position within machine culture, and that reflected the reproducibility of bodies of text and the duplicability, and thus disposability, of human beings. Seriality presented the New Woman with opportunities to engage with discourses of bodily violence, sexuality and modernity, to capitalise on the periodical press and its own preoccupation with the 'serially' damaged female body as exemplified by the Ripper case.

For Seltzer, the figure of the serial killer embodies the tensions between traditional forms of seeing and understanding the body and violence, and the modernity that brought these bodies and that violence to an expanding public audience through mass publication, thus

by 1900 the wound is by now no longer the mark, the stigmata, of the sacred or heroic: it is the icon, or stigma, of the everyday openness of *every* body. This is a culture catered on trauma [. . .] a culture of the atrocity exhibition, in which people wear their damage like badges of identity, or fashion accessories. (Seltzer 1998: 2)

If the wound is itself emblematic of an increasingly traumatised industrial population with a growing appetite for violent spectacles, then literary accounts of bodily damage might reflect the very aetiology of wound culture. In the late nineteenth century, not only does the damaged body become subject to public exhibition, but so too do fictional accounts of self-harming. Roger Luckhurst envisions trauma as a social mechanism that 'violently opens passageways' between such previously well-defined spheres as the physical and psychological. The site of the wound attests to a collapse in the distinction between public and private, making trauma a 'piercing or breach of a border that puts inside and outside into a strange communication. It violently opens passageways between systems that were once discrete' (Luckhurst 2008: 3).

Self-Harm in New Woman Writing is, at its core, concerned with connections between the inside and the outside, the internal, private, psychological world and its relationship to the external world of the public, of the body. The 'strange communication' – the moment of symbolic transformation of the wound from sacred signifier to exhibition of traumatised identity – that makes serial killing a persona also opens a discursive space for its converse. The self-harmer turns her aggression not on others, but on herself, asserting control of her own identity and body through actions of self-damage as self-preservation. Unlike serial killing – a largely 'masculine' act – self-harming is a distinctly feminine pathology, one that reflects women's internalisation of suffering according to gendered norms that understood female violence as unthinkable. Violent women were a contradiction in terms in Victorian culture. Their transgression of clearly demarcated gender roles positioned them – through emerging discourses of criminology and sexological 'inversion' – as highly masculine, outside of normativity and, resultantly, other than female (Seal 2010: 23–9).[26]

With no option to direct their feelings towards the external world, women who would otherwise have been marginalised by science and medicine, as well as the law, were more likely to enact violence on their own bodies than men. I argue that New Woman writing engaged with the imagery of self-harm as a means by which to publicise the traumatised female psyche. In doing so, the fictional exhibition of the suffering female body allowed the New Woman as both fictional character and proto-feminist writer to wear her wounds like a badge of identity, threatening the status quo by effecting a breakdown of the distinction between the public and private spheres upon which it relied. Furthermore, I assert that the dramatisation of self-harm in these texts represents a complex and self-destructive response to the particular conditions of their production. In depicting the imagery and rhetoric of self-damage, the New Woman writer arguably participated in a dangerous practice of self-harm and self-marginalisation through the very publication of her work.

The Damaged Body as Text

As the locus of desire in narrative throughout the Western philosophical tradition, the body was expected to signify in legal and fiduciary contexts as well as in fiction produced and consumed by a Victorian society increasingly fascinated by the spectacle of trauma. As Roland Barthes has persuasively argued, the body is itself text, a complex palimpsest of narrative symbols and meanings inscribed by the individuals' experience within their culture, teaching them how to read themselves and others. For Barthes 'the goal of literary work [. . .] is to make the reader no longer a consumer, but a producer of the text' (1990: 4). Reading is itself a process by which narrative is fashioned, thus the reader is always a text – in reading one's self and one's culture the body can be made to produce endless textual signs. The body is thus a site of convergence between meaning and the symbolic field, the 'sole object' from which our ideological structures 'derive [. . .] unity' (Barthes 1990: 24). According to Michel Foucault, the body is an artefact of culture determined and constructed by a variety of organising forces seeking to position it in relation to self-regulating boundaries of normativity. Critical of these forces, he singles out both the institutions that came to prominence during the Victorian period, and the observational tactics registered and internalised by a society seeking to control deviation from the mainstream.[27] Extending the claims of Barthes and Foucault, Judith Butler views the body as entirely the product of cultural construction, as a collection of performative gestures that reinforce – or place the subject in opposition to – normative identity. Thus 'acts, gestures, enactments, generally construed, are *performative* in the sense that the essence or identity that they otherwise purport to express are *fabrications*, manufactured and sustained through corporeal signs and other discursive means' (2006: 185).

Unlike Butler, who is largely unwilling to acknowledge the body's biological as opposed to linguistic semantic possibilities, Peter Brooks views it as a combination of both cultural and organic signs linked to the desire for knowledge implicit in the act of reading. For

Brooks 'epistemophilia' (1992: 96) – the desire to know and there-fore possess the body through observational processes – underpins the Western narrative tradition and places woman at the centre of this drive. In *Reading for the Plot*, Brooks notes of the heroes of the novel that they 'may regularly be conceived as "desiring machines" whose presence in the text creates and sustains narrative movement through the forward march of desire' (1992: 39). Meanwhile, their female counterparts reflect 'the formation of an inner drive toward the self-assertion of selfhood in resistance to overt and violating male plots of ambition, a counter-dynamic which [. . .] is only superficially passive' (1992: 39). Through signification, the body is made to com-municate both the desiring plots of masculine ambition and women's resistance to them. These master plots rely on the fact that

> identity, and its recognition, depend [. . .] on the body having been marked with a special sign, which looks suspiciously like a linguistic signifier. The sign imprints the body, making it part of the signifying process. Signing or marking the body signifies its passage into writing, its becoming a literary body, and generally also a narrative body, in that the inscription of the sign depends on and produces a story. The signing of the body is an allegory of the body become a subject for literary narrative – a body entered into writing. (Brooks 1993: 3)

Like Barthes, Foucault and Butler, Brooks attests to the decipher-ability of the body as a system of codes that needs to be read, as an object of modern culture, as a body of text. However, as Brooks explores in *Body Work: Objects of Desire in Modern Narrative* (1993), this body is represented in the eighteenth- and nineteenth-century novel as an explicitly female form to be watched, explored and known. In this way, the narrative bodies in which damaged bodies were represented, exploited, contained or displayed reflected the organising structures of dominant discourses largely position-ing women as objects of desire and men as entitled to the epistemic perspective, since

> that which is to be looked at, denuded, unveiled, has been repeat-edly personified as female [. . .] Sight, knowledge, truth, and woman's body: such a nexus intertwines central and highly charged attitudes and gestures of our culture. Man as knowing subject postulates wom-an's body as the object to be known, by way of an act of inspection which claims to reveal the truth – or else makes that object into the ultimate enigma. Seeing woman as other is necessary to truth about the self. (Brooks 1993: 96–7)

The act of inspection is extended both by the desiring male 'machines' who scrutinise female characters and by the reader who must view the female body through the lens of phallocentric desire. This process of seeking the truth – the secret at the heart of the text – reinforces masculine power through a process either of knowing or of othering, by which that which cannot be known, controlled or understood is exoticised and made abject. As critics like Susan Lanser have recently shown, the history of Western literature is at once a history of narrative form and of the body as subject to the heteronormative project of dominant Christian culture. The form of a narrative must be considered as content itself, in that it reflects (particularly in the case of the realist novel) both the attempt at, and complete failure of, the assertion of heteronormative discourse (Lanser 2009: 497–9).

The New Woman writer of the *fin de siècle* deployed narrative form as content, making her bodies of text speak in some way for the bodies of the women whose self-harm they fictionalise. In the New Woman novel, submissive forms of self-damage indicate the acceptance of masculine modes of narration even when attempting to assert a specifically female literary tradition. Yet, in the poems and short stories of the 1880s and 1890s, form comes to represent the erasure of passive-aggressive and predominantly silent protest, and facilitates the emergence of violent acts that both reinforce and subvert traditionally female responses to trauma. The form chosen by New Woman writers is imbued, however unconsciously, with meanings relating to issues of gender, sexuality and female self-expression. However, the New Woman's engagement with self-harm as both subject matter and literary process simultaneously challenges and inscribes notions of feminine inferiority. New Woman writers subverted traditional modes of expression, by publishing short stories, poems and essays, but also opted to write traditional three-volume novels like those of their predecessors and contemporaries.

As New Woman writers sought new and more psychologically driven modes of literary representation, they were increasingly able to depict the suffering female body through ambiguity and metaphor, in ways that would have been more difficult in other modes. Where the popular novel tended to be plot driven, developing its characters slowly and at length, the short story offered a snapshot contained within a much smaller number of pages that was often indistinct and open to interpretation precisely due to its length. The dominant realist mode of the novel necessitated lengthy description to satisfy readers of its authenticity or claim to truth. It required resolutions that reflected orthodox standards of morality, in which deviance from the accepted norm was punished and removed from the narrative, and compliance rewarded with the chance of social assimilation. However, nineteenth-century poems and short stories operated in a much less constrained fashion, in which, without the narrative space to resolve social anxieties, the reader could be asked to question rather than merely accept the established boundaries of normativity.[28]

New Woman literary production progressively turned to less conventional forms of writing as a way of dramatising the marginalisation of those who failed to conform to increasingly outdated, yet culturally pervasive, social expectations. In doing so, texts written by and about New Women attempted to resist women's categorisation as merely 'to be looked at, denuded, [or] unveiled', subverting the expectations of femininity outlined and legitimised by social and religious codes. However, in experimenting with tropes of self-harm such as self-starvation, excessive drinking and self-mutilation, largely through or in opposition to Christian teachings, these writers displayed women's bodily damage at the hands of patriarchy in spectacular fashion. New Woman writing about self-harm at times over-emphasised and eroticised the suffering female body, inviting rather than deterring the epistemophilic gaze. The acts of self-harm undertaken by the heroines of New Woman fiction represent a central conflict that these writers, at least in part, set out to disavow. This conflict, between forging a new tradition of their own, and relying upon the prohibitive forms and frameworks of male literary practice, is embodied in the self-nullifying exercises of characters who bravely deny the roles forced upon them by society, yet exemplify the lack of options available to women with the courage to do so.

The New Woman in Wound Culture

Despite an escalation of interest in the wounded body during the late-Victorian period, such interest revised and reinforced mid-century scientific discourses surrounding the management of unruly female bodies. Michel Foucault notes that Victorian medicine participated in the

> hystericization of women's bodies: a threefold process whereby the feminine body was analysed – qualified and disqualified – as being thoroughly saturated with sexuality; whereby it was integrated into the sphere of medical practices, by reason of pathology intrinsic to it; whereby, finally, it was placed into organic communication with the social body. (Foucault 1990: 140)

By the end of the century, the wounded female body was no longer a figure confined to medical and scientific debate. Rather, it became both an erotic spectacle and an exhibited specimen, destined to be socially, culturally and politically dissected by discourses produced and maintained by Victorian institutional powers. Female sexuality had been transformed from a taboo subject in the early part of the century to one debated by medical and scientific communities, as well as the press and writers of fiction, with increasing regularity as the century proceeded. As Elaine Showalter notes in *The Female Malady* (1993), 'hysteria' became the blanket term applied to an array of symptoms related to female sexuality. The Victorian female body became a site of medical exploration, observation and penetration, with new and often invasive procedures prescribed for the treatment of anything from the onset of puberty to sexual desire and even menopause.

During the mid-nineteenth century, the most drastic, although comparably rare, of such treatments was the cliterodectomy, performed most frequently by Dr Isaac Baker Brown between 1859 and 1866 (Showalter 1993: 74–6). This brutal procedure attempted to control the minds of women who refused to embody what Lyn Pykett has termed the 'proper feminine' (2006: 9), by surgically removing parts of the female sexual organ. For twentieth- and twenty-first-century feminists, the procedure has come to symbolise the penetrative techniques employed by Victorian patriarchy to assert control over disruptive female bodies through the twin phallocentrisms of medicine and science.[29] Responsible for gynaecological medicine, doctors were increasingly at liberty to exercise male will over the female (sexual) body, and although by the end of the nineteenth century the treatment of female patients had become less invasive, it continued to be prescribed in terms of male observation and influence. Emphasis on watching, regulating and even gaining access to the recesses of the female body remained a crucial part of treating 'hysterical' women. Later, the rest cure advocated by Dr Silas Weir-Mitchell became a comparatively less intrusive option than other treatments, yet it still required compulsory bed rest, observation and occasional forced feeding.[30]

By the *fin de siècle*, hysteria had become synonymous with the emergent New Woman figure as the very embodiment of feminine rebelliousness and an anarchic threat to the ruling order. She was categorised as unwomanly, feeble and hysterical, and her writing was considered the root cause of this infirmity (Showalter 1991: 40). Orthodox science and 'respectable' bourgeois publications were quick to publicise the perceived link between women's literary output and their inability to reproduce, or to live long and healthy lives. Through Spenserian limited-energy conservation theories drawing on the First Law of physics, Victorian scientists asserted that the body could only expend finite quantities of energy. Therefore, women – possessed of smaller amounts due to their correspondingly small bodies – needed to devote their meagre reserves to childbirth and motherhood. Women who pursued education were perceived to be unnatural; their expenditure of intellectual energies was understood to detrimentally affect their ability to perform their most sacred duties. The deaths of the female authors Constance Naden and Amy Levy (both in 1889) did nothing to dispel this characterisation, especially since Levy had dramatically committed suicide by carbon monoxide inhalation.

After her death Levy's body was 'read through other texts about degeneration and female weakness' (Randolph 2010: 216), a practice exemplified by Max Nordau's *Degeneration* (1892) which aligned New Women with Decadent male writers, arguing that

> the physician, especially if he has devoted himself to the special study of nervous and mental maladies, recognises at a glance, in the *fin-de-siècle* disposition, in the tendencies of contemporary art and poetry, in the life and conduct of men who write mystic, symbolic and 'decadent' works, and the attitude taken by their admirers in the tastes and aesthetic instincts of fashionable society, the confluence of two well-defined conditions of the disease, with which he is quite familiar, viz. Degeneration (degeneracy) and hysteria [. . .] (Nordau 1993: 15)

Nordau drew attention to the femininity of male authors by connecting their intellectual pursuits to hysteria. In doing so, he tapped into established cultural and pseudo-scientific debates surrounding the correlation between the overdeveloped brain and the underdeveloped, feminine body. In the ailing bodies of the neurasthenic, Decadent artists, Nordau saw proof of the weakening forces of (implicitly sexual) degeneration, just as Hugh Stutfield would later do when he famously framed the New Woman as 'sex-maniacal' (2001: 234) in his 1895 *Blackwood's* article 'Tommyrotics'. Nordau's scathing criticism of perhaps the most infamous fictional account of Decadence and Aestheticism in Joris-Karl Huysmans's novel *À Rebours* (1884) both confirms his views on so-called hysterical male authors and points to his engagement with the same limited-energy theories through which New Woman cultural production was also perceived as degenerate.

Followers of Darwinian models of essential sex-difference warned that the education of women produced an incalculable strain on the reproductive organs, threatening the eugenic health of the nation (Richardson 2008: 40–1). An increase in asylum admissions during the mid-nineteenth century encouraged rigorous psychological investigation of the relationship between mind and body, whilst prevalent evolutionary thought asserted the importance of the interplay between them. Scientific naturalists such as Huxley, Pearson, Galton and Darwin had attempted to ground the psyche in the natural world, connecting each symptom of mental deterioration with an equal and opposite physical cause. Exemplary of this thinking was the observation made by the relatively pro-New Woman writer Grant Allen in 'Plain Words on the Woman Question' (1889) that 'both in England and America, the women of the cultivated classes are becoming unfit to be wives or mothers. Their sexuality [. . .] is enfeebled or destroyed' (1889a: 456).

The New Woman was lampooned as weak, selfish, hysterical and sterile by a male-run popular press that depicted her as a dangerous figure bent on the destruction of the traditional family (Shapiro 1991, Wallis 2002). In response, a huge range of novels, short stories, essays and poems produced by women writers asserted the health and vigour of the female intellectual. Others depicted the impossibility of female strength under the very male-dominated system of education and economics that set women up for failure. Despite their different political stances and literary strategies, many of these writers had something in common: a desire to represent the traumatised female psyche under patriarchy through images of bodily self-harm. Thus, the damaged female body was written into the narrative of nineteenth-century 'feminist' agitation – made to signify 'the mark, the stigmata, of the sacred or heroic: [. . .] the icon, or stigma, of the everyday openness of *every* body' (Seltzer 1998: 2). However, women's self-harm was represented in different ways: in novels that critiqued classical philosophy yet valorised conventional religion; in poems that camouflaged women's frustrations as those of men; and in short stories that explored violent images of self-wounding, but framed them in ways that undermined the impact of their gynocentric counter-discourse.

It was not merely for medical or literary purposes that wounded bodies became part of public discourse during the shift in cultural attitudes that followed both new medical advances and the Whitechapel murders. In her work on the Victorian freak show, Lillian Cranton explains that the Victorian relationship to images of physical difference was 'complex, marked by conflicting impulses to reject, exploit [and] celebrate the odd body' (2009: 2). As part of a popular display of odd bodies the Victorian freak served a distinct purpose, reinforcing normative culture by representing the damaged body as other. Developing Mikhail Bakhtin's assessment of the carnival as a means by which to distract and control the working classes (1984: 10), Cranton positions the freak show within Foucauldian parameters as both a spectacle and ideological weapon (2009: 2–3). The alterity of the odd and often damaged body allowed for a breakdown of the strict rules regarding class – since visitors from all classes occupied the same space – and gender, because naked or semi-naked female bodies could be examined. The freak show provided a space in which the female body, as well as the male, could be displayed, discussed and objectified; in which the collapse of usually well-defined boundaries facilitated cross-class and cross-gender observation that could not be sanctioned elsewhere. The capacity for these bodies to conflate gender distinctions (among others) demonstrated a potentially subversive 'ability to inhabit two categories at once, and thus challenge the distinction between them' (Durbach 2010: 5–6).

While not all bodies exhibited in freak shows were damaged or wounded, the work of disability scholars like Cranton (and Nina Durbach) makes the case for the centrality of the damaged body as a tool with which to challenge the complicated class and gender ideologies of the period. The ability of the wounded body to transgress the boundaries that served to fasten Victorian identity to clearly defined traditional – and largely Christian – morality presented a threat to the society that gazed upon them. One key component of this threat was the public display of the female body, a sight usually confined to the domestic space. Like the odd or deformed body, the New Woman figure also resisted clear definition; she often inhabited the interstitial spaces between culturally constructed identities, resisting delineation even to this day. Her work provided a space, not unlike the freak show, where the display of self-harming female bodies allowed her to straddle the margins of gender and sexuality. New Woman writing about self-harm exhibited atrocity as an act of rebellion against normative hierarchies of masculine power, yet also in some ways – consciously or not – reproduced these very hierarchies.

Theorising Female Self-Harm

To impose contemporary models of self-harm on nineteenth-century documents is unhelpful, since language and conceptual frameworks differ according to the historical context, and retrospective diagnosis is notoriously fraught with contradictions. Furthermore, while self-harm may be a widespread historical, cultural and medical phenomenon, its meaning is neither homogeneous nor universal (Chaney 2017). For the purposes of this study I use the term 'self-harm' loosely, and for ease of reference, to discuss a range of behaviours that appeared in late-nineteenth-century fiction long before self-harm appeared as a diagnosis in the twentieth century (Millard 2015). I also refer to recent research into self-harm in theorising some of the behaviours examined in Victorian fiction, but not to apply a diagnosis or to suggest that nineteenth-century women experienced their bodies in the same way as twenty-first-century anorectics, addicts or self-harmers. There is little historical evidence underpinning the assumption that self-harm was either a standardised medical category or commonly practised behaviour outside of the asylum context. Despite this, as I show, self-harm constituted a major site of political tension and interpretive inquiry in fictional writing about women's bodies at the *fin de siècle*.

Twenty-first-century medicine recognises distinct psychological behaviours that constitute a broadly defined spectrum of self-harming activities in widespread use (Nock 2012). However, the understanding and diagnosis of self-harming behaviours as separate conditions largely unrelated to suicide has been the result of centuries of psychiatric advancement, knowledge that has developed most rapidly and significantly during the past three decades. Contemporary culture is inundated with images of self-harm, from abnormally thin models and celebrities lining the pages of fashion magazines to the self-help guides that have flooded the literary marketplace in an effort to help those who starve, burn, cut, poison or otherwise deliberately injure themselves.[31] Theoretical frameworks for understanding self-harm differ depending on the form it takes, and contemporary models will be considered alongside Victorian research in each of the forthcoming chapters. Both Victorian and contemporary psychiatric understandings do, however, emphasise the importance of childhood development and traumatic experience in the formation of self-destructive behaviours.

Twentieth-century psychoanalytic models of self-harm (including self-starvation and self-neglect) operated (roughly) within the boundaries of the Freudian Oedipal paradigm, through which 'deviation' (2001b: 185) in early childhood development accounts for the formation of the abnormal drives facilitating 'perversions' such as self-injurious behaviour. In Freud's *Beyond the Pleasure Principle* (1920), the self-harmer withdraws from human connections and retreats into a narcissistic position, silently driving themselves towards death.

Freud emphasised that it is only through the activity of the life instinct that this death-like force is projected outward as destructive impulses (2001c: 7–66). Although Freud's work identifies certain integral elements of the condition years before his contemporaries, it does not account entirely for instances of behaviours that develop before or after the Oedipal phase. For example, Freud's centralisation of the Oedipal stage in the development of self-destructive drives does not consider earlier experiences of infantile trauma, nor the culturally constructed or performative nature of certain cases.

While instances of self-harm in patients unable to identify specific traumatic events from childhood or to trace them to childhood might attest to the unreliability of Oedipal dynamics, attachment theory addresses this in part. Arguing that early infantile traumas manifest in a warped sense of maternal attachment in which 'events from childhood [. . .] appear to get "stuck" in the memory' (Adshead 2010: 73), twenty-first-century attachment theories draw upon Donald Winnicott's psychoanalytic model of maternal 'holding' (1989: 26). Maternal care, if preoccupied by trauma, disinterested or dismissive, imprints upon the infant a sense of detachment from the self, a 'failure of mentalization' (Adshead 2010: 74); this in turn is reasserted through actions that put the self and the body into a narrative correspondence that is often violent. 'Deliberate self-harm is a symptom of internal distress, which has both a private and a public message' (Adshead 1997: 111), thus the body is made to signify that which has been unspoken, the failure of the self to accurately or fully narrate its psychic traumas.

For women who self-harm, frustration is turned against the self in a typically female expression of anger because

> [w]hile men tend to cope with anger by directing it outward, viewing themselves as the victims of injustice in a harsh and punitive world, women often blame themselves, and take responsibility for wrong done to them. When memories of abuse or feelings of anger threaten to overwhelm them, and destroy their conciliatory stance in relation to aggressors, they turn anger inwards [. . .] (Motz 2008: 139)

Self-harmful expressions of anger against a punitive world in which women's horizons are limited and controlled by men appear, on the surface, to be an entirely self-defeating enterprise. However, the self-harmer fails to care for herself or enacts violence on her own body as an act of survival rather than of suicide, a distinction that Victorian medicine did not recognise. For Freud, self-harm was part of the drive towards death that served to reaffirm life. For twenty-first-century clinicians, acts of self-harm display a desire to cope with overwhelming feelings of pain and anger, temporarily deferring the urge to die and allowing the sufferer to live (Klonsky et al. 2013). Self-harm is 'a powerful, silent language [which] communicates states of mind to others, inscribing a narrative on the body itself' (Motz 2009: 15) and a 'frantic attempt to assuage overwhelming trauma that an individual cannot process' (Kleinot 2009: 119). Self-harm is thus a paradoxical gesture, one that both damages and preserves, feeds and yet mitigates desperation, temporarily giving voice to the otherwise silent protests of those living in a world in which either their gender or other markers of identity are non-normative.

Some contemporary clinicians approach self-harmful behaviour as a form of addiction, and treat it similarly to alcoholism, gambling or drug addiction (Turner 2002); others refute the importance of gender and focus wholly on abuse history as a predictor of self-harm (Gomez et al. 2015). In this study I consider addictive behaviours as examples of self-harm, as opposed to self-harm as itself an addictive act. I also imagine self-harm as both a form of symbolic language and a coping mechanism, taking into consideration the preponderance of women who self-harm, and the cultural factors that contribute to the gender imbalance in reported instances. To inscribe the body, to make external the internal through acts expressing unvoiceable traumas, is both to resist and yet ultimately to succumb to Western patriarchal and Christian ideologies of the soul as separate and superior to the body. The paradox of self-damage and self-preservation inherent in acts such as self-starvation, excessive drinking and self-mutilation is dramatised in New Woman writing. It is no surprise, given the preponderance of self-harming amongst twenty-first-century women, that the novels, poems and short stories written by women at this time represent some of the most detailed and accessible examples of these practices.

Self-Harm in the Victorian Context

Women typically locate their sense of identity in their bodies, as the woman's private sphere of influence, the cultural weapon with which to assert, or the blank canvas upon which to inscribe, female experience. With restricted influence outside the domestic space, the Victorian woman might arguably have turned on her own body to express feelings of disappointment or anger. Like the twenty-first-century women whose self-harming is now the subject of psychiatric as well as sociological research, the Victorian woman was equally, and indeed more, encouraged by cultural norms to look to herself for blame and to take responsibility for her inadequacies. Victorian expectations of ideal femininity required women to embody qualities such as passivity, submission and, most importantly, silence on matters of emotional concern. Women who failed to adhere to expectations of angelic femininity were demonised as improper, and self-harming strategies arguably expressed, yet also concealed, female anger at the limited options available to women who raged against their situation. I argue that, given the socio-historical context of women's political disenfranchisement, Victorian women had reason to resort to self-harming behaviours as much as, or even more than, their twentieth- or twenty-first-century counterparts.[32]

Little evidence of the rates of self-harming in middle-class Victorian women exists today, and even in the case of institutionalised women records are comparatively scarce. This is largely due to the dearth of official records kept during a time in which female violence (even against the self) was a taboo and disturbing subject. Recorded incidences of female self-harm in twenty-first-century Britain are highest amongst populations of women incarcerated in penal or mental health facilities. According to Ann Lloyd, self-harm among female prisoners is ignored by a system viewing violent women as 'doubly deviant' (1995: xvii) owing to both their institutionalisation and their rejection of gender norms. As Olive Anderson's research demonstrates, records of suicides and attempted suicides – and what Anderson characterises 'parasuicides' – by women were unreliable and emerge from sources (such as police, hospitals and coroners) with their own, often conflicting, social and political agendas (1987: 263–417). Some of the only data on potential examples of female self-harm comes from the mostly incomplete and inconsistent records kept by medical staff at prisons, workhouses and asylums. In the Victorian prison system suicides by women were not as common as by men, yet were recorded as such even when attempted and failed on numerous occasions, because those who examined survivors were unable to differentiate between self-harm and attempted suicide (Priestly 1999: 74). Victorian women prisoners were prone to acts such as food refusal or self-injury (Higgs 2007: 98) and often sustained bodily damage during the act of 'breaking out', a type of riotous behaviour that took the form of smashing furniture and frenzied self-injury (May 2006: 34–5). However, while it was generally and anecdotally observed that female prisoners committed these acts, the logging of injuries was neither thorough nor consistent.[33]

Victorian workhouse records were more detailed, owing in part to their reliance on parish funding and regulation. However, little information as to the physical condition or mental state of boarders upon admission or release is noted, and the 'remarks' box at the end of the admission log provides the only space for additional comment on the subject's condition (*Register of Admissions to Hampstead Workhouse 1893–1896*). In over three thousand samples of workhouse registers at Hampstead Workhouse between 1893 and 1896, there is not a single female occupant who warrants comment in the 'remarks' box. This omission indicates that the information was not considered important in the case of pauper and working-class bodies, or that abnormalities in the physical conditions of the inmates either did not exist or went ignored. The workhouse Register of Deaths is not much more helpful, in that it supplies only the inmate's name, age, parish and place of burial as well as the date of death. The cause of death is absent from these records, and they supply no further information to suggest workhouse inmates were self-harming to the point of suicide (*Shoreditch Workhouse Register of Deaths 1871–1889, Register of Deaths at Hampstead Workhouse 1893–1896*).

Workhouse infirmary records supply detailed accounts of the bodily condition of vulnerable patients and include: date of the log, name of patient, time when presented, address of patient, name of medical officer, name of relieving officer, disease and termination of the case (*St Pancras Workhouse Infirmary Log 1890, Parish of Hampstead Register of Patients in the Workhouse Infirmary 1854–1896*). Common diagnoses of injuries include 'laceration of leg' and 'injury to leg' (*St Pancras Workhouse Infirmary Log 1890*) but are not more specific and give no indication as to whether injuries were self-inflicted. In all two thousand entries in the log at the St Pancras Workhouse Infirmary between 1889 and 1890, there is no reference to injuries to the wrists or arms, although there are several records of injuries to the legs. No indication is given in the register as to the cause of the various diagnoses; in the case of one patient who had been 'scalded' (*St Pancras Workhouse Infirmary Log 1890*) it is impossible to ascertain whether this was of the patient's own volition.

Similarly, the Register of Lunatics in the Workhouse solicits a 'result of examination on admission' and advises those completing the record to 'say whether [there are] bodily defects, bruises, marks, old scars or the like' (*Woolwich Union Workhouse Register of Lunatics in the Asylum 1897–1899*). While the condition of many female patients warrants comment, such comments do not indicate body-focused repetitive behaviours or otherwise significant indicators of self-harm. Examples include single instances of bruising (*Woolwich Union Workhouse Register of Lunatics in the Asylum 1890–1895*: 5–7, 15–17, 31, 62) but, more often, gynaecological symptoms were noted, for instance 'vaginal discharge', 'lactation' (*Woolwich Union Workhouse Register of Lunatics in the Asylum 1897–1899*: 5, 28, 72) and 'menstruation' (*Woolwich Union Workhouse Register of Lunatics in the Asylum 1890–1895*: 64). Some instances of women's bodily wounds are, however, noted in these documents. For example, in 1892 Edith Grace Duck exhibits 'scratches on right hand' (*Woolwich Union Workhouse Register of Lunatics in the Asylum 1890–1895*: 31); in 1894 Jane Durrant is described as 'suicidal' with 'slight burns on arms' (55), and Naomi Lucy Wake is – rather ambiguously – called 'a danger to herself' (71). However, in the records available, there are no signs that injuries were repeated, nor of any patterns, suggesting that self-harm in workhouses was neither recognisable nor prevalent within the population at this time, or that incidences were deemed too insignificant to record. Admissions to asylums from the workhouses were recorded, but in contrast to private asylum admissions, no information was given as to the physical or mental condition of the patient upon transfer to the asylum. At the Royal Holloway Sanatorium at Virginia Waters in Surrey, admission logs indicate diagnosis upon admission, as well as the occupation, marriage status and physical condition of the patient (*Register of Admissions to Royal Holloway Asylum at Virginia Waters 1825–1900*: 1–15). Similarly, at Bethlem Royal Hospital the records are much more detailed and include the diagnosis, and the physical and mental condition of residents upon arrival and throughout their stay (*Bethlem Royal Hospital Casebooks 1860–1884*).

From approximately 1850, a diagnosis of 'suicidal tendencies' in both male and female patients is noted with increasing frequency in the register of patients for both Royal Holloway and Bethlem.[34] Of the 600 patients admitted to Bethlem between 1859 and 1900, twenty-one women were institutionalised for suicide-related illnesses, or presented with suicidal tendencies. Of these women, all are described as a 'gentlewoman' or the 'wife of' a professional man (*Register of Admissions to Bethlem Royal Hospital 1859–1881*). There appears to be no differentiation between patients admitted to these facilities for suicide attempts and admissions for self-injurious activities. Where suicide was attempted, the suicide method is omitted from the record entirely. As Sarah Chaney notes, the term 'self-injury' was used to refer to acts from food refusal to attempted suicide in nineteenth-century psychiatric contexts (2011a: 280). This meant that a variety of behaviours were categorised as self-injurious when they may not have constituted a pattern of deliberate self-damage, and were instead indicative of isolated incidences of violence or disobedience. Records were usually ambiguous, and while some did specify that self-destructive activities had been observed in female patients, the lack of detail makes it impossible to ascertain whether they denoted any particular pathology. For example, at Bethlem in 1868, Eliza Staffens suffered with 'suicidal mania', Eliza White with 'delusions of burial alive', and Eliza West, Constance Savoy, Frances Beardswell and Mary Mitchell 'refuse[d] food' at intervals between 1874 and 1879. In 1878 Caroline Walker 'fell from [a] window' and in 1880 Marion Liddel is described as having 'bruises on arms' and 'cuts on elbows' (*Register of Admissions to Bethlem Royal Hospital 1859–1881*). Meanwhile in 1898, a lunatic admission to the Woolwich Union Workhouse is described as 'constantly pulling her face' (*Woolwich Union Workhouse Register of Lunatics in the Asylum 1897–1899*: 15).

In both pauper and working-class psychiatric institutions, as in the workhouses and prisons, little was recorded of self-harm among female patients or prisoners, and surviving records are limited to the question of whether the patient presented as 'disposed to suicide, or otherwise self-injury' (*Bethlem Royal Hospital Casebooks 1860–1884*). In the case of the working classes, this may have been due to disinterest concerning the bodies of the poor, and in the case of private institutions, to hesitancy on the part of medical professionals to make this behaviour a matter of public record. Self-harming behaviours were new to Victorian psychiatry, and while the phenomenon emerged as a troubling facet of certain disorders in the latter half of the nineteenth century, it would be decades before recognition of, and adequate treatment specific to, each type would follow.

Nineteenth-century alienists were particularly interested in the psychology of those who self-harmed, and developed a language (including the term 'self-mutilation') that drew on literary examples as well as case studies (Chaney 2011a: 281). By the late nineteenth century psychiatry had begun to concern itself with the most sensational and inexplicable of self-harming behaviours, those that most violently disrupted the tissues of the body. However, as the most violent expression of self-harm, self-mutilation alone warranted entry into *A Dictionary of Psychological Medicine* (1892), which does not include an entry on self-harm or self-injury in general

(Tuke 1976: 1147–52). Psychiatric research did not directly connect self-harming behaviour to passive or less overtly violent acts like self-starvation or excessive consumption of alcohol or drugs. Rather, it focused on the sexual element particular to violent self-harm – a fact anecdotally evidenced by the documentation of gynaecological symptoms in lunatic patients – that both Richard von Krafft-Ebing and Sigmund Freud were to identify in their respective works on masochism and sexual sadism.

In *Psychopathia Sexualis* (1886), Krafft-Ebing describes masochism as 'pleasure from reckless acts of violence [. . .] from the most abhorrent and monstrous to the most ludicrous and absurd' (1909: 53). While Krafft-Ebing makes note of the violence attending acts of deliberate self-harm, he connects it entirely to sexuality – what he terms the 'voluptuous sensation of coitus' (1909: 53). In *Three Essays on the Theory of Sexuality*, Freud describes the passive acceptance of violence from an external agent in which 'satisfaction is conditional upon suffering physical or mental pain at the hands of the sexual object' (2001b: 158). Nineteenth-century asylum psychiatrists frequently encountered and recorded cases of self-injury, but usually read them through then-prevalent theories of sexual self-mutilation (particularly self-castration) or as related to suicide or mania (Chaney 2017: 66–111). As such, James Adam – the Medical Superintendent of the Crichton Royal Institution in Dumfries, and the Southern Counties Asylum – writes in 1883 that

> although instances of attempted self-injury are not infrequent, it will be found as a rule on inquiry that the intention in their infliction is suicidal in character – whereas instances of wilful self-mutilation, for its own sake, are much more rare [. . .] The task of investigation becomes easier, however, when we find the mutilative act the direct result of hallucination or delusion affecting the special senses. [Patients] will readily tell you that the act has been committed owing to hearing a voice from heaven commanding them to do it; or by a terror at seeing a vision [. . .] (Adam 1883: 213)

As a senior psychiatrist and published author on psychiatric subjects, Adam exemplifies the authoritative late-Victorian medical discourse surrounding self-harm.[35] Firstly, he asserts that self-injury is not infrequent, but chooses to discuss only the most spectacular form of bodily self-harm from a range of less violent or dramatic acts with which his work might have brought him into contact. Secondly, his discussion largely excludes deliberate self-injury as an exercise unrelated to either suicidal drives or episodes of psychosis. Adam's research was rooted in the study of institutionalised patients who self-harmed in response to both mental illness and incarceration. Despite this, the notion that self-harming could be a form of self-preservation – a formulation that would only begin to emerge at the end of the following century – does not occur to him.

Interestingly, Adam refers to a female self-harmer in his article on self-injury, which cites a rare case study of a patient at the Crichton Royal Institution who became intent on disfiguring herself. He describes one Mrs B, a forty-five-year-old married woman and former governess who 'had attempted self-violence by various means, and was deluded on religious subjects' (1883: 215). Adam describes from his case books her

> greatly reduced, exhausted, and emaciated frame – a cachectic, hollow, and worn facial appearance, the right eye is wanting, the hair is grizzled and grey, and there are marked facial lines; the cause of the repeated mutilative attempts of which she has been guilty, and to which she still has a determined tendency, is hallucination of the senses, both of hearing and vision [. . .] She hears voices commanding her to do the acts referred to [. . .] She says she feels she is not worthy to live, because she is so diseased and wicked [. . .] (Adam 1883: 216)

As an ex-governess, Mrs B is respectable but probably not middle class; however, she is not described as a pauper as in other such records of female asylum patients. Significantly, the language used by Adam to frame the female lunatic, and by which she is also said to frame herself, betrays the deeply encoded expectations of gender at play in Victorian psychiatry. She is described as having lost that which signifies her femininity; her skin, hair and body are testament to her 'guilt', implying that she is culpable not only for her lunacy, but for the erasure of expected gendered traits. She calls herself 'diseased and wicked', drawing on the rhetoric of sin and fall implicit in biblical constructions of femininity, which is perhaps unsurprising given the religious nature of her hallucinations.

Few Victorian case studies of female self-harmers such as Adam's can be accessed today, and records suggest little about how much (if at all) self-harm was committed by those who were neither incarcerated, deluded nor suicidal. Although documents relating to rates of Victorian alcohol consumption do exist, they are anecdotal at best, and represent a wider project of documenting the conditions of the poor in Victorian cities. Similarly, accounts of Victorian anorexia are available yet they almost exclusively document cases of wealthy female patients examined by male doctors, and are unlikely to reflect accurately either the prevalence of self-starvation or the experience of women in the period. Fictional texts remain the only substantial documents relating to various self-harming behaviours amongst middle-class women for which all the conditions for widespread practice were at work at the *fin de siècle*. This study does not set out to prove that Victorian women were prolific self-harmers, but rather to suggest that the lack of official material relating to female self-harm does not accurately reflect the imaginative execution of bodily self-damage as a major tropological concern in women's writing. It examines corporeal spectacle and display in New Woman fiction; it references the female body as a communicative tool upon which the language of both protest against and submission to Western patriarchal (and predominantly Christian) ideologies is inscribed. It questions the extent to which these strategies both subvert and propitiate Victorian cultural mores, and whether through their very expression they challenge traditional representations of bodies, and traditional bodies of text. The New Woman writer's rejection of conventional narrativisation emerges alongside her preoccupation with the increasingly violent behaviours enacted by her heroines. The paradoxical gestures of self-control and self-display negotiated by the heroines of New Woman fiction, in turn, reflect the marginal cultural and national position occupied by female authors who fought against an all-male literary canon yet aspired to inclusion within it.

Chapter 1 provides a socio-religious framework within which to read self-harm in New Woman writing, positioning Christianity as a major contributing factor in both the recourse to and expression of self-harm by women. It examines four texts written by two New Woman authors: *The Wing of Azrael* (1889) and *The Daughters of Danaus* (1894) by Mona Caird, and *The Woman Who Didn't* (1894) and *Anna Lombard* (1901) by Victoria Cross. Caird was a major player on the *fin-de-siècle* British literary and political scene, publishing extensively on contentious issues and inciting debate in key areas.[36] In contrast, Cross spent barely any time in Britain; she published fiction featuring New Woman characters, yet did not officially contribute to the public debate surrounding the Woman Question. My discussion of these texts demonstrates the extent to which very different New Woman writers critiqued and yet internalised Christianity despite their respective tirades against religious conventions like marriage. My second, third and fourth chapters examine three forms of self-harm in New Woman fiction: self-starvation, excessive drinking and self-mutilation, all of which share psychological and representational characteristics, yet are essentially distinct and with their own symptoms and origins.

In Chapter 2, I discuss self-starvation in the work of Sarah Grand. I position self-starvation in Grand's novels as a response to the Cartesian duality implicit in Western philosophical understandings of the body.[37] I also show how the triple-decker novel form, in which the majority of Grand's novels were published, works to bind the bodies of its heroines to both conventional narrative and passive-aggressive strategies of feminine resistance. To this end, I examine three of Grand's novels: *Ideala: A Study from Life* (1888), *The Heavenly Twins* (1893) and *The Beth Book* (1897). In Chapter 3, I explore representations of excessive drinking in texts written by and about the New Woman, including George Gissing's *The Odd Women* (1893), George Egerton's 'Gone Under' and 'Wedlock' (1894), and Mary Angela Dickens's 'An Unprincipled Woman' and 'So as by Fire' (1896). I show how the bodies of women who consume excessively can be considered alongside the starving heroines of Grand's fiction, as the frightening converse of Cartesian dualism. I argue that the female characters examined in Chapter 3 drink to excess in an effort to disrupt the established dichotomy of women as either angels or demons, saints or sinners, private bodies or public figures. In my fourth and final chapter, I consider the most violent form of self-harm deployed by the New Woman writer. I discuss the use of the imagery and rhetoric of self-mutilation in the poetry of Amy Levy, and four short stories by George Egerton that feature self-mutilating heroines. I propose that self-mutilation in these texts functions as an act of feminine self-preservation, and I situate the violence of opening up the body as a metaphorical rupturing of public and narrative spaces by the New Woman writer.

In all four chapters, I consider the relationship between New Woman cultural production and representations of the damaged female body in art and literature by men. I explore the New Woman's use of self-limiting symbolism, and suggest that her subversive displays of female self-harm both disrupt and ultimately reify the masculine ideologies and gender binaries against which she protested. In doing so, I argue that the New Woman enacted the complex position she inhabited, both on the margins of dominant culture and at its centre, as both a writer of popular fiction between 1880 and 1900, and a figure forgotten and excluded from literary history.

Notes

1. 'The New Aspect of the Woman Question' was published in the *North American Review* in 1894. Ouida refuted most of Grand's claims in her own contribution entitled 'The New Woman' in the same year.
2. For example, the Pickering & Chatto (now Routledge) series *New Woman Fiction 1881–1889* includes editions of earlier texts and seeks to expand the New Woman canon.
3. See Sutherland 2015, Gagnier 2010, Richardson 2008, Ledger 1997, Heilmann 2004, and Gardner and Rutherford 1992 for discussion of the failure of New Women to agree on key issues.
4. See Grand's 'The Modern Girl', published in the *North American Review* in 1894, in which she outlines the need for education so that girls can defend themselves against unworthy men. Grand suggests that marriage is not itself a problem, and that the blame is on the parents of young girls (reproduced in Forward and Heilmann 2000a: 30–6).
5. See Caird's 'A Defence of the "Wild Women"' (1897), in which she compares motherhood to military service (2010a: 173), and her article 'Marriage' in the *Westminster Review* (1888).
6. Both Viola Sedley in *The Wing of Azrael* and Hadria Fullerton in *The Daughters of Danaus* are tempted to initiate extramarital relationships (neither do) and both are punished for transgression.
7. Although rare, images of violent self-harm by women did exist in mid-Victorian writing by men. For example, in Dickens's *Dombey and Son* (1848) Edith Dombey reacts to Mr Carker kissing her hand by striking it 'on the marble chimney-shelf, so that, at one blow, it was bruised, and bled; and held it from her, near the shining fire, as if she could have thrust it in and burned it' (2002: 558).
8. For example, Matthew Lewis's *The Monk* (1796), in which the naked, tortured body of Agnes de Medina is displayed in the dungeon below the convent in which she lives.
9. This study does not argue that New Woman writers committed acts of self-harm. Anecdotal evidence does, however, suggest a correlation between New Woman authorship and self-harm. For instance, in his highly problematic biography of the New Woman author Olive Schreiner, S. C. Cronwright-Schreiner describes how she would, when anxious, 'bang her head against the wall until she was almost senseless' (1924: 68).
10. Very little is known about Caird's mother; sources cite that she was possibly Australian, German or Danish.
11. Mary Angela Dickens's father Charles Dickens Junior was the eldest son of the Victorian novelist Charles Dickens. Mary Angela's aunt Mary (Mamie) Dickens published a collection of her reminiscences about her father entiled *Charles Dickens by His Eldest Daughter* (1885) and edited his letters with her aunt Georgina Hogarth. Mary

Angela's father Charles Dickens Junior edited his father's periodical *All the Year Round*, to which she contributed.

12. See Ashcroft et al. 2002 (originally published in 1989), which addresses the ways in which colonially marginal authors 'wrote back' to the centre of the British literary canon.

13. Seltzer's work examines American culture, which witnessed very different displays of mass atrocity to those of nineteenth-century Britain. However, Seltzer locates the birth of wound culture in British modernity. I apply Seltzer's terminology cautiously with an understanding of these different contexts.

14. See Daly 2004 for exploration of the train as a symbol in Victorian narrative.

15. See the American Psychiatric Association's *Diagnostic and Statistical Manual of Mental Disorders Volume 5* (2013: 27) for a recent definition of PTSD.

16. See Mee 2010 for an account of Dickens's railway accident and consequent health problems.

17. See Foote's discussion (2013) of Louise Mallard's death (and her husband's presumed demise) as a warning about technology which anticipates twentieth-century literary Modernism.

18. See Bronstein 2008 for an exhaustive account of industrial accidents in Victorian Britain; Pick 1993 refers to the introduction of mechanised guns as the 'deranged machinery of war' (205); see Gannon 2003 for discussion of mechanised guns in British and American fiction of the nineteenth century.

19. See Leys 2000 for discussion of Freud's role in researching military hysteria and trauma.

20. See 'My Views on the Part Played by Sexuality in the Aetiology of the Neuroses' (1909), in which Freud lists the symptoms of traumatic neurosis (Freud 2001a: 271–82). Freud struggled to reconcile his theorisation of traumatic neurosis with his earlier work on neurosis which was unrelated to war.

21. The Battle of Alma (1854) was the first conflict of the Crimean War, and lists of the dead and wounded were published in local and national newspapers. See 'Battle of the Alma' in *The Huddersfield Chronicle and West Yorkshire Advertiser*, 4 October 1854, and 'Victory of the Alma' in *The Morning Chronicle* of the same date.

22. 'Self-Mutilation by a Soldier', p. 3.

23. 'Another Shocking East-End Murder', p. 126.

24. A serial killer is an individual who has killed three or more people over a period of more than a month, with a 'cooling-off period' between the murders, and whose motivation for killing is usually based on psychological gratification. See Renzetti et al. 2013 for further in relation to gender.

25. See Weedon 2003 for discussion of the Victorian printing press.

26. In *Women Who Kill* (1980), Ann Jones notes that the nineteenth-century 'father of criminology' Cesare Lombroso had argued that women were trained to 'inflict their disappointments on themselves, to become not angry and aggressive but depressed and self-destructive' (2009: 368).

27. See Foucault 1990, 1995 and 2001.

28. Nineteenth-century women's short stories were not always devoid of a moral message, neither were they always 'unconventional'. Early-nineteenth-century stories often mirrored religious tracts in their development of a single, unambiguous (usually Christian) theme or lesson. See Killick 2008 for discussion.

29. See Heilmann 2002, Bronfen 1998, Showalter 1993, and Gilbert and Gubar 1984.

30. Charlotte Perkins Gilman became perhaps the most vocal critic of the rest cure following her own treatment, which is dramatised in 'The Yellow Wallpaper' (1892).

31. For examples see Turner 2002, Hollander 2008, and Chapman and Gratz 2009.

32. Although little is known about the prevalence of Victorian self-harm, twenty-first-century records are also not exhaustive. Self-harm continues to go largely unreported, and often incidences cannot be distinguished from attempts at suicide by twenty-first-century clinicians.

33. For examples see the *Directors of Convict Prisons* taken at Millbank prison in 1853.

34. Standardised admission papers at Bethlem began to ask this from approximately 1844 (Chaney 2011a: 280).

35. Adam was a major contributor to *A Dictionary of Psychological Medicine* (1892), the official reference guide to psychological disorders during the late nineteenth century.

36. Caird's 1888 article 'Marriage' was the first of her writings to be published under her own name and called marriage a 'vexatious failure'. London's *Daily Telegraph* quickly responded with a series entitled 'Is Marriage a Failure?' (1888: 2), which drew a reported 27,000 letters from around the world and continued for three months.

37. Descartes conceptualised the body as both separate from and inferior to the mind or soul. His *Meditations on First Philosophy* set out his argument that the essential self was to be found within the thinking mind and soul, and not the physical body (2008: 9–20).

Chapter 1

Saintly Self-Harm: The Victorian Religious Context

The Politics of Suffering

New Woman writing is replete with images of sacrifice, martyrdom and masochism. Just like the pioneering mid-Victorian women writers who preceded them, *fin-de-siècle* 'feminists' often chose to imaginatively interconnect their political message with religious allegory, privileging self-sacrifice as representative of saintly virtue. As Jan-Melissa Schramm notes, 'the suffering Protestant protagonists of the Victorian novel stand in a complex relation to the Christ who died for the sins of mankind: they seek to appropriate his example but they appreciate the hermeneutic complexity involved in the reading of his life' (2012: 8). Multifaceted textual interpretations of the Bible meant that Christ's example was understood in diverse and nuanced ways during a period in which religious certainties were under threat. Victorian images and discourses of self-sacrifice negotiate the subtle distinction between the physical and vicarious forms of suffering found in differing biblical interpretations. Often these distinctions are blurred, with physical pain the consequence of women's fictional attempts at catharsis, their understanding and enactment of sacrifice. Simultaneously, women's denial of bodily needs endorsed the Cartesian duality inscribed by Western, Christian ideologies – the separation and sublimation of the body in favour of the mind or soul, a dualism explored in detail in Chapter 2.

Scholars of Victorian women's writing have noted the revolutionary potential offered by figures of female divinity, and the ways in which Judeo-Christian mythology could empower and enable female authors (Houston 2013: 1–3). Others have read self-sacrifice as a strategy of self-assertion, as part of a subversive dynamic of feminine power through which women gained authority and asserted influence (Gray 2010: 7–8). However, women's spiritual superiority and increased powers were usually limited to the domestic sphere, restricting the potential for sacrifice as an effective political manoeuvre (Jenkins 1995: 66, Melnyk 2003: 144). However, I argue that gestures of saintly martyrdom and feminine self-denial were expressed in fiction at the *fin de siècle* through images of increasingly violent self-harm. As I demonstrate in subsequent chapters, the self-destructive imagery that began to be deployed in the New Woman novel was adapted to more dramatic effect with the adoption of innovative and less restrictive narrative forms throughout the 1890s. This period not only signalled a transition towards literary Modernism, but simultaneously facilitated an evolution in Victorian thinking about religiously sanctioned suffering.

The Victorians were 'a society outwardly aligned with Christian principles but increasingly reliant on science and material evidence to validate "truth"' (Moran 2007: 1). Thus, perspectives on pain walked an imaginary line between the empiricism of the new sciences and the non-quantitative figure of an omnipotent God. Christian justifications for pain that had been largely accepted for centuries were 'widely seen to be inadequate, while physiological understanding was not yet advanced enough' (Bending 2000: 5). Despite great advances, doctors had yet to gain a full neurological understanding of the ways in which the body responded to suffering and to the new techniques available for its abatement. Methods of pain relief extracted from opiates had been used in Western medicine since the classical period (Brownstein 1993). However, it was the Victorian medical establishment that oversaw the development of reliable pain relief, and its industrial capabilities that facilitated the mass production of analgesia. The hitherto accepted belief that pain was necessary to human experience faced a profound challenge with little evidence of a downside to contradict it, directly calling into question religious philosophies concerning the transformative value of suffering.

The masculine self-sacrifice that had been required in the interests of national prosperity during both the Crimean War and continuing colonial projects slowly became less convincing to the mind of the Victorian public, as the salvific qualities of death were reassessed. The Benthamite utilitarianism of the early nineteenth century had operated on the assumption that the sacrifice of a single citizen might be justifiable in the interests of many. However, from the mid-nineteenth century, popular Victorian fiction explored the ways in which individual worth could not be so easily determined and substituted. Charles Dickens, for example, demonstrates the instability and impracticality of utilitarianism in both *Hard Times* (1854) and

A Tale of Two Cities (1859). In the former, Thomas Gradgrind's system of human classification is exposed and undermined by the singular importance of Sissy Jupe, who resists reduction to a calculation of functionality. In the latter, the dissolute Sydney Carton dies in place of the more socially useful Charles Darnay, yet through sacrifice Carton proves his social value. Dickens's attitude towards utilitarianism is, however, complicated by the ways in which the unnecessary sacrifice of the individual allows the communities they leave behind to flourish in many of his texts.

Dickens's literary ambivalence towards the value of altruistic sacrifice was equalled by public and political reaction to a variety of humanitarian crises during the mid-nineteenth century. The Irish Famine that began during the 1840s and killed over a million people, and the numerous outbreaks of cholera in both Britain and its colonial outposts, galvanised thinking about human misery as an unnecessary threat to imperial strength and integrity.[1] However, bodily suffering in Ireland, the colonies and even the slums of nineteenth-century London was easy for the Victorian middle classes to ignore. At a turbulent time during which doctrinally sanctioned pain was called into question as a convincing justification for unendurable agony, the New Woman frequently adopted motifs of self-flagellation and poses of religiously framed self-sacrifice in her fiction. Her return to the image of the martyred female body at a time when martyrdom itself was viewed as a sacred yet rather outdated practice suggests a motive more in line with subversive politics than a sincere attempt at allegorical didacticism.

Although belief in the importance of Christ's sacrifice remained significant, the day-to-day struggle faced by Victorian women meant that secularism was slowly gaining ground. The pseudo-religious image of the domestic Angel had been introduced and legitimated by popular Victorian art and literature, and remained a ubiquitous model of femininity both aspired to by middle-class ladies and denigrated by those women who perceived the impossibility of its example. New Woman writers exploited growing religious dissent, problematising the theologies that underpropped women's self-negating response to a variety of patriarchal brutalities. In rewriting or reimagining historical sacrifice, New Woman writers demonstrated a dissatisfaction with the judicial and political mechanisms of contemporary society. Representing society's 'atavistic processes that recapitulate those of human sacrifice' (D. Hughes 2007: 2), they often drew parallels between nineteenth-century and classical, medieval or biblical acts that encoded political power dynamics.

Sex, Sacrifice and the Male Gaze

Sacrifice operates as a complex codex of conflicting cultural meanings, at times contradictory in its aim of expressing a straightforwardly selfless or spiritual bodily act (Carr 2003: 3–5). Arguing that sanctity and sexuality are perennially connected, Virginia Burrus reminds us that,

> [a]t most, ascetic eros – encoded as a yearning for God – may be seen as the residue of an imperfectly sublimated sexuality. Better yet: it is a merely metaphorical expression for a purely desexualized love. Worse still: it reflects pleasure derived from practices of self-denial rooted in pathological hatred of the body. (Burrus 2007: 1)

A horror of the flesh, and a pathological desire to harm it, is encoded to variable degrees in all the New Woman texts examined in *Self-Harm in New Woman Literature*. If the destruction of the body and its desires cannot be entirely divorced from acts of Christian asceticism, self-denial or self-abnegation, then the deployment of religiously motivated self-harm can be read through a variety of psychoanalytic frameworks, including Freudian masochistic fantasy and post-Freudian theories of the gaze.

Freud's early work on masochism focused on the role of the Oedipus complex, in which the human subject's unsuccessfully repressed guilt led to feelings of self-directed rage (Glick and Meyers 1993: 4–5) transforming sadistic aggression into masochism. Post-Freudian psychoanalysis continues to question, reassess and re-present the Freudian model, but until relatively recently few clinicians or critics had departed from the pleasure/pain dichotomy as the basis of the condition. In 'Coldness and Cruelty' (1989), Gilles Deleuze challenges Freud's belief that masochism is sadism turned upon the self, arguing that

> Masochism is characterized not by guilt feelings but by the desire to be punished, the purpose of masochism being to resolve guilt and the corresponding anxiety and to make sexual gratification possible [. . .] The process of turning around upon the self may be regarded as a reflexive stage ('I punish myself') but since masochism implies a passive stage ('I am punished, I am beaten') we must infer the existence in masochism of a particular mechanism of projection through which an external agent is made to assume the role of the subject. (Deleuze 1991: 104–6)

Given Deleuze's assertion that masochism enacts a resolution of guilt through bodily punishment at the hands of a higher power, it is not difficult to connect the masochist's behaviour to internalised religious codes requiring penance for un-Christian thoughts and actions. Considering the importance of sexual gratification as a component of masochistic self-harm, acts of Christian mortification and their representation can be understood (broadly) within a quasi-masochistic framework.

Victorian religion and eroticism also interacted through the authoritative gaze of masculine institutions. The Church, for example, which formalised and legitimated the Victorian family and its relations, also kept watch over subversive bodies, desires and sexualities (Foucault 1990). Competing and conflicting interpretations of the gaze have appeared in (amongst others) Freudian, Lacanian and Foucauldian theoretical models during the past century. Literary and historical criticism on the subject has expanded Freudian and Lacanian notions of the gaze as, respectively, sexually charged looking (Freud 2001a) or a field of vision producing awareness in the subject that they are incomplete or other (Lacan 1998). Later theories imagine the gaze as a disciplinary act underpinning institutional and social control, or the masculine desire to visually appropriate the body (Irigaray 1985, Foucault 1990, Brooks 1993). Feminist interpretations of the penetrative male gaze in Luce Irigaray's *Speculum of the Other Woman* (1974) and Laura Mulvey's 'Visual Pleasure and Narrative Cinema' (1975) have been much complicated by twenty-first-century criticism, which deconstructs the gendered binaries of a passive, watched female and an aggressive, watching male. Beth Newman's recent discussion of the function of the gaze within the visually charged economy of the Victorian marriage market attempts to reconcile Freudian, Lacanian and Foucauldian perspectives, arguing that

> what this conflict mirrors may in fact be *different* ways that desire – no simple thing reduced to Freudian drive [. . .] or Foucauldian mirage produced in the heat of subjectification – works on subjectivity. Desire, unlike drive, involves meaning, and therefore is always inherently social. It is what happens to drive when it attaches itself to one or more specific bodily sources (the eye being one of them) and then settles, however fleetingly, on an object that has already been invested with meaning. (Newman 2004: 13)

As objects invested with meaning, (often damaged) female bodies formed the central focus of narratives of self-sacrifice in the classical and biblical traditions, as well as in the medieval poetry crucial to the work of writers and artists of the mid- to late-Victorian period. As my subsequent chapters show, New Woman writers were involved in an uneasy dialogue with Victorian artists that often implicated them in the patriarchal gaze in complicated ways. The New Woman writer's position regarding religiously motivated self-harm was an ambivalent one, critical of women's bodily pains, yet inexorably bound to discourses that were misogynistic and highly exploitative. She challenged the status quo, and imagined new social, educational and cultural spaces for women. However, in fictionally displaying the wounded female body, the New Woman writer also contributed to a culture in which the act of looking, or reading, was a gesture of 'symbolic violence' (Bordieu 1991: 242) that placed women at the centre of male-oriented narrative drives, as objects to be inspected and demystified.

Pained Pleasure: Masochism and the Holy Virgin

Often deploying the dual feminine archetypes of the Virgin Mary and Eve, Victorian visual and literary culture drew upon deep-rooted (largely) Christian models for representing women that were, in part, borrowed from medieval tradition. The inherently contradictory and unachievable standards of perfect femininity exemplified by Mary as a mother, virgin and saint were internalised by women, and are exemplified by the self-harming heroines of New Woman fiction. The centrality of the figure of the Virgin in the Marian art of Roman Catholicism, in her four central incarnations as perpetual virgin, mother of God, vessel of Immaculate Conception, and citizen of Heaven, attests to the conflict between embodiment and spirituality implicit in the feminine ideal. While Mariology began as a Catholic practice, worship of the Virgin diffused into English Protestantism despite the efforts of the Protestant Church to malign Mary as a feminine deity (Herringer 2008: 1–5, Vanita 1996: 16–17). Mary appeared in a variety of guises in fictional texts throughout the nineteenth century, and the complications inherent in her example were explored by late-Victorian artists and writers, who depicted the Mater Dolorosa in all her contradictory glory.

'Our Lady of Pain' was a preoccupation of many writers of the Victorian Decadence who did not stop at representing the conflict between Mary as at once maternal, virginal and saintly.[2] A figure of motherly grief, the Lady of Sorrows became a symbol of masochistic self-denial, imagined as heavenly and disembodied, yet simultaneously of flesh, desiring and pained. The European poetic tradition significantly influenced British artistic and literary production during the nineteenth century, and found its way into a wide variety of textual artefacts, including Decadent art and poetry and New Woman writing. The most prominent proponent of this tradition was Charles Baudelaire, whose *Fleurs du Mal* (1857) encouraged and inspired a generation of Decadent artists and writers. In Baudelaire's 'À une Madone', Mary is by turns both the dominant and the submissive partner in a sadomasochistic relationship in which her body is both wounded and worshipped, and grief is a source of eros.[3] Like the New Woman, the Madonna embodied the conflicting identities open to Victorian women, as well as the restrictions placed upon the female body as an object to be 'looked at, denuded [and] unveiled' (Brooks 1993: 97) by traditional forms of seeing and writing.

In Algernon Charles Swinburne's poem 'Dolores' (1866), the Madonna is a sinful woman: sterile, savage and cruel, not the pure and virginal mother of Christ, but the sadomasochistic woman.[4] In the poem's refrain 'Our Lady of Pain!' Swinburne turns liturgical incantation into masochistic affirmation, subverting Catholic transubstantiation into sexual pleasure through the poem's form, which resembles the structure of the intercessory in the Anglo-Catholic Mass. Unlike Eucharistic consumption, in which the flesh and blood of Christ are made incarnate through audible prayer, the speaker metaphorically consumes the Madonna, drinking of the flesh and blood of the demonic woman in a scene of orgasmic cannibalism (lines 31–2). Dolores is both a consuming and consumed woman, whose

> [. . .] ravenous teeth that have smitten
> Through the kisses that blossom and bud,
> By the lips intertwisted and bitten
> Till the foam has a savour of blood,
> By the pulse as it rises and falters,
> By the hands as they slacken and strain,
> I adjure thee, respond from thine altars,
> Our Lady of Pain. (lines 113–20)

In rendering his Mater Dolorosa a divine whore, whose hungry mouth violently devours those who kneel before her, Swinburne mocks the Catholic belief in Mary as the chaste and innocent mother of the Church, and indeed belief in the Church as the 'bride' of Christ.[5] Swinburne parodies the ritualism of Catholicism through a process that Margot Louis has termed 'Eucharistic murder' (1990: 38) by which the contradictions inherent in the body of the Holy Virgin are transposed into sacramental violence and masochistic fantasy.

As Ruth Vanita notes, the body of the Virgin has been discursively and culturally linked to both pain and eroticism, through her interest in the salvation of prostitutes and mothers of illegitimate children (1996: 34). Swinburne extends this connection by aligning the body of the female saint with the pleasures and pains of self-flagellation, depicting the eros of both Christianity and self-harm.[6]

Swinburne's interest in masochism, religion and self-harm can be traced to his preoccupation with medieval culture, and the nineteenth-century revisions of medievalism that permeate some of the New Woman writing explored in the chapters that follow. The Middle English lyric poetry that inspired late-Victorian writers like Swinburne, and so often engaged with the transgressive possibilities of the gaze, is a particularly rich site for examining the ways in which the sacrificial body could depose, yet equally reinforce, male observation and dominance.[7] In her exploration of Middle English lyrics of the Passion, Sarah Stanbury recognises that the role of the Virgin Mary is 'shaped by the intersected trajectories of multiple lines of sight', including those of the viewers within the lyrical narrative space, and those of a culture that 'politicizes the act of viewing' (1991: 1086). The gaze of the Virgin upon the wounded body of her martyred son is emphasised by lyric poetry in ways that both undermine the primacy of masculine observation and merge maternal compassion with eroticism. 'The male body is laid out, naked – one might even say nude – limp, surrounded by women who not only grieve but stare and touch as well' (1991: 1086); their gaze is 'legitimized by maternity and eroticized by its transgressive sexuality' (1991: 1087).

Despite the empowerment of the feminine through the Virgin's gaze, it is impossible to ignore the fetishisation of the Madonna in the art and culture of the Middle Ages. While the Virgin provided one possible answer to what Gail Turley Houston calls 'mother-god-want' (2013: 1) in Victorian women's fiction – the need to construct a female deity and connect with a radical tradition – such a connection was fraught. The Virgin epitomises 'the problematic of the female body as an object of the gaze [. . .] given a prominent role in a narrative as she was immobilized as icon; but even so, ideology was at work to deny her agency' (Caviness 2001: 2), refusing her a position outside of domesticity. Similarly, the self-harming fictional heroines discussed in the chapters that follow formed spectacles of bodily damage and subverted the separate sphere ideology that denied women agency, yet their power to disrupt patriarchy was limited by their exploitation as objects of desire in much the same way as the Holy Virgin.

Broken Bodies in Nineteenth-Century Culture

For centuries, religious literature and art has examined the relation-ship between the tortured body and those who gaze upon it. These works implicate subject, object, viewer and reader in an exchange whereby the sacrificial body is imbued with competing impulses of compassion, desire, glorification, politicisation and exploitation. Sarah Beckwith notes of Christ that he 'was eaten in the Eucharist. He was also looked at, identified with, imitated, violated, played with in an almost alarming variety of shifting social roles' (1993: 4). It is clear that these roles fit the specific needs of a given culture. Whilst, like the potentially empowering Christ figure, women's bod-ies remained a potent commodity in Victorian society, the damaged female body became temporarily marginalised in art, literature and cultural discourse until the late nineteenth century. Throughout his-tory the female body in art had been subject to regulatory powers that shifted in relation to socio-political factors and fluctuating religious and moral codes. After the mass destruction of Catholic art during the Reformation, the Puritanism of the 1640s Civil War period finished what had been started by King Henry VIII. The nude emerged again in Renaissance painting, which began to influence British painters as post-Reformation links with Europe were slowly repaired during the seventeenth and eighteenth centuries, and attitudes towards religious paintings changed (Graham-Dixon 2009: 80).

Once an example of the post-Reformation sensuality of Catholi-cism and the immorality it implied, by the nineteenth century painting the naked body had become one of the most fundamental artistic skills taught at the Royal Academy (Beisel 1993). However, throughout the Victorian period, censorship of paintings that showed the naked or semi-naked body remained strictly regulated for fear of offending public decency or promoting sexual indiscretion. Yet these regula-tions were cultural rather than legal, since laws surrounding obscen-ity applied only to the written word and later photographic pictures, whereas the showing of artworks was principally controlled by muse-ums. The female nude could be shown in art through 'certain dis-tancing devices regarding time, place, and treatment' (Smith 1996: 4) that legitimised the naked female form. Strategies included draping, amorphous gender, or the use of historical and mythical settings. Public debate concerning the propriety of displaying religious paint-ings featuring torture was ongoing, and concerned the possibility that the public could become sexually aroused by images of women in pain, however sacred or devotional (Moran 2004: 475).

While images of suffering women were displayed, their religious context and educational message had to be emphasised to be deemed proper. Propriety could be secured by underscoring the transcendence of religiously motivated sacrifice, as opposed to the realistic physical agonies of self-immolation. Paintings frequently depicted tortured virginal bodies of female saints, which conformed to nineteenth-century ideals of passivity and submission. Women's bodies had to be framed by nineteenth-century art in ways that sanctioned 'the containment and regulation of the female body' (Nead 1992: 6). The beauty and docility of female saints was accentuated by emphasising their white, untainted bodies, and their expressions of meek acceptance conveyed the admirable nature of sacrifice. While Christian art stressed the separation of spirit and body that martyrdom entailed, its iconography risked uprooting the ideological disembodiment of its female saints.

The narrowly demarcated boundaries between eroticism and spiritual didacticism made permissible the display of female bodies in biblical contexts, by painters whose message was often far from moralistic. In John William Waterhouse's *Saint Joan* (1872) and later his *Saint Eulalia* (1885) the bare white breasts of the martyr's body are displayed, yet their sexuality is downplayed by the emblematic virginity of both women. In *Saint Eulalia*, the twelve-year-old martyr lies dead in the gladiatorial arena, surrounded by drifts of the symbolic snow said to have been sent from God to cover her nakedness, yet her breasts remain exposed. The implicit eroticism of Eulalia's bare and tortured body – a body violated by the Roman spear after being forcibly stripped of her clothes – went (largely) unnoticed by the viewing public. So too did the necrophilia implied by the display of her beautiful corpse, because the snow and the inclusion of white doves encoded her chastity and suggested how the picture should be read. In Dante Gabriel Rossetti's *Joan of Arc* (1882), the martyr is depicted as a voluptuous figure, in a composition that does more to contradict than to accentuate the purity of its subject. Joan's wild, flame-coloured hair and red lips, as well as the sensuality of her pose and the opulence of the surrounding drapery, suggest a sexual availability that undermines the admissibility of the painting. So too does the fact that Joan was modelled on Jane Morris, the wife of Rossetti's fellow Pre-Raphaelite 'brother' William Morris, with whom Rossetti was rumoured to have been having a romantic relationship (De La Sizeranne 2008: 90–9).

As well as biblical subjects, the Pre-Raphaelites were heavily influenced by, and interested in, medieval culture; like the classical nude or the Christian martyr, historical scenes and folkloric figures offered another representational outlet. Medieval Christian culture 'gave ready expression to sadism and masochism by dwelling upon its tortured dead' and made 'appeals to its devotees to identify with the sufferings of the martyrs as if they were their own' (Caviness 2001: 35). Thus, the adoption of medieval images by Victorian artists and writers contributed to a late-nineteenth-century cultural saturation with the rhetoric of martyrdom, and, more generally, a glamorisation of self-denial. Christ's example was epitomised by the figure of the domestic Angel, and images of saintly self-sacrifice became so culturally pervasive that they were echoed and reflected by New Woman writers despite their disapproval of masculine representational strategies. Sarah Grand was a vocal critic of men's sensuality in art and literature, critiquing masculine cultural production in 'The New Aspect of the Woman Question' (1894), and depicting Decadence, Naturalism and Aestheticism as forms of masculine sexual deviance in her fiction. Similarly, Vernon Lee in 'Lady Tal' (1892), Ella Hepworth Dixon in *The Story of a Modern Woman* (1894), Ménie Muriel Dowie in *Gallia* (1895), Ella D'Arcy in 'The Pleasure Pilgrim' (1895), and Lucas Malet in *The Wages of Sin* (1890) and *The Carissima* (1896) respectively lampoon the figure of the male artist and/or aesthete. While critical of artistic exploitations of the female body, New Woman writers also developed modes of expression that ensured that the private female body, in all its tortured glory, was publicly consumable. As a product of Freudian drives attached specifically to bodily sources invested with social meaning, the damaged female form was the pivot around which women's continued fight for the right to control their own bodies revolved. It eventually took its place as an object of desire and metaphorical tool in New Woman writing, in ways that were significantly different, both formally and thematically, from those adopted in mid-century women's writing, and in *fin-de-siècle* works by men.

Unlike the Gothic texts of the previous century which had displayed the female body for erotic consumption, the New Woman's spectacle of feminine self-damage constituted a deliberately gendered and politically motivated exhibition of suffering. The broken body had been made spectacle in eighteenth-century Gothic fiction, whose melodramatic display of torture undercut the body's potential as a political signifier (Bruhm 1994: 92–3). Arguably, nineteenth-century Gothic texts that developed eighteenth-century displays of the tortured body did so with a view towards the 'ruination of the human subject' (Hurley 1996: 3). They highlighted the impossibility of transcending the grotesquery of human corporeality, at a time when labelling and controlling the body had become increasingly difficult for the Victorian establishment. Of the nineteenth-century Gothic, Kelly Hurley argues 'one may read its obsessive staging and restaging of the spectacle of abhumanness as a paralysis [. . .] as the human body collapses and is reshapen across an astonishing range of morphic possibilities' (1996: 4). New Woman fiction often featured elements of Gothicism that corresponded to its melodrama and sensationalism, yet it represented the horrors of women's experience in a way that had not been seen since the previous century, and then usually in novels by men.[8]

In the religiously framed, and often Gothic-tinged, fiction produced by the New Woman, the broken bodies of self-sacrificing women are often denied 'morphic possibilities'. Rather than staging abhuman spectacles, these writers attempted (yet often failed) to emphasise the humanity of their subjects, and, paradoxically, to deny their corporeality altogether. In self-harming, I argue that the heroines of New Woman fiction attempt to elude classification as objects to be looked at, by undermining outdated and restrictive constructions of femininity found in both eighteenth- and nineteenth-century writing on the damaged body. As opposed to the 'paralysis' of which Hurley writes, New Woman writing about female martyr figures represented and indeed effected movement, between, and through the centre of, the rigid categories of public and private that defined and limited femininity. These pioneering writers adopted motifs of self-mortification and self-abnegation to downplay the primacy of the female sexual body, and thus to resist the proprietary male gaze. However, their own works fell into the trap of displaying and over-emphasising their characters' bodies as erotic spectacles.

The use of self-harm as a narrative trope in Victorian women's writing is significant precisely because it is (paradoxically) both an unconventional and a traditional representation of female corporeality. Texts that represent acts of martyrdom often 'encompass the orthodox and the radical simultaneously' (Moran 2004: 478) and in doing so enable the formation of oppositional yet coterminous readings. Since the Victorian ideal of femininity required that self-interested display was eschewed in favour of quiet, domestic obscurity, the tendency for New Woman texts to dramatise, idealise and hyperbolise women's bodily suffering signals the complexity of martyrdom and religious self-sacrifice as tropes. The dichotomy of impropriety and permissibility, inherent in the act of viewing the wounded female body, created a psychological space in which (as with martyrdom and masochism) disinterested spirituality and violent sexual desire competed and coincided. Thus, Victorian imagery of martyrdom and religious self-harm often expressed the instability of the boundaries between the private interior world of the spirit and the erotic spectacle of the broken body in which it resided. Towards the end of the century, as Victorian understandings of the relationship between body and soul began to fluctuate, and ultimately transform, the correlation between the private body and the public space became similarly altered. Texts that depicted the traumatised body through religious imagery did so by legitimising the radical, subtly eroding the boundaries between what could and could not be publicly displayed.

In my introduction, I discussed Mark Seltzer's notion of a Victorian wound culture in which 'the private and natural body has, in unprecedented ways, become publicly relevant' and 'the body has insistently become relevant as spectacle and representation – and, most insistently, as spectacle or representation of crisis, disaster, or atrocity' (Seltzer 1998: 35). The New Woman writer's use of religiously framed tropes of self-damage operated in ways that attempted to make the broken female body publicly relevant, to exhibit as atrocity the wounded feminine psyche and to erode the margins between the public and private spheres. However, as this chapter and those that follow will show, this strategy was sometimes problematised by the use of highly conventional constructions of gender, class and sexuality. Such constructions limited the New Woman's radicalism and in many ways abnegated (or, as I argue, self-sabotaged) her own proto-feminist projects. Furthermore, in relying upon well-established moral and religious structures through which to dramatise self-harming acts, the New Woman limited her challenge to patriarchy, at times internalising self-reproach just as much as some of her unfortunate heroines.

Martyrdom, Self-Wounding and the Erotics of Self-Abasement

Historically, martyrdom was a strategy through which honour could be attained in bodily suffering, in a paradoxical act that redefined power relations between the sacrificed and the executioner. In a society that privileged heroism, Christians offered up to torture transcended their lowly position as traitors through bravery in the face of avoidable death (Barton 1994: 41). In the Roman tradition self-destruction was 'the supreme form of munificence, the extremes of largesse and deprivation at once' since 'their stories of vindication of honour are designed not to elicit pity, not to reveal a victim, but to reveal an unconquered will' (Barton 2002: 27). The gladiator or executioner who faced the Christian martyr did so in command of great power, yet, by their own violent renunciation of the self, the martyr could achieve a similarly honourable and authoritative status by their death, in the eyes of the republic as well as a Christian God.[9]

By the Victorian era, the martyr figure had become culturally diffuse and was based on the recurring model of the martyrdoms of Jesus Christ and the medieval saints. In a society rapidly developing new challenges to the notion of an omnipotent God and to the centrality of humankind in the workings of the universe, Christian iconography remained surprisingly fashionable. Victorian scientific naturalism, particularly the work of Charles Darwin – and later Herbert Spencer – on evolution and natural selection, presented a challenge to the concept of man created by God in his own image. Despite this, religious art was hugely popular. William Holman Hunt's *The Triumph of the Innocents* (1876–9/1883–4), depicting the Holy family's flight from Bethlehem (Matthew 2: 16–18), prompted the critic John Ruskin to call it 'the greatest religious picture of the century' (Hilton 2002: 742). The popularity of images such as Hunt's was partly due to women, since 'the commercial religious business both exploited [. . .] and catered to her, restricted the dimensions of her identity and endowed her as a privileged customer' (Carpenter 2003: xvii). Since women's personal interests were often limited to maintaining the family and the household, their identification with Christ's trials made Victorian housewives voracious consumers of religious images and texts who contributed to the cultural potency of martyrdom.

The Catholic and Orthodox Christian faiths had assimilated images of sacrifice into their respective places of worship through sculpture, tapestries, paintings, relics and architecture. However, representations of Catholicism, and, more generally, the ritualistic elements of Christian custom, were sensationalised in eighteenth- and nineteenth-century fiction through tales of confinement, torture and sexual deviance. Horace Walpole's *The Castle of Otranto* (1764) and Matthew Lewis's *The Monk* (1796), as well as later texts such as Bram Stoker's *Dracula* (1897), exemplify the range of possibilities available to writers willing to engage with religious ritualism. The ascetic and ceremonial performances that characterised the Church of Rome were a combination of both seductive spectacle and deviant oppositional force in Victorian culture, and 'presented as fantastic but real, a metaphor for the unorthodox [. . .] a significant imaginary space, embracing the unfamiliar, but also challenging the Victorian *status quo*' (Moran 2007: 17). The figure of the martyr served as a recurrent trope in the Victorian creative imagination, as a symbol of the conflicting loyalties of State and Church, self and family, moral conscience and the law. This accounts in some part for its enthusiastic adoption by Decadent writers and artists, both as subject matter and as metaphorical tool (Hanson 1997).

Maureen Moran's observation that both Catholic and anti-Catholic rhetoric adopted 'emotive diction, melodramatic and morbid stories, and extravagant images of horror' (2007: 6) is borne out by the popularity of works that imagined the broken bodies of martyred figures. While this 'propaganda' demonstrated Victorian Protestantism's attempt to extricate itself from Catholic influence, the allure of such images was furthered by popular Victorian literature and art. Among the literary characters were Elizabeth Gaskell's heroine in *Ruth* (1853), Charles Dickens's Stephen Blackpool in *Hard Times* and Sydney Carton in *A Tale of Two Cities*, George Eliot's Maggie Tulliver in *The Mill on the Floss* (1860) and Dorothea Brooke in *Middlemarch* (1872), and Thomas Hardy's protagonist in *Tess of the D'Urbervilles* (1891). Popular images included Frederick Sandys's *The Boy Martyr* (1862), Edward Burne-Jones's *St Theophilus and the Angel* (1863–7), John Everett Millais's *The Martyr of the Solway* (c. 1871), Charles Mitchell's *Hypatia* (1885), and John William Waterhouse's *Saint Eulalia* (1885), all of which took martyrdom as their subject matter.[10] Despite the fact that images like these often represented the naked female body in postures of submission and torture, they were considered devotional and thus acceptable because the purity of the subject was stressed, and a historical distance was maintained.[11]

Victorian religious works embodied tensions between the spirituality of self-sacrifice and the erotics of self-abasement. In the case of historic martyrdom, these tensions manifested in acts of watching, during which the damaged body (often female) became public spectacle. For example, during the martyrdom of Felicitas and Perpetua – executed at Carthage during the third century – the crowd demanded that 'their eyes could share the killing as the sword entered the flesh' (Castelli 1996: 33). The gaze of the martyr was equally important to that of the crowd, and, as Carlin Barton underscores in her discussion of Saint Perpetua's *Passion* (2002), martyrdom is particularly rich in the language of observational defiance. For instance, Perpetua 'advanced with a luminous face and calm step [. . .] casting down the stare of the crowd with the power of her gaze' (Musurillo 1972: 73), subverting her role as object. The nature of the public execution as mass spectacle created a sense of community centred on a shared voyeuristic and fetishistic desire for the penetration and destruction of the body. Irigaray has shown in her reassessment of both the Freudian and the Lacanian gaze that observation constitutes a substitution for the sexual act in which watching functions as 'power over the genitals/woman/sex [. . .] the penis eye, the phallic look' (1985: 134). Arguably, the crowd's excitement is located not in the spiritual righteousness of the act of punishment, or indeed self-renunciation, but in the vicarious corporeality of surveillance. As Seltzer asserts, this strategy became commonplace during the late-Victorian period as 'the exhibition and witnessing, the endlessly reproducible display of wounded bodies and wounded minds in public', increasingly appeared in its literature and culture.

Scenes of self-sacrifice were nothing new to nineteenth-century women's writing, and discourses that considered and even tentatively combined religious devotion and sexual experience were widely read. Both the valorisation of sacrifice and the erotic potential of self-destruction were perhaps best represented in one of the most well-read poems of the day: Christina Rossetti's 'Goblin Market' (1862).[12] Rossetti's poem tells a seemingly simple, biblical tale of temptation, fall and redemption through sacrifice that, to a certain extent, guarded against strict Victorian moral censorship. Since Rossetti – an unmarried spinster with a blameless reputation – wrote of sisterly love and Christian salvation, the troublingly homosexual and incestuous connotations of 'Goblin Market' went mostly unnoticed by Rossetti's contemporaries. Rossetti's consciousness of the poem's metaphorical association of self-sacrifice with sexual pleasure continues to be the subject of critical debate.[13] However, her work underscores the prevalence of such links in the cultural imagination of Victorian women writers, heralding a trend towards exploring the sacrificial female body in ways that struggled to bifurcate the religious from the sensual.

Women writers regularly associated their social position with the sufferings of Christian martyrs, identifying with Christ in particular as a feminised figure. As Simone de Beauvoir notes in *The Second Sex* (1949), 'for many women writers, all women are Christ; whether for good or ill. The image of Christ, so often negatively applied, might prove a more salutary symbol for women if they chose to identify with the aspect of power rather than martyrdom' (2010: 316). Victorian art and literature often struggled to make a clear distinction between the sacred and the sexual in their depictions of a suffering yet androgynous Jesus Christ. A. J. L. Busst's essay on the figure of the androgyne recognises the universal popularity of an androgynous and feminised Christ. In describing the pessimism of late-century images that displayed 'demonality, onanism, homosexuality, sadism, and masochism' (1967: 39), Busst makes the case for a shift in the representation of religious figures during the Victorian Decadence. He notes that writers and artists of the *fin de siècle* were also inspired by Leonardo da Vinci's highly feminised rendering of *St John the Baptist* (1513–16) and that they continually reproduced and reimagined this image.

Busst's observations are borne out by well-known Victorian paintings that imagined Christ's androgynous body as subject to particularly feminine forms of submission. In William Holman Hunt's painting *The Light of the World* (1854), Christ is shown holding a lamp and knocking at an overgrown and long-unopened door. Like Hunt's *The Triumph of the Innocents*, *The Light of the World* was praised by Ruskin, who described it as 'one of the very noblest works of sacred art ever produced in this or any other age' (Ruskin 1854: 9), and the painting was well received by the public. However, the history of the painting's composition exemplifies its subversion of gender and sexuality, since the androgynous face of Christ was inspired by Christina Rossetti, while the hair was modelled for by Dante Gabriel Rossetti's wife Elizabeth Siddal (Andres 2005: 9). As Nina Auerbach points out, femininity haunts this painting, making femaleness 'a hidden alter-ego' (1982: 77) of Hunt's Christ figure. Connecting *The Light of the World* to Hunt's *The Awakening Conscience* (1853), the woman is 'the fallen soul at whose door Christ is knocking' (1982: 77) and both images are a transmutation into a 'peculiarly Victorian typology of domestic female divinity' (1982: 78). Once rendered feminine, images of saintly suffering take on an erotic significance that accounts, in part, for the inability of writers like Christina Rossetti to clearly delineate self-sacrifice and sexual pleasure. Feminine qualities that encoded Victorian gender binaries are emblematised by the martyrdom of Christ; selflessness, patience, forbearance, sacrifice, submission and beauty were characteristics associated with women, yet were repeatedly reproduced in images of the crucifixion.

Christ's maternal nature was persistently stressed by scripture and nineteenth-century contemporary culture. As Simon Richter observes, the Christian tradition deploys metaphors of Christ as a 'lactating mother' (2006: 46), aligning the 'Word made flesh' of the Book of John with a maternal transmutation between spiritual and literal nourishment from Christ's bosom.[14] Similarly, critics and historians like Busst, Irigaray and, more recently, Amy Hollywood and

Constance Furey have argued that Christ is feminised by the wound to his side – a metaphorical representation of female genitalia. The wound of the crucified Jesus Christ was understood in medieval Christianity as having 'given birth' to the Church. Thus – as both Busst and Irigaray propose – it mirrors the reproductive organs of the Virgin Mary.[15] In the same way that her body was to be wounded by mankind in giving birth to Christ, Mary's son was similarly wounded in an act aligned with maternal suffering and self-sacrifice. Christ's side, penetrated by masculinity signified by the phallic spear, has a long and rich representational history as having been wounded by sexually charged violence. As 'tomb, womb, and vagina' (Furey 2012: 336), Christ's suffering body signifies the ecstasies of female martyrdom and self-sacrifice in a way that can be traced in the art and literature of the *fin de siècle*, including New Woman texts that represent the wounds of female experience. The New Woman writer adopted the rhetoric and symbolism of religiously motivated self-harm, Christ-like suffering and martyrdom. She expressed her dissatisfaction with the pain that patriarchy expected women to bear, yet continued to venerate biblical figures as the ultimate examples of strength and goodness.

Christianity and Sacrifice in Mona Caird's *The Wing of Azrael* and *The Daughters of Danaus*

In her extensive discussion of the novels of Scottish author Mona Caird, Ann Heilmann notes the use of classical, pagan and biblical images that challenge the primacy of male-oriented mythological constructions of femininity. In Caird's *The Pathway of the Gods* (1898) – in which the heroine is framed as a martyr both by the fantasies of the male narrator and by her self-destructive actions – Caird expounded 'a fierce delight in exploding the euphemistic apologia of violence' and 'a feminist critique of the patriarchal strategy to contain the New Woman in and through myth' (2004: 160, 170). Attacking the 'sacrificial' (Caird 1987: 556) woman in a much-quoted 1889 letter to Lady Jane Wilde, Caird complained about the self-destructive women who frequently appeared in both mid-Victorian novels and the work of her New Woman contemporaries. Caird makes the case for the futility of religiously framed self-sacrifice by women, deploying Christian iconography and images in her writing to destabilise the authority of the Church and protest against the limited roles offered to women both New and Old.

Caird argued publicly for the abolishment of traditional forms of marriage as well as what she saw as socially enforced motherhood. Thus, in *The Daughters of Danaus*, Caird's heroine describes the image of a young mother as a 'symbol of [. . .] abasement' (1894: 248). Caird specifically blamed the conflation of Christian notions of divine surrender with the bodily duties required by marriage and motherhood for the misery endured by her heroines. Despite this, her frequent depictions of martyrdom and religiously determined self-sacrifice attest to the Victorian cultural saturation of Christian mythology, and, in even the most radical of women writers, an investment in images that imbued the tortured body with erotic and cultural capital. Caird's novels are deeply critical of Christianity, yet they also revel in the rich linguistic possibilities proffered by images of martyrdom, and comprehensively exhibit the tortured bodies of female victim-characters. In two of her best-known novels, Caird interrogates the internalisation of Christian principles adopted even by women who tried desperately to resist one of the most hallowed of sacraments. In both texts Caird's heroines are forced to adopt self-harming strategies; one woman commits suicide, and the other sacrifices her mental and physical well-being to survive. In the readings that follow, I extend Heilmann's discussion of the martyr image in *The Pathway of the Gods*, in which Anna Carrington's construction by the male narrative voice allows Caird to critique patriarchy and undermine the homogeny of New Woman identity (Heilmann 2004: 170). Using similar imagery to different effect, Caird dramatises women's indoctrination into bourgeois religion and morality, but struggles to transform martyrdom from a gesture reinforcing male dominance, and does not offer an alternative to self-sacrifice.

The Wing of Azrael concerns the unhappy marriage of Viola Sedley to the cruel Philip Dendraith. Despite her burgeoning love for her distant relation Harry Lancaster, Viola is pressured into marrying Dendraith to secure her family's financial future. Eventually, Viola murders her husband in self-defence and the text strongly implies her death by suicide. As in many New Woman novels, the feeble mother of the ill-fated protagonist is blamed for perpetuating and reinforcing the standard of wifely submission against which her daughter rages.[16] In the case of Mrs Sedley these ideals are 'ascetic' (Caird 2010b: 8) and reflect the self-abrogative characteristics of her marriage to Viola's father:

> Mrs Sedley with her still, dutiful ways and religious principles had irritated [her husband] from the first day of her meek reign [. . .] Mr Sedley, by nature, was blustering and self-indulgent [. . .] His wife's tendencies,

on the other hand, were ascetic. Her conscience never let her rest until she had made things as unpleasant for herself as circumstances would permit, and by long practice in the art, she had now achieved a ghastly power of self-suppression. (Caird 2010b: 8)

Mrs Sedley possesses 'unfailing submissiveness' and 'meek and saint-like endurance' and, by her 'perpetual self-effacement', she encourages her husband's wrath, accepting it as 'another Heaven-sent trial to be borne without murmuring' (2010b: 9). Through Mrs Sedley's unfulfilled, monastic life, Caird illustrates the senselessness of women's religiously motivated self-denial. Positing it as a form of self-harm whereby submissiveness in fact effects a worsening of marital discord, Caird derides the poor example Mrs Sedley sets for her young daughter, who 'accepted this without question' and 'absorbed this teaching readily' (2010b: 10).

As the text proceeds to show, Viola is taught by her mother's behaviour to interiorise meekness and passivity, to perform a 'subordination of the self' (2010b: 10) resulting in self-reproach for her inability to adhere wholeheartedly to her Christian faith, or to save herself from the misery she endures. Viola's mother unwittingly offers her up for sacrifice, yet, we are told,

> Suffering, which Mrs Sedley had borne herself without a murmur, made her terrible when it threatened her child [. . .] She was ready, with hands that trembled and quailing heart (but she was ready), to give that nerve-thrilled being to the flames – for Duty's sake – and quickly that insatiate woman's Idol was advancing to meet his victim. (Caird 2010b: 67)

Despite Mrs Sedley's reservations about Viola's impending marriage, she rationalises her daughter's sacrifice as a pious offering, metaphorically placing Viola on the pyre in worship of (as Caird's novel suggests) a false and voracious God. As a consequence of her upbringing, Viola is deeply religious – and, like many of the New Woman heroines I discuss, punishes herself for acts that fall short of a Christ-like standard of goodness. We are told that Viola

> passed through a phase of fervent religious feeling, during which she rivalled in devotion and self-mortification many a canonised saint. Her mother had some trouble in keeping her from doing herself bodily harm, for in her new-born zeal she preferred tasks that gave her pain, and never thought it possible to be well employed unless the occupation was severely distasteful. (Caird 2010b: 66)

In marrying Dendraith, Viola takes her self-harming tendencies to their logical conclusion, in a relationship that reproduces the dynamic of her parents' domestic misery and ends in suicide. Unlike Mrs Sedley, Viola cannot so easily justify her ill treatment at the hands of her husband, and comes to question the value of suffering and the necessity of her own pain. Constantly oppressed by the internal conflict between religious and social expectations and her own desires, Viola's only hope of salvation is her love for Harry, and the influence of his friend – the infamous Sibella Lincoln.

A New Woman of the most obvious type – educated, financially independent, and the only character unafraid of Dendraith – Sibella encourages Viola to follow in her footsteps. While Sibella has defied custom by repudiating her adulterous husband, choosing a lover, and pursuing a life of independence and self-fulfilment, Viola inwardly rages against the sacrifices required of her by marriage, yet outwardly submits to Philip and to social expectations. Face to face with the 'wicked' Mrs Lincoln, Viola finds she is calmed by Sibella's presence and stirred by her words, yet ultimately remains unconvinced by the New Woman thinking she espouses. Drawing on Christian imagery, Mrs Lincoln distorts and undermines the principles to which Viola desperately tries to adhere, and the idol worshipped by Mrs Sedley, explaining that

> [w]e have both been taught, as we imagined, to worship God. I fear that we have really been taught to worship the devil! We are trained to submission, to accept things as they are, to serve God by resignation – yes, even the resignation of our human dignity – whereat the devil laughs in his sleeve, and carries off the fruits of miserable lives to add to the riches of his kingdom [. . .] And so are the virtues and the martyrdoms of good women in vain. (Caird 2010b: 228–30)

As her oracular name suggests, Sibella uncannily foretells Viola's fate, since she senses the depth of religious feeling that renders impossible Viola's contravention of Mrs Sedley's beliefs.[17] Unlike Sibella, Viola cannot accept that the teaching of the Church, and the adherence to its creed by generations of women, can be entirely wrong. Instead, she attempts to survive her unhappiness by conflating her pains with those of the saints and martyrs of Christian mysticism, implementing the principles of submission taught to her by her mother. Viola never manages to fully reconcile religion with her desire for personal happiness, and the plot resolves this conflict with her death. Ultimately, and radically, Caird shows that self-sacrifice is not only pointless but also unhelpful to each new generation of women who follow in the footsteps of their antecedents. However, despite her suggestion that women must break the cycle of internalised self-criticism, Caird likewise represents the futility of any attempt to do so. Although comparatively free, Mrs Lincoln is a social pariah, unwelcome and disapproved of, and Viola commits both murder and suicide. Caird proposes no plan for combining religious feeling with feminine empowerment, suggesting the incompatibility of the two and denying her heroine the positive powers associated with faith.

The irreconcilability of duty and self-fulfilment in Christian marriage is also explored in Caird's most well-known and controversial novel *The Daughters of Danaus*. Appropriately named after the Greek myth of fifty sisters forced to carry water through sieves for eternity as punishment for their rebellion, the text is concerned with the similarly futile experience of trapped female genius.[18] As in *The Wing of Azrael*, Caird fictionalises the sacrificial woman, in a critique of the bourgeois family as the locus of patriarchal control over the female body. Caird's novels attempt to rewrite Western mythologies 'in order to dismantle the foundation stories which defined women as objects of exchange [. . .], willing martyrs [. . .], and bodies for slaughter' (Heilmann 2004: 158). By aligning classical mythologies with nineteenth-century Christian moral directives, Caird puts religiously motivated self-sacrifice at the centre of her critique of nineteenth-century society.

Featuring two New Woman heroines, *The Daughters of Danaus* closely examines the relationship between individualism and free will, the incompatible claims of family and self, and the damage resulting from conflict between these oppositions. Algitha Fullerton is a comparatively successful example of the New Woman – strong-willed and independent, she leaves her family home and refuses to marry, preferring to work than be dependent on her father or any future husband. Algitha is eventually rewarded for her brave yet socially transgressive actions with a happy marriage and professional success. Her younger sister Hadria is the embryonic New Woman – robust, adventurous, politically aware, intellectual and talented – and her poor opinion of marriage and its restriction of female potential establishes her as an advanced heroine. Conspired against by the social system and contrary to her own best judgement, Hadria is coerced into marrying and beginning a family, slowly eradicating her musical talent under the weight of household concerns and maternal obligation.

Caird's choice of name for her central heroine immediately establishes her as a Scottish rebel figure, aligning her with the Emperor

Hadrian, who marked the limit of the Roman Empire with the construction of his wall. Since Caird's text concerns an unhappy marriage between a controlling Englishman and a wild and spirited Scot, her heroine's name can be read as symbolising the metaphorical walls she both demolishes and constructs, as well as the relationship between the conquering colonial force and his conquered subject. The English Hubert Temperley, along with his sister, lays siege to Hadria, using a range of persuasive methods to capture her as his wife. Despite the walls she constructs to resist their advances, Hadria is eventually conquered and made to give up her music, a talent connected directly to her sense of Celtic identity and the landscape that encodes her (initially) untameable nature. This loss of identity through marriage is associated with the historic invasion and colonisation of Scottish lands, and with the loss of cultural heritage associated with the imperialism of Caird's own century.[19]

In an analysis of the Emersonian optimism naively proffered by her brother Ernest, Hadria argues that women's ability to overcome developmental restrictions has yet to be tested, since any deviation from tradition signals the destruction of women's powers. She explains that 'Obstacles may be of a kind to stimulate one person and to annihilate another' (Caird 1894: 6). Hadria laments the futility of the lives of women whose talents and individuality of character have been surrendered because of such obstacles. She explains that 'pale hypotheses, nameless peradventures [. . .] lie in forgotten churchyards – unthought of, unthanked, untrumpeted, and all their tragedy is lost in the everlasting silence' (1894: 8). The closing sentences of George Eliot's *Middlemarch* praise the goodness of Dorothea Brooke, whose talent and potential are never fully realised, one of many women 'who lived a faithfully hidden life, and rest in unvisited tombs' (Eliot 2008a: 688). Caird paraphrases this final line in a critique of Eliot's politics of female renunciation, yet despite clear censure of Eliot's sacrificial heroine, Caird's Hadria Fullerton is to meet a much worse fate. Manipulated into marrying unhappily, Hadria contravenes social expectations and leaves her husband and children for a satisfying creative life in Paris. However, she is forced by her sense of familial duty to return to him when her parents are left destitute and her mother develops a nervous illness. Forced into a life she despises, Hadria increasingly imagines her sufferings as forms of martyrdom.

Both Fullerton sisters deploy the language of religious sacrifice in conflicting ways, demonstrating the opposing experiences and viewpoints of a healthy and independent, fully realised New Woman and, contrastingly, a morbid, self-destructive sacrificial woman made prematurely Old. Hadria's failed attempts at self-determination are figured within the rhetoric of Christian mortification, emphasising Caird's clear critique of Christianity as a hypocritical and counter-productive social force. The acknowledgement of the necessity of female sacrifice is expressed by Algitha at the outset of the text, who explains that 'if one is unjustly restrained [. . .] it is perfectly right to brave the infliction of pain' (Caird 1894: 9). However, Algitha refers not to the endurance of one's own pain in the pursuit of noble aims, but the pain of others that naturally occurs as a by-product of social deviance. While Algitha is to reconcile herself to the pain she causes her parents by her unconventional step, Hadria is positioned to repeatedly suffer self-inflicted pains as the remaining daughter upon whom the Fullertons place their hopes.

Hadria envisions the pain of others in strict relation to her own body, in an image of corporeal interconnectedness based on Darwinian models of organic interdependence but also on vivisection, a topic of debate in which several New Woman writers were engaged.[20] Of women's inability to develop professional or artistic lives outside the boundaries of marriage and motherhood, Hadria explains:

> she has to tear through so many living ties that restrain her freedom [. . .] to have to buy the mere right to one's liberty by cutting through prejudices that are twined with the very heart-strings of those one loves! Ah that particular obstacle has held many a woman helpless and suffering, like some wretched insect pinned alive to a board throughout a miserable lifetime. (Caird 1894: 9–10)

In describing women's inability to disconnect from the double bind of domestic and public duty, Hadria imagines social tradition as a bodily system that relies upon connections of flesh and blood. In attempting to free herself from this system, a woman must metaphorically cut through those sinews; she must wound herself as well as the bodies of all those that make up the wider organism of the family and the body politic. The alternative is to suffer by different, yet potentially more destructive means, as the victim of torture pinned alive by tradition. The reference to an insect tortured alive and pinned to a rack is both etymological and distinctly Christian. While it is suggestive of scientific advancement through dissection and study, Caird devalues any intellectual gains made through vivisection. Instead, she evokes violent images of martyrdom from the

Middle Ages during which Christians were forced to renounce their beliefs or die slowly and painfully, often by crucifixion.[21] Offering the example of Mrs Fullerton, whose intellectual potential has been thwarted by her own marriage, Caird demonstrates the effects of slow physical torture. Mrs Fullerton's wasted gifts have no outlet, and consequently her mental and physical health decline, culminating in a terminal illness towards the end of the novel. In centralising the wounded and tortured body as an emblem of nineteenth-century female sacrifice, Caird establishes a progressive and pervasive subtext of martyrdom throughout her novel, undermining the temporary gains made by sacrificial women but also hyperbolising, and thus potentially limiting, the impact of her message.

Before her removal to Paris and eventual return, Hadria refuses to be made to commit any act of self-renunciation or self-harm, explaining:

> They must take the trouble to provide the instruments of death from without; they must lay siege and starve me; they must attack in soldierly fashion; I will not save them the exertion by developing the means of destruction from within. There I stand at bay. They shall knock down the citadel of my mind and will, stone by stone. (Caird 1894: 152)

Again, Hadria expresses her determination as an act of both saint-like perseverance and bodily sacrifice. Although she acknowledges that she may be defeated by the weight of centuries of tradition, she is (at this stage in the novel) unwilling to sacrifice herself without a fight. Describing the passivity of women in their acceptance of masculine rule, Hadria uses similar language, describing how the submissive woman

> goes to the stake smiling. She swears the flames are comfortably warm, no more [. . .] She smiles encouragement to the other chained figures, at the other stakes. Her reward? The sense of exalted worth, of humility; the belief that she has been sublimely virtuous [. . .] She has done her duty, and sent half a dozen souls to hell! (Caird 1894: 213)

Caird recalls the image of a female martyr who had reached the status of canonised saint and folk heroine by the nineteenth century. Joan of Arc was put on trial for charges of 'insubordination and heterodoxy' (Warner 2013: 5) following her leadership of the French army to a number of victories and her capture by pro-English forces. Fresh interest in her execution for heresy by burning at the stake was awoken during the nineteenth century, when transcripts of the trial of Joan of Arc were released to the French public.[22] The transcripts revealed that Joan was not only exceptional in her position as a female leader and military strategist, but also capable of confounding her male inquisitors with her clever responses.

Like the Catholic Saint Joan, Hadria Fullerton is an exceptional young woman, and despite her impatience with women's submission she clearly identifies with the subversive components of martyrdom. As Casey Cothran suggests, Hadria deploys violent imagery of bodily damage in order to subvert patriarchy and realise 'self-actualization' (2009: 68). The death of Joan of Arc is satirically reimagined by Hadria, who, while drawing a parallel between herself and other female martyrs, recognises the long-term futility of female submission to masculine law. Ironically, society is saved the exertion of destroying Hadria, because when she is forced to return home she lays siege to her own body and starves herself, harming herself through guilt and self-incrimination. It is Hadria who (metaphorically) joins the martyred women at the stake, and damns the souls of others, by her renunciation of her happiness for the betterment of family and society.

Eventually Hadria 'commenc[es] the attack on herself' (Caird 1894: 259) following the announcement of her mother's illness and her father's financial ruin, and she imagines this attack in religiously determined language. She describes 'the injury from without, and then the self-injury, its direct offspring; unnecessary yet inevitable' (1894: 264), and Caird draws on Greek mythology when her narrator explains that

> [i]t was as inevitable as that the doom of Orestes should follow the original crime of the house of Atreus. Hadria's whole thought and strength were now centred on the effort to bring about that propitiation, in her own person. She prepared the altar and sharpened the knife. In that subtle and ironical fashion, her fate was steadily at work. (Caird 1894: 264)

Paralleling her heroine's suffering with a classical myth of matricide and familial blood sacrifice, as well as pagan ritualism, and using language also associated with Christian worship (such as 'altar'), Caird situates Hadria's act of self-renunciation as owing in part to her sense of responsibility for her mother's illness.[23] Hadria's sacrifice is rendered as an act of martyrdom in the pose of Iphigenia, murdered by her father in the interests of the wider family, their health and prosperity. Like Iphigenia's, Hadria's body is sacrificed for her family's well-being as she nurses her mother, committing all her energy and time to the sickroom and severely neglecting both her music and her health.

Faced with a lifetime of sacrifice, Hadria muses that 'cutting one's throat would be the only way out' (Caird 1894: 299) yet she does not do so. Rather, she continues to critique female martyrdom despite her own continual recourse to acts of self-sacrifice, explaining that 'self-sacrifice in a woman, is always her easiest course. It is the nearest approach to luxury that society allows her [. . .] A woman will endure martyrdom with the expression of a seraph' (1894: 340). Caird's use of irony is clear here, in that Hadria's own martyrdom aligns her with women for whom she has no sympathy, who smile and gain favour by their own self-denial. Hadria's disapproval is centred upon the public nature of women's self-sacrificial activities, the display of their Christian 'goodness' as part of an economy of nineteenth-century bodily exchange. This economy, the display of broken bodies 'like badges of identity or fashion accessories', however distasteful to Caird's heroine, is one in which Caird herself participates through her writing. Heilmann has argued that Caird's use of mythological rewriting works to downplay patriarchal strategies to 'dampen insurgent spirits by hyperbolising the ghastly punishments meted out to the revolting daughter' (2004: 158). However, in many ways it is the spectacular overemphasis of women's self-punitive responses to nineteenth-century phallocentricism on which Caird's message depends. Her martyred heroines are indeed needlessly sacrificed, their bodies broken by the demands of family life, yet even Caird's happier female characters also fail to escape seemingly tortuous social imperatives.

In displaying the bodies of sacrificial women in religiously framed narratives of self-harm, Caird attacks the system that requires such dangerous concessions, yet also promulgates the spectacularisation of the damaged body as a cultural and economic commodity. Cothran observes that Hadria's bodily sacrifice works as a form of protest that 'bring[s] to fruition new paths for other women' (2009: 64) by drawing attention to the bodily pain and endurance sanctioned and demanded by an unfair society. However, while Cothran explores how Hadria can be seen to 'visibly dramatize her suffering' in order to encourage others to 're-envision the roles of all women in late Victorian culture' (2009: 64), I would argue that this tactic fails within the economy of the novel. While Hadria's suffering elicits sympathy from those around her, her experiences are kept hidden within the family and the narrow social sphere in which Hadria operates.

Unlike the heroines of many other New Woman texts, Hadria does not transform her experiences into productive strategies that publicise the problem of women's position, such as public speaking or authorship. According to Sally Ledger, Caird 'takes on the dominant discourse and is finally defeated by it' and is, on occasion, 'radically limited' (1997: 28–9) when critiquing such discourses only through their own language and structures. Caird's strategic exploitation of late-century wound culture, of the 'excitations in the opening of private and bodily and psychic interiors' (Seltzer 1998: 253) that underpin her stories of self-abnegation, at times not only implicates her in the very system she sets out to condemn, but also minimises the revolutionary potential and precautionary value of her texts.

Eroticised Sacrifice and Gender-Bending in Victoria Cross's *The Woman Who Didn't* and *Anna Lombard*

More sensational even than Caird's writings was the work of Victoria Cross, who published more than twenty novellas and several volumes of short stories across a four-decade-long career. Her early works, including a satirical response to Grant Allen's *The Woman Who Did* (1894) entitled *The Woman Who Didn't*, reveal Cross as a major contributor to the New Woman oeuvre. Cross contributed to Henry Harland's infamous *The Yellow Book* in 1895 and published her shockingly seditious novella *Anna Lombard* in 1901. The novel was a huge success, was considered morally objectionable by an indignant reading public, and is the only one of Cross's many novels to remain in print today.[24] As Gail Cunningham notes in her introduction to the most recent edition of *Anna Lombard*, remarkably little is known about the author's personal life, since she distanced herself from late-Victorian literary circles as well as public politics (2006: vii). Cross's real name was Anna Sophie Cory, although she published under a variety of gender-ambiguous monikers including V. C. Griffin and Cory Griffin. Her regular pseudonym references both the female monarch and the Victoria Cross medal – the highest award given for acts of British (masculine) military valour – and hints at the subversion of gender stereotypes that feature in her work.

Cross spent most of her life abroad, and despite being educated in England travelled extensively in Europe and grew up in what was then British India. Her marginality, both as a female writer of sexually 'explicit' stories and as writing for a British readership from India, accounts in part for the fact that so much of her work has been lost or forgotten. Cross defied the strict expectations of her gender, representing cross-cultural and gender-bending sexual encounters in her fiction, but she also wrote back to the imperial centre from a perspective of cultural hybridity that gave her writing an exotic and distinctly non-English flavour. The male narrators of both *The Woman Who Didn't* and *Anna Lombard* are Englishmen working in India, and both are involved with the British military. Both texts dramatise (albeit very differently) extramarital relationships, referencing martyrdom in discussion of both the male and the female protagonists. In both cases, Cross sets most of the action of the plot outside of the reach of the British homeland, exploring both the innate freedoms of colonialism and the restrictive morality of English life.

The Woman Who Didn't explores the relationship between a male narrator, known only as Evelyn, and his ideal woman Eurydice Williamson.[25] The two meet on board an Egyptian steamer travelling from India to England, find they are two halves of a perfect whole, and fall deeply in love, only for the hero to learn that his heroine is already married to a philandering husband. The novel questions whether the dissolution of a marriage through divorce or abandonment, even when socially justifiable, can be morally right. Ultimately, while Evelyn reconciles himself to a step that he views as akin to fraud and theft, Eurydice's firm belief in the sanctity of marriage stops her from embarking on an affair that would secure her happiness. Unlike Grant Allen's heroine Herminia Barton, who chooses to live in a free union and conceives an illegitimate child, Eurydice decides not to act on her desires; Herminia commits suicide, but Eurydice lives and suffers. Like several of the texts I examine in subsequent chapters, the heroine's strength of character and internalisation of Christian teachings prevent her from committing a grave sin. However, unlike in the work of social purity novelists like Sarah Grand, who warned against the consequences of sexual transgression and rewarded her heroines for refusing their fleshly desires, both of Cross's characters are left miserable. While Eurydice asserts the angelic self-denial of a martyr and finds minor consolation in her abstinence, she fails to find earthly reward, and the male narrator's eroticisation of her suffering intimates the problems inherent in women's adoption of such postures.

Evelyn imagines his heartache as torture, describing Eurydice's initially perfunctory attitude towards his attentions as 'sabres unsheathed, knives in the sunlight, and fires burnt blue' (Cross 1895: 12), and his devotion to her as 'the rack to which I was bound' (1895: 41). Like Caird's Hadria, Cross's protagonist envisions his

pains as torture, explaining that he is a 'passive and suffering martyr' (1895: 48). However, Cross's treatment of Evelyn's complaints
is ironic, since his tortures are of his own making, and pale in comparison to those of the heroine. Following their separation, Eurydice
bravely bears the burdens of her vanquished hopes, admirably obey-
ing her duty to her husband while remaining true to the memory of
her unfulfilled love. Meanwhile, Evelyn spends six months in Paris
acquiring as many carnal pleasures as possible, describing the guilt
of such bodily desecrations as 'hosts and legions of uncomfortable
thoughts' that 'came in squadrons [. . .] continually supplemented
by detachments of recollections' (1895: 49). Picturing his torment as
that of an invading legion, Evelyn's reference to the Roman torture
of Christian martyrs is extended, yet the reader is left suspicious of
his melodramatic response to his own dissipation, inconstancy and
male indulgence.

Evelyn's most significant use of the martyr image is in his conceptualisation of his heroic lover, whose laughter incites his desire:

> That laugh of hers, full of bravely repressed and hidden pain, and ring-
> ing with mockery and cynical philosophy, stirred and roused my admira-
> tion. She was of the material of which martyrs are made. An untamable,
> unbreakable spirit, that laughed in the face of Fate and mocked its own
> pain, fired the blood in those smooth veins. (Cross 1895: 44)

> She looked at me, with the familiar mocking laughter on her brilliant
> face, which was her mask for everything. I had seen it drawn down over
> pain, weariness, and despair, and she would meet the fear and horror of
> death with that same careless smile. (Cross 1895: 54)

Eurydice's laugh, a gesture encoding both resilience and despair,
evokes admiration but also desire in Evelyn. He is both 'stirred' and
'roused' by the mask she deploys, and such arousal is supplemented
as he overwrites her sufferings with his own fantasies of female heroism and self-sacrifice. His assertion that she would meet death with a
'careless smile' evokes Caird's critique of the woman who goes to the
stake smiling in *The Daughters of Danaus*, published a year previously. The metaphor is extended when, after a period of separation,
Evelyn embarks on a friendship with Eurydice, who fights against
her love for him to stay pure, and thus

> the pallor and dense fatigue had fallen like a mask from her face. The
> power and force of intellect seemed set upon her brow, looking out of

her eyes, playing like sudden light all over the transfigured countenance. Opposite me, in this hum-drum drawing-room, against the white curtains, looked back at me a face gleaming with rapt enthusiasm, as a martyr's and saint's may have looked up from the stake to heaven, or across the flare of the kindling faggots. (Cross 1895: 67)

Not only is Cross's heroine intelligent and powerful, but, in her martyrdom, she is the image of the inviolate Saint Joan staring unconquered from the pyre as she burns alive. The juxtaposition between the humdrum living-room and the heroic scene foregrounds the banality of the everyday self-sacrifice endured by women, and suggests the pointlessness of this tradition. However, Cross narrates female sacrifice through the eyes of a male narrator whose reverence is conflated with sexual excitement. In doing so, she condemns patriarchy, lampooning the weakness of the male sex, and subtly destabilising Evelyn's authority by exposing the eroticism implied by his reading of the suffering female body. Cross valorises self-sacrifice in Eurydice, who is a far more likeable character than her narrator, yet also leaves her trapped in an unhappy marriage. In offering her heroine no chance of escape, Cross critiques Victorian social and moral norms but, like Grant Allen before her, suggests no workable trajectory for women's emancipation.

Six years later, Cross developed the metaphors of self-sacrifice she had included in *The Woman Who Didn't* to more dramatic and subversive effect. Like her short story 'Theodora: A Fragment' (1895), *Anna Lombard* explores the erotic potential of relationships that blur the boundaries between class, race and gender.[26] The novella follows the romantic aspirations of Gerald Ethridge, a British Assistant Commissioner in India, who falls in love with the eponymous heroine, only to be sent away to a remote corner of the country before admitting his feelings to her. Despite her romantic love for Gerald, who has seemingly deserted her, the English Anna embarks on an interracial relationship with an Indian servant working in her father's house. When Gerald unexpectedly returns and proposes to Anna, she informs him of the intense sexual and emotional bond she has formed with Gaida Khan, and Gerald selflessly agrees to become engaged to her until she is strong enough to end her other relationship. Eventually, Gaida dies during an outbreak of cholera, and when Anna finds she is pregnant with Gaida's child, Gerald agrees to marry her to cover up her indiscretion. The text culminates in infanticide, when Anna smothers her mixed-race child, since her love for it threatens to alienate the man to whom she owes so much.

In *Anna Lombard*, Cross undertakes to address a number of modern social issues, making the argument for a new type of masculinity to respond to an emerging New femininity at the *fin de siècle*. Anna is strong, intellectual, sexually liberated and unfettered by conventions of race and class, or by traditional moral scruples. Conversely, Gerald is patient, kind, passive and submissive, loyal and devoted – an angel in the house and the personification of Victorian domestic perfection. Characterised as Christ-like, Gerald represents a highly feminised masculine ideal, whose womanly qualities allow him to assume the self-flagellative role usually reserved for the typical Victorian heroine, turning New Woman novelistic convention on its head. In this text it is not the socially transgressive, suffering New Woman heroine who must bear the trials and sacrifices forced upon her by convention. Instead, the sorrows of the painfully traditional male narrator are imagined in the language of Christian sacrifice, in a novel that is otherwise entirely secular. Other than references to martyrdom and self-sacrifice, little mention is made of Christianity in *Anna Lombard*, and the images I discuss, like those in Caird's novels, are often conflated with Greek or pagan mythologies. Cross deploys the transgressive aesthetic devices of literary Decadence, combining Hellenism with Victorian Christianity in her exploration of non-normative gender and sexuality.

At the outset of the text Gerald responds to a friend's lamentation on British women's poor physicality when he asks 'and what about the girls? Are the men made to suit them?' (Cross 2006: 5). The comment encapsulates Cross's challenge to what was seen as a crisis in nineteenth-century masculinity catalysed by the evolution of the New Woman. Cross's work unashamedly subverts gender stereotypes, and attempts to imagine what will be required of the New Man once women are political, economic and social equals. She adopts similar rhetoric to that used to describe Eurydice's 'martyrdom' in *The Woman Who Didn't*, but instead martyrs the body of her male narrator. However, despite her reversal of the gender dichotomies which reinforced Victorian moral and religious values, Cross's feminisation of Gerald relies entirely upon the same inflexible and reductive binaries. In her use of religious images of self-harm, Cross sacrifices the body of the male-narrator-as-female-martyr, but in doing so she commits to traditional and well-established discourses on the need for feminine self-sacrifice, simultaneously blurring the boundaries between martyrdom and masochistic pleasure.

We are told by Ethridge himself that he is 'usually considered good looking, [his] features were straight and perfectly regular, the skin pale and clear, the eyes large' (Cross 2006: 12). Although Anna expresses her admiration for Gerald's 'beautiful face and those beautiful eyebrows' (2006: 55), he does not supply further description of himself beyond these strikingly feminine facial characteristics and his height of six feet. Gerald is conspicuously disembodied, a man whose sexual desires are sublimated to his emotional need to belong to the woman he loves. When Anna offers Gerald her 'soul and heart and brain', he rejects them as 'hardly enough for me' (2006: 54) – yet these are all Gerald is to have of Anna, because she continues to be sexually satisfied elsewhere. Contrastingly, the exotic body of Gaida Khan is central; his sheer physicality is overwhelming to Anna, who describes his 'wonderful neck' (2006: 56), and to Gerald, who envisions him as 'a king' (2006: 64). Gaida's raw, physical masculinity unnerves Gerald, who feels insubstantial by comparison, since Gaida 'was of great height, and his form evidently, from his motions, as perfect as the perfect face', understanding that '[a] woman whose eyes had been once opened [to his body] would never be free' (2006: 64). While Cross's narrator devotes several paragraphs to describing the native's body, about his own he is largely silent. Gaida is 'almost superhuman' with 'perfectly straight features', is 'statuesquely beautiful' and a 'marvel of humanity' (2006: 65), yet Gerald's masculinity is subject to a narrative fissure. Gaida, related to the ancient Greeks by way of his Pathan genealogy (Brittain 2001: 81), is a Hellenic God, and his Apollonian body bestirs erotic (and homoerotic) desire, while Gerald's body is simply missing. In failing to narrativise Gerald's body and focusing only on his face, Cross feminises Gerald, contrasting the forbidden body of the native with the sexual ineffectiveness of the pale English gentleman hero.

Of Anna we are told much more. According to Gerald she is incongruous with the century in which she lives, and her divergence in thought and her bravery of action are affiliated with ancient acts of heroism. Upon hearing her name for the first time Gerald explains that 'it sounds somehow to me medieval, a middle-age sort of name' (Cross 2006: 6), and later he expands:

> her character and mind belonged rather to a more stirring time, when personal courage was at a premium [. . .] she said things and expressed opinions that gave me a faint, peculiar sense of her extreme independence and of something wonderfully strong in her character – something large, larger than the nature of most women, something also extremely courageous, that called for a heroic age to find its natural exercise. Amongst the other things I had studied, the history of the Middle Ages

had always possessed a great fascination for me, and now I was suddenly drawn again towards it by the girl I loved, and by the peculiar timbre of her nature that seemed familiar to me and came to me as an echo from the past. (Cross 2006: 41)

Like Evelyn in *The Woman Who Didn't*, Gerald idealises his fault-less woman as brave and virtuous, identifying in her the courage of conviction demonstrated by the martyrs of the Middle Ages. Like Caird, Cross represents her heroine as a Joan of Arc figure, an unruly woman condemned for her refusal to adhere to strict gender codes. Anna is viewed not only as a suffering martyr, but also as the epitome of chivalric virtues aspired to by the knights of Arthurian legend. The language Cross uses in relation to her heroine is grandiose: her independence is 'extreme', she is 'wonderfully strong', 'courageous' and 'heroic', and although these are qualities associated with classical masculine heroism, Gerald finds them sexually appealing. Reversing the traditional roles played in courtly romance, Anna represents the knight who in adherence to the rules of courtly love finds himself in love with more than one lady. Meanwhile, Gerald assumes the role of an obedient and honourable romance heroine ready to stand by his lover and face any challenge, despite her wavering commitment to him.[27]

Any comparison with Joan of Arc is unconvincing and short-lived in Cross's text, since, unlike the chaste heroine of French legend, Anna's body is corrupted by her relationship with Gaida, who fathers her illegitimate, mixed-race child.[28] As Melissa Purdue notes, Anna's eventual infanticide restores racial boundaries by eliminating a potential threat to British eugenic purity, yet it also disrupts gender expectations (2012: 131), satirising fears about women who refuted maternity as their natural state. Similarly, when Anna is cast by Gerald as Caterina Sforza in a game of *tableaux vivants*, the text signals that she is not to be read as a typical female martyr. Since Sforza's murder of numerous men, women and children was motivated by the secular concerns of protecting her property and land, Cross's rendering of Anna in this way connotes a lack of Christian morality in her heroine. Gerald's choice of *tableau vivant* indicates his unconscious acknowledgement of Anna's potential for moral ambiguity, and her success in the role further hints at her impending social and sexual misconduct. While Anna is thus depicted less as a martyr figure and more as a femme fatale, Gerald becomes increasingly feminised by his Christ-like sufferings, during which he assumes the role of a martyred heroine much more convincingly than Cross's central female character.

When Anna confesses to her relationship with Gaida, Gerald is 'wounded, sore and cut to the quick' yet his voice 'was tender instead of stern' (Cross 2006: 54), and when Anna repents her actions yet refuses to stop, Gerald describes how 'the touch of her hands seemed to burn into my flesh' (2006: 55). Despite the physical pain Anna inflicts, Gerald commits to endure it, offering his body up to sacrifice in a variety of self-flagellative postures that ensure his emotional survival 'whatever [his] pain and suffering and ultimate reward' (2006: 9). Although Gerald imagines his sacrifice as Christian martyrdom and expects the resultant spiritual reward, his submission is also decidedly erotic and, indeed, masochistic. Having decided to endure the pains of Anna's continuing relationship with Gaida, Gerald reasons that

> I knew not one pang of mine, not the smallest sacrifice would pass unnoticed and unweighed, or fail to bring me more than five times its value in gratitude and love. What hardship is there in serving such a mistress? To me none. There are instances recorded, or at least supposed to exist, when men have poured out a life-long devotion at the feet of some senseless idol that cared little for them, nothing for their suffering, and laughed at their love. Such self-abnegation seems to me degradation, and can only exist where the worshipper is as worthless as the idol. But for Anna I would give up my life as cheerfully as men in all ages have died for their gods, while and because they believed in them. (Cross 2006: 59)

Cross conflates Christian notions of earthly, bodily sacrifice for spiritual, emotional compensation with the desire inherent in a relationship of submission to a female object of masculine desire. The use of terms such as 'serving' and 'mistress' implies Cross's recognition of the masochistic drives at play here, even if only on Gerald's part. A reading of the relationship between Anna, Gerald and Gaida as masochistic is invited by a scene in which Anna forces Gerald to watch her interactions with Gaida from behind a screen, where

> a figure came into the room [. . .] I sat motionless, hardly breathing, in my chair in the shadow. This, then, was Gaida Khan [. . .] It is difficult in the slow, cold words that follow each other on paper to convey any idea of the glory of beauty that the hand of God has set upon this race. The face was of the Greek type in the absolute oval of its contour, and the perfectly straight features, the high nose, [. . .] the short curling upper lip, and the full rounded chin [. . .] I sat paralysed and gazing at him, feeling crushed and without hope. (Cross 2006: 65)

Witness to his extreme physical beauty, Gerald is emasculated by the godlike Gaida, in Cross's reinterpretation of the final masochistic tableau of Leopold von Sacher-Masoch's *Venus in Furs* (1870). Written in German but widely read in European literary circles, Sacher-Masoch's sensational text features a masochistic contract between the dominant Wanda von Dunajew and her submissive lover Severin von Kusiemski. In a scene of sexual humiliation, Wanda invites the Apollonian Alexis Papadopolis into her bedroom, forcing Severin to watch them together and to suffer punishment at the hands of her corporeally superior lover.

Papadopolis (referred to, like Gaida, as Greek) is very beautiful. He is an image of hyper-masculine perfection and 'a magnificent specimen of a man' through whom Severin is made to 'understand the masculine Eros' (Sacher-Masoch 2006: 66) just as Gerald understands the allure of Gaida's body. In a text that consciously flouts 'the kind of love which is preached by Christianity' (Sacher-Masoch 2006: 11) and eulogises paganism and Hellenism, the wounded narrator eventually finds his ideals lacking, and his body subject to Christ-like tortures. Gerald's obsessive pursuit of Anna, despite her sexual preference for Gaida, dramatises an emasculating power imbalance, similar to that of *Venus in Furs*. The relationship, which ultimately sees a saintly and suffering Gerald physically and emotionally wounded, depicts him as impotent and broken. Though I do not necessarily read Gerald as homosexual, the reversal of the male gaze, the subversion of the gendered binaries of watched female and watching male, and the homoeroticism that marks this scene work to supplement Gerald's narrative feminisation and sexual ambiguity.

When Gaida is struck by cholera and Anna is left to pray for his recovery, Gerald sees his opportunity to be free of his rival, yet does not take it. Instead, Gerald nurses Gaida, undertaking a role conventionally reserved for women in Christian tradition, instantly maternalising him. According to Simon Richter, the acts of motherly care undertaken by Christ – the washing of feet, the nursing of the sick – situate him as a maternal figure in Christian art and culture, imagery that is arguably at work in Cross's text (Richter 1992: 133). The homosocial relations between men, which ratified nineteenth-century patriarchal power, what Eve Kosofsky Sedgwick describes as 'friendship, mentorship, admiring identification, bureaucratic subordination and heterosexual rivalry' (1990: 186), also forced men on to sexually and socially ambiguous ground, undermining masculinity. Though Gerald's heterosexual desire for Anna is made clear,

Cross's treatment of Gerald gazing upon his male rival suggests a sense of sexual ambiguity and 'homosexual panic' (Sedgwick 1990: 186). This, in turn, undermines and confuses Gerald's subjectivity and increasingly signifies his role as a passive, watched object with little control over the scopic dynamics of the relationship. Unlike Anna, who watches both Gaida, in all his masculine splendour, and Gerald watching Gaida, Gerald assumes the position of the observed, despite his own observational function.

As Gerald's desire for Anna continues to be confounded by her inability to break with Gaida, he commits acts of increasingly violent self-harm. Gerald describes how he sits 'with teeth set and [his] nails sunk deep into the palms of [his] hands' in 'terrible nights of desperate pain', unable to eat because 'the excitement in which [he] lived seemed to close [his] throat against it' (Cross 2006: 73). Gerald's pains begin to manifest, metaphorically and literally, as the wounds of Christ, as he tells how '[he] carried a wound, a raw terrible wound in [his] breast' (2006: 78) and 'pain at [his] wrists and ankles' (2006: 81), and later 'a wound that [he] could not recover from, since the wound must [. . .] remain open and bleeding sore' (2006: 113). He begins to suffer from nightmares in which his wrists and ankles are attacked and in which his persecutors 'came at them with red-hot saws' (2006: 81). Waking to find he has been bound to his bed in a tableau of crucifixion, Gerald finds his wrists are 'livid and swollen' (2006: 82). Gerald's 'stigmata' echo imagery from an earlier scene in the text, in which the adolescent snake charmer Lulloo, a colonial Eve figure, wears a crown of snakes, and twirls serpents around her ankles and wrists. Her spectacle of 'crucifixion' foretells her actual death by suicide, when she hangs herself because Gerald will not take her as his native 'wife', an act that further feminises Gerald since his male colleagues treat such refusals with distrust.

After the death of his rival, and on his wedding night to a now-pregnant Anna, Gerald reflects on the extent of his sacrifice, explaining that

> I, to whom she was as sacred now from the approach of passion as before she became my own and held my name, looked upon her and realised that in self-renunciation, self-abnegation, self-denial for another, lies the keenest, purest pleasure of humanity. This was my marriage night, and what had it brought me? No abandonment to personal pleasure, no sensual delight of any sort, no gratification of the desires or the senses [. . .] only self-repression and self-restraint, a total denial of physical will. Yet out of all this rose a supreme happiness [. . .] (Cross 2006: 115)

Cross carefully reverses the archetypal roles established by Victorian novelistic tradition, forcing her central male character into the guise of the patient and subservient heroine, while her female protagonist experiences sexual fulfilment without the threat of social derision or exposure. Taking recourse to the imagery of religious self-harm and martyrdom, Gerald frames his sacrifice as a worthy act; the self-denial of his sexuality and his physical sufferings are forms of sacred, divine and transcendental reward. In representing Gerald's renunciation of physical fulfilment as an affirmation of non-corporeal, spiritual elation, Cross undertakes to satirise women's strategies of self-sacrifice, showing the waste and ineffectiveness of a man who adopts the same approach. In doing so, she critiques gender binaries regardless of the direction on which they are crossed. Despite this, since Gerald Ethridge is revealed to be the true heroine of the story – his deep and unwavering love for the questionably heroic Anna his most admirable feature – it is difficult as a reader not to sympathise with his acts of self-denial. It is challenging, even as a twenty-first-century reader, not to judge Cross's strong-willed, independent and revolutionary New Woman heroine as a disappointingly selfish and cruel character with too few good qualities by which to redeem her.

Cross is clearly critical of the prohibition of Victorian women's sexual and social freedoms as well as the internalisation of religious doctrine. However, by at times lionising Gerald's selflessness, his saintly patience and forbearance, Cross's attempt to rewrite the religiously framed script of sacrifice enforced on women falls short. While attempting to envision a reversal of gender roles, Cross in fact implements the very same binarisms against which she appears to write – her novel is about a suffering heroine whose patience and self-denial bring spiritual if not actual reward. Her depiction of a strong female character, who challenges the established order and prevails, reworks the roles of coloniser and colonised, imbuing the bodies of the native and the woman with power usually reserved for the Englishman. However, in attempting to write against convention, Cross's novel merely relies upon the tried and tested dichotomies of angel and demon, saint and sinner, Mary and Eve, found in Victorian literature and visual culture.

Writers like Caird and Cross attempted to exploit the symbolism of martyrdom and suffering in fictional texts that capitalised on the generative and didactic potential of Christian allegory. At a time when the sensuality of self-abasement was appearing in popular

Christian iconography, yet Christ's example was beginning to lose its widespread appeal, the New Woman writer challenged the idealisation of self-abnegation. However, in doing so she also perpetuated a tradition in which the damaged body of the female martyr operated as a site of erotic spectacle and thus failed to escape fully the rhetorical limitations of patriarchy. In the chapters that follow, I show how religious dictates are internalised by female characters seeking either to replicate Christ's martyrdom or to punish themselves for their inability to do so. Rites of expiation which had for centuries been controlled by male-dominated religion began to be exploited by women at a time when the influence of faith was beginning to wane, but its powerful cultural ideologies prevailed. This exploitation, however, failed to assert women's authority over their own discourse – since, as I will show, New Woman writers both reproduced male narrative traditions and committed acts of thematic self-sabotage in attempting to free themselves of those traditions. Practically speaking, in endeavouring to rid themselves of restrictive masculine modes of narration, many of the women writers discussed in the following three chapters wrote themselves out of the literary canon. Their work was disconcerting – it engaged with taboo themes that made the reading public uncomfortable, and despite some early successes, many of these stories have been lost to mainstream publishing. Writing from the doubly liminal position of both femininity and ambiguous national identity, all but one of these women writers were marginal in terms of cultural background. In this way, their self-harming literary practices correspond to an internalisation of unconventional gender and nationality that, in turn, reflected the double bind of their fictional engagement with Christianity.

To a greater or lesser extent, all the texts explored in the subsequent chapters engage with Christian iconography or are framed by the organising structures of Christianity. The self-destructive enterprises of self-starvation, excessive drinking and self-mutilation are depicted by New Woman writers as reactions to nineteenth-century masculine rule, but are often rhetorically formulated using the very philosophies of sacrifice against which they wrote. Whether directly referencing the limitations or appeal of Christ's example or more covertly undermining the authority of the Church, all the novels, poems and short stories that I discuss both denigrate and replicate self-sacrifice as a dangerous but useful strategy for feminine survival.

Notes

1. British India was particularly affected, with up to eight million deaths between 1900 and 1920. London was also hit by cholera; see Hempel 2007 for further.
2. See Farmer 2011 on various incarnations.
3. 'À une Madone' was published in 1861 in the extended edition.
4. Swinburne's *Poems and Ballads* (1866) provoked intense public criticism.
5. See Ephesians 5: 22–33 and 2 Corinthians 11: 2, in which Paul speaks of the Church as the bride of Christ.
6. Literary critics have noted that Swinburne's interest in self-harm (particularly masochism) is framed by both Christianity and Hellenism. See Richardson 1988: 29–32, Vincent 1997: 269–99, Maxwell 1997: 87–93 and Olverson 2009: 759–76.
7. See Stewart 2003 for discussion of the female gaze's disruption of gender boundaries.
8. See Horace Walpole's *The Castle of Otranto*, Lewis's *The Monk*, and, for an early-nineteenth-century example, John Polidori's *The Vampyre* (1819).
9. For example, the martyrdom of Saint Perpetua and Saint Felicitas in Carthage around 203 AD in *The Passion of Saint Perpetua, Saint Felicitas and their Companions* by Saturus. See R. Butler 2006 for a translation.
10. Burne-Jones painted *St Theophilus and the Angel* between 1863 and 1867, and again in 1868.
11. See Philip H. Calderon's *St Elizabeth of Hungary's Great Act of Renunciation* (1891) in which the female martyr is naked and bending to receive punishment at the hands of her confessor.
12. Rossetti and her brothers William Michael and Dante Gabriel were raised as High Anglicans but were all heavily influenced by the Catholicism of their father's native Italy.
13. See Waldman 2008 for discussion of the erotic undertones at work in Rossetti's poem.
14. John 1: 14 reads: 'And the Word was made flesh, and dwelt among us, (and we beheld his glory, the glory as of the only begotten of the Father,) full of grace and truth.'
15. Busst mentions this first in relation to Oskar Pfister's Freudian analysis of a painting by Ludwig von Zinzendorf (1967: 7). Irigaray notes the symbolic slippage between female genitalia and the wounds of crucifixion in *Speculum of the Other Woman* (1985: 199–200), retracting this idea in later work. See Hollywood 2004 for an examination of the sexual symbolism of the wounds of crucifixion.
16. In Sarah Grand's *The Heavenly Twins*, the submissive mothers Mrs Frayling and Mrs Beale are partly responsible for the respective fates

of their unhappy daughters. In Grand's *The Beth Book*, Mrs Caldwell submits to the will of her husband and later her brother, and ignores her husband's philandering.

17. 'Sybil' is from the Greek word meaning 'prophetess'. Her surname is also suggestive of the 'great emancipator' (Rosenberg 2010: xv), American president Abraham Lincoln.

18. In Greek mythology all but one of Danaus's fifty daughters murder their husbands and are condemned to filling a sieve with water for eternity. The only extant text in which the story features is *The Suppliants of Aeschylus* (c. 470 BC). See Walter 1987 for an English translation.

19. *The Daughters of Danaus* represents a sustained engagement with Scottish history from a New Woman perspective which, unfortunately, cannot be fully investigated within the remit of this study.

20. Caird was an active anti-vivisection campaigner, authoring *Beyond the Pale: An Appeal on Behalf of the Victims of Vivisection* (1897), and she depicts Philip Dendraith as unnecessarily cruel to animals. Fellow writers Sarah Grand and Vernon Lee were also active in campaigns against vivisection, and included negative portrayals of vivisectionists in their fictional works.

21. During the fifth century AD, Saint Aemilianus was flayed alive, Saint Benjamin was tortured by the insertion of sharp objects into his body, and Vigilius of Trent was stoned to death. The Romans routinely crucified Christians with nails. See Foxe 2009 for a Victorian account of martyred Christians.

22. Translated documents from the trial were made public in 1840 by Jules Quicherat (Heimann 2005). The first English translation was in 1932, although Caird was most likely aware of the contents in 1894.

23. See Aeschylus and Euripides for examples.

24. *Anna Lombard* sold six million copies and ran to forty editions worldwide (Dierkes-Thrun 2016: 206).

25. Eurydice was the wife of Orpheus in classical mythology, rescued from Hades by her devoted husband. The name is ironic given that her husband is unfaithful. Eurydice's married name, Williamson, juxtaposes her heroism against her husband's banality.

26. In 'Theodora' the male narrator is drawn to Theodora's sexual ambiguity, leading him to question his sexuality. The setting amongst Eastern artefacts links this desire to non-white, non-British exoticism.

27. The rules of courtly love are described in Andreas Capellanus's 'De Amore' (c. 1184–6).

28. The body of Joan of Arc is repeatedly conflated with Mary mother of Christ, both by contemporary and medieval art and literature and by the rehabilitation hearings (1450–6) during which Joan was absolved of heresy and praised as a French national heroine.

Chapter 2

Beyond the Fleshly Veil: Self-Starvation in the New Woman Novel

The Starving Victorian Body

Mid-Victorian women writers were confidently engaged in the use of self-destructive tropes, of which the most clearly identifiable was the starving heroine who featured frequently in popular fiction. Charlotte Brontë's Jane Eyre, Lucy Snowe, Shirley Keeldar and Caroline Helstone, Emily Brontë's Catherine Earnshaw, Charles Dickens's Little Dorritt and Nell Trent, and George Eliot's Mirah Lapidoth and Gwendolen Harleth are all significant fictionalisations of the starving female body in mid-Victorian literature. Attitudes towards the thin body began to change during the nineteenth century, which saw the rise of a new culture of dieting aimed at women and largely disseminated and controlled by men.[1] A variety of Victorian conduct manuals and periodicals were devoted to diet, and they stressed the importance of a slender waist by underscoring the cultural potency of the thin woman as an asset to the middle-class household. While predominantly written by women, these publications were edited and printed by men who controlled and influenced an aesthetic that valorised women who exercised self-control and disinterestedness in line with patriarchal objectives (Vigarello 2013: 197–8, Gilman 2008: 4–6).

Patmore's 'The Angel in the House' (1854) was one of the most popular poems of the mid-nineteenth century, and along with John Ruskin's idealisation of middle-class women in 'Of Queens' Gardens' (1865) had set the standard for femininity that persisted throughout the period.[2] The self-sacrificing angel-woman was embodied in popular fiction by characters like Amelia Sedley in Thackeray's *Vanity Fair* (1848), Esther Summerson in Dickens's *Bleak House* (1853), and Lucy Dean and Dorothea Brooke in Eliot's *The Mill on the Floss* (1860) and *Middlemarch* respectively, but also in periodicals aimed specifically at the middle-class housewife. *Mrs Beeton's Book of Household Management* (1861) gave diet advice, and both *The*

Englishwoman's Domestic Magazine (1852–78) and *The Woman at Home* (1893–1920) featured regular columns encouraging ladies to adhere to a plain and sparing diet.[3] Publications with such seemingly benign titles as *The Daughters of England* (1842) by Sarah Stickney Ellis and *The Art of Beautifying and Improving the Face and Figure* (1858) disparaged the greed, lack of control and domestic misman-agement implicit in eating large portions, and lauded the abstinence of the fasting woman (Silver 2002: 12).

Conversely, as scholars of Victorian print culture have shown, the overweight woman signified to the middle-class readership the moral as well as physical antithesis of the thin woman.[4] The dichotomy of virtuous slimness and immoral corpulence was class oriented, since for the working classes the well-covered body was a sign of health and affluence, while thinness signified sickness, poverty and even substance abuse. While positive examples of corpulent women appeared in Victorian culture – for instance Queen Victoria, and Peggoty from Dickens's *David Copperfield* (1850) – these were usu-ally maternal, desexualised figures: the nurse, the widow, the post-menopausal woman. In general, the woman who over-ate embodied a lack of control over her appetites that in turn threatened the suc-cess of her household, her family's social and economic prosperity, and ultimately the prosperity of the nation. The link between food and national identity was well established in the period, and notions of Englishness – and by implication colonial strength – were both reflected and distorted by Victorian fiction (Parsons 2014: 337–42, Cozzi 2010: 1–18). The female body was 'often depicted as a reposi-tory for ideology, the nation in miniature' and thus 'not only vulner-able, but edible' (Cozzi 2010: 16).

Tensions between the body as a representation of Britain's health, and the excessive and degenerate appetites that threatened its vigour, were played out across female bodies in Victorian literature. Body norms that had been relatively consistent throughout the preceding two centuries were subject to the shifting cultural values of a cen-tury in which advances in science, medicine, psychology and print culture were central to debates about the body politic. Towards the end of the nineteenth century, these shifts opened a space both cul-tural and narrative, within which New Woman writers could both explore the thin female body as a textual signifier and contradict negative representations of New Women in the periodical press. One such writer was Sarah Grand, who depicted thin, virtuous her-oines who starved themselves to protest against separate sphere ide-ology, or to demonstrate their intellectual and spiritual superiority. Other supposedly 'new' women writers depicted starving heroines;

Caird's Hadria Fullerton, Ella Hepworth Dixon's Mary Erle in *The Story of a Modern Woman* and Olive Schreiner's Lyndall in *The Story of an African Farm* (1883) are all described as thin at one time or another. However, this chapter primarily examines Grand's Morningquest trilogy (1888–97) – the most extensive dramatisation of self-starvation in the New Woman novel. Grand's trilogy responds both to the cultural climate of late-Victorian wound culture in which the eating disorder anorexia nervosa appeared, and to discourses situating the New Woman as deliberately unhealthy, unwomanly and threatening.

Throughout the latter half of the nineteenth century, definitions of the emerging disease of anorexia nervosa were developing alongside each other in a variety of Western medical contexts. Self-starvation was not a Victorian phenomenon but had been widely practised for centuries, most often in politico-religious and ascetic forms (Vandereycken and Van Deth 1994: 4). While evidence of food-refusing exists within the history of most cultures, it was the Victorian evolution in medical knowledge and authority that facilitated the emergence of a definable pathology in England, France and America during the 1870s (Brumberg 2000: 6). Coined by the British physician William Gull in 1873, *apepsia hysterica*, later to become anorexia nervosa, was defined by a set of symptoms still partly in use in twenty-first-century diagnosis and treatment.[5] Victorian doctors identified gender-specific symptoms that 'implied a moral or mental aberration rooted in the nervous system' (Brumberg 2000: 111).[6] Describing a patient who 'complained of no pain, but was restless and active', displaying 'peevishness of temper' and 'jealousy', Gull posits that 'it seemed hardly possible that a body so wasted could undergo the exercise which seemed agreeable' (Acland 1894: 307). His comments suggest that he considered the physical manifestations of anorexia as behavioural as much as psychological or physiological. Gull advocated a regime of control and regulation in which 'wilful patients' were placed under 'moral control' (Acland 1894: 311), corresponding to his reading of disobedience as detrimental to feminine well-being. Diagnosis and treatment were formed around the assumption that the female body required responsible management, and that nonconformity represented a challenge to health and vitality. Bound up with Gull's clear criticism of female unruliness was the notion that anorexia was, in part, the product of women's attempts to manage their own bodies.

For Ernest Charles Lasègue – whose research on anorexia was published in the *Archives générales de la médecine* (1873) and was more detailed than Gull's – the psychological workings of the condition were key to understanding its treatment. Lasègue, rather astutely, viewed anorexia as a strategy by which 'to avoid pain, which, although hypothetical, is dreaded in advance' (Vandereycken and Van Deth 1990: 904) and noted that anorexia appears in a young woman who 'suffers from some emotion which she avows or conceals' (1990: 904). However, as with Gull's account, Lasègue's observations framed the female anorectic through bourgeois imperatives, emphasising the 'moral element' (1990: 905) in treating anorexia. Lasègue's insistence on the language of morality demonstrates the extent to which his observations are imbued with naive assumptions about women in much the same way as Gull's.

The Victorian medical establishment did not connect women's food refusal to the ideology of self-sacrifice deeply rooted in Christian asceticism or in Christ's example, even if women did. Like the medieval martyrs or fasting saints, starving Victorian women attempted to assert control over their own bodies, and to rend them from the masculine forces that would master them. Doctors did not correlate the political motivations of religious ascetic practices with women's social or political demands; they understood self-starvation as the reverse of Christian ideals, as a selfish act. The insistence on the moral management of the female body highlights the medical scopic drive – the desire to know and possess the female body through acts of observation which constituted and reinforced masculine diegesis is identifiable in the clinical observation and narration of Victorian patients. Despite their efforts to help 'cure' the new disease of self-starvation, Gull and Lasègue failed to acknowledge the complex cultural factors at play in women's resistance to their own bodies.[7] Neither physician situated food refusal as part of a wider framework of self-harming behaviours that were exacerbated, rather than cured, by male intervention.

Masculine cultural discourse can be read through psychoanalysis as placing women at the centre of the castration complex, as the primary image of phallic lack, in other words a

> signifier for the male other, bound by a symbolic order in which man can live out his phantasies and obsessions through linguistic command by imposing them on the silent image of woman still tied to her place as bearer of meaning, not maker of meaning [. . .] In their traditional exhibitionist role women are simultaneously looked at and displayed, with their appearance coded for strong visual and erotic impact so that they can be said to connote to-be-looked-at-ness. (Mulvey 2010: 57)

The determining male gaze of the Victorian medical establishment, which interpreted the story of anorexia nervosa as the moral failure of selfish, petulant women, imposed fantasies of female submission and castigation upon the anorectic. The predominantly observational nature of the work carried out by Victorian doctors styled the female anorectic as the embodiment of feminine ideals of weakness and passivity exemplified by Patmore's fictional Angel and Ruskin's middle-class women, yet also as a threat to these ideals. Thus, Gull and Lasègue fail to emerge untainted by the implicit eroticism of their clinical work with young women. Their emphasis on the appraisal and moral judgement of the women in their care implicates both men in a system that exploited, degraded and devalued women's bodies as bearers of meaning, tied to their place and exempt from making meaning. This chapter examines the behaviours of fictional heroines who attempt to transgress the boundaries of their place in a masculine culture. These women, and the authors who wrote them into discourse, rejected the female body through self-starvation, attempting to make their own meaning in a culture that sought to make their bodies its semantic bearers.

Theorising Self-Starvation

The anorectic of the Victorian period was not subject to the same diagnostic frameworks as twenty-first-century patients, since such frameworks were formed by distinct socio-historic and cultural factors. For example, neither Gull nor Lasègue mentions body image, nor do they connect anorexia nervosa to the new Victorian culture of dieting, or the mass dissemination of media images and guides to weight management. Because of the impossibility of retrospectively applying a contemporary medical diagnosis to the literature of a period during which self-starvation was only beginning to take its place as a pathology, I use the term 'anorexia' cautiously in the readings that follow. There is no way to know how many Victorian women may have suffered from a disease that has become both widely recognised and extensively researched in our twenty-first-century context. While anorexia nervosa says much about the cultural values of contemporary society, these values have been, and continue to be, fluid and changeable, making it a difficult, and not always useful, terminology to apply.

Nineteenth-century conceptions of food refusal were in many ways different to those of the contemporary moment. However, the apparatus that operated to restrict, control and scrutinise the starving female body reflected those which New Woman writers sought to dismantle, and which remain in place even today, in the philosophical tradition that underlies modern Western culture. Therefore, it is useful to apply at times the terminology of Gull and Lasègue, and to look cautiously towards twentieth- and twenty-first-century theoretical models to try to understand certain food-refusing behaviours. Where I use the term 'anorexia' in relation to nineteenth-century fictional women, I do so with a view towards bridging the gap between the silences about women's self-harm that marked the Victorian period and the narratives about the damaged body in which we are, by now, well versed. Many of the self-harming hungry heroines of the texts examined in this chapter would not be considered anorexic by twenty-first-century standards. However, I am keen to stress what I see as a link between the ideological structures that framed, and continue to frame, the disease and the nineteenth-century values that privileged abstinence and abhorred bodily desires, which are still so culturally entrenched.

As Michel Foucault has argued, the body is an artefact of culture, determined and constructed by its scientific, medical and 'moral' context. The damaged body, a biologically and culturally constructed space, can thus be made to signify in a world where, as Elaine Scarry points out, there is no language for physical pain but that which is spoken by the body itself (1985: 2). Through self-starvation, then, the anorectic inscribes his or her body with a web of complex discourses, mapping personal psychological experience through a process of traumatic signification to which the human form testifies. According to Maud Ellmann, an abundance of signifiers accumulates around the starving body, paradoxically providing somatic substance to the insubstantial, increasingly coding the body when its own lack of corporeality fails to signify (1993: 1–7). For the anorectic 'hunger is a form of speech; and speech is necessarily a dialogue whose meanings do not end with the intentions of the speaker' but are 'enmeshed in social codes that precede [. . .] and outlast [. . .] its consciousness' (Ellmann 1993: 3). Curiously, the disappearing act of self-starvation, itself so often verbally undisclosed, is frequently the locus around which narrative gathers and through which political and social discourse or 'speech' is played out. For example, for very different reasons, the bodies of the hunger strikers of both the early-twentieth-century women's suffrage and twentieth-century Irish nationalist movements became sites around which narrative collected, stories became embodied, and political battle lines were drawn.[8]

The Victorian triple-decker and traditional realist novels respectively represent the artefacts par excellence of women's starvation literature, and the excess of words that cluster around the bodies of her heroines implicate the New Woman novelist in exploiting the starving female body as political capital. This chapter examines the use of behaviours that I will at times term 'anorexic', as both a thematic motif and a form of literary and political tactic by which to force a confrontation between (and thus an interruption of) the private and public spheres. In late-Victorian wound culture 'the excitations in the opening of private and bodily and psychic interiors' signalled an 'endlessly reproducible display, of wounded bodies and wounded minds in public' (Seltzer 1998: 253). By making public the private story of women's self-starvation, I argue that the New Woman attempted to collapse the separate sphere ideology that bolstered the rigid codes of Victorian femininity against which she fought. However, in making the thin body central to her body of narrative, the New Woman novelist practised a paradoxical strategy of self-effacement, erasing and making incorporeal her heroines, and subscribing to troubling and ultimately counter-productive patriarchal doctrines in a self-sacrificial strategy not dissimilar to the hunger protest itself.

Hunger and Femininity

Most feminist critics view eating disorders as symptomatic of our culture's unequal gender-relations – the position of women as economically dependent and politically impotent can be seen to have fostered their emergence.[9] Drawing on de Beauvoir's *The Second Sex*, Morag MacSween cites the recognisably Victorian ethos of self-negation as the primary cause of self-starvation (1993: 52–87) – one that provokes a conflict between femininity and individuality (1993: 4). Joan Jacobs Brumberg accounts for anorexia as

> an inevitable consequence of a misogynistic society that demeans women by devaluing female experience and women's values; by objectifying their bodies; and by discrediting vast areas of women's past and present achievements [. . .] our society's exaltation of thin, weak women expresses the inner logic of capitalism and patriarchy, both characterized by the sexual division of labour and female subordination. (Brumberg 2000: 35)

For Brumberg, social institutions limit and confine women as both labourers and commodities within a male-dominant economy, with this dynamic figuratively reproduced in women's self-starvation. Susan Bordo points to the importance of normalising (particularly visual) culture in both historical and contemporary experiences of eating disorders, noting that images of slenderness 'offer fantasies of safety, self-containment, acceptance, immunity from pain and hurt' (2003: xxi). Self-destructive behaviours are thus a response to deeply implanted and often unacknowledged cultural imperatives, intrinsic to any society in which the hegemonic power structures reflect masculine economic and social dominance. The contextual framework of Victorian print culture differs widely from the twenty-first-century media that Bordo cites. However, the 'fantasies of safety, self-containment, acceptance, immunity from pain and hurt' offered by contemporary media have evolved out of the very system of bourgeois patriarchal ideologies that fostered similar fantasies for the Victorian anorectic. My readings of self-starvation in late-nineteenth-century women's writing consider food refusal as performative in nature, as an enactment of both identity and protest and a dichotomy of rebellion and submission within a culture of clearly defined and inflexible gender expectations.

For late-Victorian and early-modernist women writers, hunger was to become an established and highly recognisable mode of political protest only a few years into the new century. Women prisoners detained on charges relating to the campaign for universal suffrage were denied the status of political prisoners and, in response, some elected to refuse food during their incarceration. The hunger strikes began in 1909, and were followed by forcible feeding that caused public outcry and furthered sympathy for the women's plight (Wingerden 1999: 89–92). Once again the medical establishment undertook to marshal and systematise unruly female bodies, replicating the processes of bodily invasion by which it had attempted to control Victorian women at the end of the previous century. Feminist commentators have long noted the similarities between forcible feeding and rape, suggesting that the actions of the all-male government metaphorised acts of sexual aggression against the female body at a time when bringing it into line seemed paramount.[10]

Although the emergence of the New Woman pre-dates the hunger strikes, a number of the texts referred to in this chapter attest to the concerns of women writers with the processes of masculine incursion into the female body that prefigure the forced feeding of suffragettes. These concerns are often formulated through the imagery of rape, but also of cannibalism, necrophilia, imprisonment, traumatic collapse and religious sacrifice. Clearing a path for future generations of women to articulate and protest their disenfranchisement through the trope of hunger, the New Woman novelist also literally 'wrote the book' on how to make the starving body speak. Through images of thin but politically aware heroines, writers like Sarah Grand (whose work this chapter primarily examines) conjured the figure of the female hunger striker long before her arrival on the British cultural and political landscape. However, in doing so, writers like Grand also set a dangerous precedent by valorising the new disease of anorexia, and romanticising self-sacrifice as a form of activism.

In late-Victorian Britain, as medical research into anorexia increased, so too did a consideration of the disease in the emerging sciences of psychoanalysis and psychiatry. Since medicine remained a male-dominated arena, studies of anorexia positioned the disease within long-established discourses of female frailty and hysteria (Showalter 1993: 74–100). In 1895 Freud wrote that 'the famous anorexia of young girls seems to me to be melancholia where sexuality is underdeveloped' (Masson 1985: 272). Freud saw the refusal of food as closely linked to a denial of other bodily appetites and understood anorexia as a strategy by which to slow or stop the onset of sexual maturity (Freud 2001b: 106). Indeed, certain twenty-first-century understandings of anorexia continue to subscribe to Freudian theories, although with less emphasis on a specifically sexual control of the body.[11] Psychoanalysis proposes that culture 'provokes, exacerbates, and gives distinctive form to an existing pathological condition' (Bordo 2003: 51). However, this fails to account adequately for the disproportionately high instances of anorexia in women, and the escalation in rates of anorexia since the onset of the Industrial Revolution (Bordo 2003: 49–50). Control of the body is a fundamental tenet of self-starvation, and sufferers frequently internalise the pervasive cultural images and ideologies that encode the subordinate role required by the society they inhabit. As it manifests in the New Woman novels of Sarah Grand, self-starvation functions as a defence against a lack of control stemming from this position, enacting a resistance to the femaleness of the body and a punishment of its physical needs and perceived shortcomings.

In Chapter 1, I discussed the ways in which the renunciation of the flesh was required to satisfy Christian ideologies of female sacrifice. In Christian asceticism, 'bodily, earthly desires were vicious and had to be curbed in favour of the sublime, pure soul' (Vandereycken and Van Deth 1994: 18). This model reflected – and continues to reflect – prevailing religious and philosophical conceptualisations that view the body and soul as separate entities. In his *Meditations on First Philosophy* (1641), René Descartes first conceives of the notion of dualism in the relationship between body and soul, clarifying how

> by body I mean everything that is capable of being bounded by some shape, of existing in a definite place [. . .] for to have power of moving itself, and also of perceiving by the senses or thinking, I judged could in no way belong to the nature of the body [. . .] I am therefore, speaking precisely, only a thinking thing, that is, a mind, a soul, or an intellect [. . .] I am not that framework of limbs that is called a human body; I am not some thin air infused into these limbs, or a wind, or a fire, or a vapour, or a breath, or whatever I can picture myself as [. . .] (Descartes 2008: 19–20)

Leslie Heywood's *Dedication to Hunger* theorises contemporary and historical eating disorders as the product of an unremitting dissemination of Cartesian doctrine, the 'anorexic logic' (1996: 8) of the Western patriarchal tradition. Thus, anorectics 'enact with their bodies the process that Western logic inscribes: they physically demonstrate its subtext, the horror of the female flesh that is often the unconscious of discourse' (1996: 8). Undermining Cartesian notions of the body as an inferior vessel, and the mind or soul as capable of transcendence from corporeality, Heywood highlights how Western ideologies identify the flesh and its intrinsic desires and corruptions as female. Conversely, the realms of philosophy, knowledge and culture are designated male, and women's hunger for knowledge is repeatedly associated with the temptation of Eve – with the corrupt bodily desires that initiated the fall of humankind. In the case of the anorectic this logic is endorsed by escaping the confines of corporeal being, believing that the flesh does not adequately represent the essential 'self'. Citing also Plato, Hegel and Freud, Heywood critiques classical philosophy, explaining that

> in their relentless process of designating the soul, the mind, subjectivity, and civilization as masculine, these 'figures' have formed a tradition that some women [. . .] internalize in an attempt to enter the magic inner circle of culture and become something other than the bodies, sexualities, loves, and flesh with which this tradition equates them. (Heywood 1996: 28)

Although the masculine philosophical tradition designates women as fleshly and desiring, the various identities offered to women by this tradition represent a much more complex dichotomy than that of simply masculine knowledge or feminine carnality. During the

Victorian period, these binarisms demonstrated the conflicted attitudes towards femininity produced by a culture that lauded the bodiliness required by motherhood yet demonised female sexuality, and praised the passive ethereality of women yet refused to acknowledge their intellectual gifts.

Women have continually occupied two central categories throughout Western culture, the angelic and the demonic. In the period concerned, these categories expanded in response to the cultural climate and to nineteenth-century bourgeois morality, to include the archetypes of the old maid and the fallen woman. Stressing the futility of any attempt to assess the cultural proliferation of these categories as separate, Nina Auerbach views them rather as 'fluid boundaries' placing women at 'the junction between the social and the spiritual, the humanly perishable and the transcendently potent' (1982: 63–4). Heywood's notion of anorexic logic is useful in reading food refusal in New Woman writing, when considered alongside Auerbach's interpretation of the angel/demon dichotomy embedded in Victorian understandings of femininity. For Heywood, modernist texts best express anorexic logic, the 'point of convergence [. . .] between the artificiality of gender constructions that mark an unstable cultural system' (1996: 14). However, the *fin de siècle* witnessed a significant period of instability in cultural systems that in turn produced texts engaging with the same logic at a moment of both diegetic experimentation and political and social crisis in British history.

Despite a lack of reliable evidence surrounding rates of Victorian anorexia, I suggest that the *fin-de-siècle* culture that paved the way for literary Modernism in late-Victorian Britain facilitated the rise of the condition both psychologically and textually. Heywood's theorisation of 'convergence' echoes Seltzer's claim that the *fin de siècle* facilitated a clash between the public (masculine) and private (feminine) spheres producing 'excitations in the opening of private and bodily and psychic interiors' (Seltzer 1998: 253). In drawing attention to the artificiality and permeability of these boundaries – like those of the angel/demon dichotomy – the starving heroine of Victorian fiction began to evolve rapidly during the final decades of the nineteenth century. In doing so, she began to express this instability at a time when the increasingly blurred distinction between gender roles threatened the status quo.

This chapter examines the convergence between the female body and the bodies of proto-feminist narratives that centralised the starving female form within late-Victorian gender debates. The starving, self-harming bodies of New Woman heroines are depicted in ways that represent and respond to conflicting notions of women as incorporeally pure and yet, paradoxically, dangerously fleshly. According to Luce Irigaray the male gaze is 'the penis eye, the phallic look' (Irigaray 1985: 134), and to Peter Brooks the epistemophilia driving the novelistic tradition. Brooks's reading of the novel form has curious implications if we consider the fiction of the New Woman oeuvre, and, most particularly, the polemic novels of the 1890s that aimed to refute gender double standards and educate a female readership. This chapter argues that the close relationship between narrative form and the female body is expressed, and ultimately complicated, through the fictional trope of self-starvation. New Woman anorexic fiction attempts to counteract women's portrayal as objects of desire or bodies incapable or undeserving of access to the masculine realms of culture and knowledge. However, in challenging women's designation as purely corporeal yet subject still to the example of saintly disembodiment encoded in Christian ideology, it also enacts the very disappearance from existence against which its heroines fight. In attempting to deny the bodiliness of the female body, New Woman writers often produced huge bodies of text whose narrative locus was the disappearing body itself.

Within the predominantly masculine literary world, the triple-decker novel had dominated the marketplace and represented the height of writerly achievement. Despite this, and perhaps because of it, not all New Woman novels adopted Realism, and towards the end of the century the literary Modernism of subversive female authors including Lucas Malet, Vernon Lee and even George Egerton (who primarily wrote short stories) began to challenge novelistic convention from within the novel form.[12] However, for the purposes of this chapter I focus on the novels of Sarah Grand, an influential and well-known figure in the so-called New Woman movement, whose social purity novels relied on literary Realism. In both emulating their male counterparts and attempting to claim their own distinct tradition, writers like Grand produced enormous bodies of text that reduced the female body to a narrative absence. Grand's New Woman novels relentlessly return to the starving body as a site of textual meaning, dedicating pages and pages to its display, curiously cooperating with, and participating within, both wound culture and epistemophilia. They distort, yet ultimately reflect, the masculine literary tradition, at a time when new 'feminist' forms were emerging to replace it.

Victorian Anorexic Fiction and the New Woman Novel

Women writers often dramatised their powerlessness at the hands of patriarchy through fictional accounts of anorexic heroism and self-sacrifice in the face of illness; there is 'scarcely a Victorian fictional narrative without its ailing protagonist, its depiction of a sojourn in the sickroom' (Bailin 1994: 5). Through food refusal female characters could metaphorically express women's mental and moral starvation, enacting an 'extreme manifestation of the feminine role, flaunting her martyrdom, literally turning herself into a "little" woman' (Showalter 1993: 128). Feminist theorists have been quick to observe that Victorian notions of hunger were widely interpolated with sexuality, in a reimagining of the temptation of Eve.[13] Narratives that privileged the disappearing female body directly engaged with the rhetoric of fall implicit in women's hunger, and warned against the immorality of consumption as a highly irreligious act. Furthermore, decades of popular fiction characterised the feminine ideal as passive, frail and silent; Jane Austen's sickly Fanny Price in *Mansfield Park* (1814) and the invalid Miss Williams in Charlotte Yonge's *The Clever Woman of the Family* (1865), as well as several Dickensian heroines (Houston 1994: 39–41), all exemplify this ideal.

Within the boundaries of domestic 'perfection', women who faced disappointment or failed to be satisfied with their lot found themselves unable to express outwardly feelings of anger and disillusionment. Sandra Gilbert and Susan Gubar explain that 'any young girl, but especially a lively and imaginative one, is likely to experience her education in docility, submissiveness, self-lessness' as 'sickening' (1984: 54). Through her training in domesticity 'the girl learns anxiety about – perhaps even loathing of – her own flesh' (1984: 54). As the moral centre of the Victorian home, the middle-class woman was expected to conform to a stereotype of feminine spirituality and disinterested affection in line with the examples set by the Christian martyrs, Mary and Jesus Christ explored in Chapter 1. In doing so, women were 'urged to downplay every aspect of their physicality, including (but not limited to) their sexuality' and encouraged to 'demonstrate their incorporeality through the small appetite and correspondingly slender body' (Silver 2002: 9). This cultural model, in which anxiety was to be resolved strictly within the margins of one's own borders, encouraged the focusing of rage not outwards towards the public or even domestic sphere, but inwards towards the self. Thus, throughout some of the best-known fiction of the period, the trope of self-starvation as either political gesture or repressive control of anxiety can be clearly mapped.

In *Victorian Literature and the Anorexic Body*, Anna Silver explains that 'the anorexic woman's slender form attests to her discipline over her body and its hunger', signalling 'her discomfort with or even hatred of her body and its appetites' (2002: 3). For the mid-Victorian woman writer, then, the starving heroine ironically became the embodiment of repressed desires, represented and yet simultaneously effaced within her story. Women characters were 'prisoners of their own gender [. . .] who attempt to escape, if only into nothingness, through the suicidal self-starvation of anorexia' (Gilbert and Gubar 1984: 86). Published eighteen years after Gilbert and Gubar's *The Madwoman in the Attic*, Silver's work cites numerous examples of popular fiction in which the female anorectic appears. Gilbert and Gubar suggest, perhaps reductively, that anorexia in women's writing represents a tried and tested symbolic protest against patriarchal restrictions and confinement (1984: 390–1). However, Silver's work demonstrates that figurations of starvation were by no means homogeneous in Victorian fiction, nor did they always represent the precise same system of cultural codes (2002: 82).

Mid-century writing by men and women regularly portrayed moral ascension through physical starvation in female characters, subtly delineating and reinforcing class boundaries through depictions of beautiful, inactive, middle-class (and thus ideal) feminine bodies.[14] I would argue that this practice persisted but also developed during the late-Victorian period. The anorectic heroine continued to feature in women's writing but by the 1880s had evolved into a highly complex and troubling stock character. Unlike most of the wasting women in earlier texts, the starving New Woman heroine did not always disintegrate in silence in an act of self-effacement that internalised and concealed enforced Victorian gender codes. Where self-starvation in earlier Victorian fiction had been a central yet largely covert trope, New Woman anorexia demonstrated a much more extreme and violent pathology of Victorian femininity.[15] In this later writing, food refusal is no longer fictionalised as a solitary disorder, nor one obscured in part by narrative conventions, but is symptomatic of a more violent and disturbing range of self-destructive bodily and textual practices. The narrativisation of these practices 'function[s] as a way of imagining and situating our notions of public, social, and collective identity [. . .] as a way of imagining the relations of private bodies and private persons to public spaces' (Seltzer 1998: 21).

In the hotly contested battle for access to the public space, the New Woman attempted to effect a dramatic change in the way that notions of public and private were formulated and sustained. She depicted hungry heroines whose bodies, as inescapably participant in the libidinal economy of patriarchy, are traumatised, dramatised, and ultimately sensationalised as public spectacle. In doing so, she forced a wedge between the hitherto clearly defined boundaries between public and private, male and female. However, she did so within a framework of anorexic logic (a term I borrow from Heywood throughout) and the highly conventional form of the realist romance plot, somewhat undermining her cause. Expressed through the traditionally dense medium of a nine-hundred-page text, the New Woman novel attempted a tactical – if not always a formal – departure from the writing of both its male and female predecessors.[16] Of this new brand of authors, the writer most engaged in the use of the anorexic trope was Grand, whose Morningquest trilogy signals a significant preoccupation with self-harm in general, and self-starvation in particular.

Literary critics have noted the ways in which Grand's novels continually reference both food and female appetite. Tina O'Toole (2013), Abigail Dennis (2007), Ann Heilmann (2004) and Heather Evans (2000 and 2001) have written extensively on the uses of food and famine in Grand's writing, showing the ways in which it highlights just one of the many seemingly oppositional ideologies at play in her work. Grand's journalistic altercation with Ouida in the *North American Review* established her as a major player in the Victorian debate surrounding the Woman Question. However, despite Grand's militant stance against sexual double standards and the insufficiency of women's education, her attitude towards both marriage and motherhood is revealed in the conservatism of her social purity subtexts. Her fiction enacts a variety of traditional, and often conflicting, beliefs that served to reinforce, rather than to disrupt, the rigid gender codes that her writing attempted to dislocate. Angelique Richardson shows how Grand's work engages with eugenic discourses which enforce imperialist notions of race and class (2008: 95–131). Similarly, inconsistencies in Grand's work placed her 'always in the centre of New Woman debates even when marginalising the radical ideas she had helped put in currency' (Heilmann 2004: 13). Additionally, while Grand's social purity novels were highly polemical and, at times, stern and moralising in tone, her short stories were often comic and far less pessimistic, especially in their discussion of food and hunger. Clearly, for Grand, the social purity novel allowed her to sermonise in a way that would have been trickier in a less prescriptive form.

In 'The New Aspect of the Woman Question' Grand describes women as 'healthy hungry children' (1894: 271). Characterising the New Woman as physically robust and with a healthy appetite, Grand here summarises the attributes of her most successful fictional heroines. Despite the various tortures from which they eventually emerge, Grand's protagonists largely escape self-destruction (except for *The Heavenly Twins*' Evadne Frayling and Edith Beale), becoming socially useful as well as healthy and hungry. Ideala returns from the East '[s]traight as an arrow, young-looking and fresh' (2008: 187), whilst Angelica Ilverthorpe is a 'splendid specimen of hardy, healthy, vigorous young womanhood' (2007: II, 309), and despite her self-starvation Beth Caldwell's huge appetite never dissipates. Even the heroine of Grand's later novel *Babs the Impossible* (1901) demonstrates a ravenous appetite for both mischief and food. Negative portrayals of artificially thin women also appear in Grand's writing, notably her scathing critique of a mother whose insistence on a nineteen-inch waist during pregnancy leaves her infant chronically underweight in 'The Baby's Tragedy' (1897). Nonetheless, while Grand proclaims the importance of women's health and the fulfilment of appetites both physical and intellectual, this is at times undermined by the treatment of self-starvation in her novels.

Although some of her heroines evolve through pecuniary and mental starvation, it is Grand's idealisation of food refusal that suggests the complex and paradoxical nature of her attitude towards food, starvation and the suffering body. Through the deployment of motifs of martyrdom and sainthood discussed in the previous chapter, Grand defends the anorexic experience by suggesting it is essential to the moral and spiritual growth of her characters. This growth, enacted across the abundant pages of both the three-volume and shorter novel forms, reflects an ideology of the body corresponding directly to anorexic logic, and around which clusters an excess of signifiers. For Grand, the realist novel provided a body of text expansive enough to thoroughly endorse the disembodiment of her heroines, whilst drawing attention to processes of female self-effacement through a dramatisation of these same bodies. As I will show, this paradox of textual excess and bodily lack exemplifies a dangerously self-effacing strategy at play in the New Woman social purity romance.

I explored in my introduction the ways in which the realist mode required novelists to impose a sense of social cohesion in their texts, a plot requirement to which Grand subscribes by rehabilitating or excising the bodies of dissolute and philandering men within, or from, the social order. However, Grand's adoption of Realism meant that the bodies of women had to be assimilated into that same order, to be married off and made mothers, despite the inherent dangers of these enterprises. As Marilyn Bonnell notes, Grand attempted to 'legitimize women's reality as a literary mode, to champion an ethic of care over an enterprise concerned solely with artistic expression' (1995: 124). However, Grand's female bodies are subject to the same textual dictates as the men's, making Grand's use of the novel less revolutionary than its content might suggest. Although *Ideala: A Study from Life* (the first of Grand's Morningquest novels) was not published in the triple-decker form, a close reading of this novel makes possible the mapping of textual and thematic developments in Grand's anorexic logic, as well as her use of self-starvation as a literary strategy.

Transcending the Body: Sarah Grand's *Ideala: A Study from Life*

In 1888, Frances Elizabeth Bellenden McFall published her first novel with her own money following separation from her husband, completing her transformation into Madame Sarah Grand (Youngkin 2008: vii). Born and raised in Ireland, Grand left for England aged seven, but retained fond memories of her time in Ireland and a keen sense of affinity with the Irish (Forward and Heilmann 2000b: 1). Grand drew on Irish landscapes and culture in her writing, and her support for British colonialism is evidenced by her ambivalent literary and political approach to nationalism (O'Toole 2013: 17–42). Although Grand lived in England and abroad for most of her life, her engagement with Irish concerns, both in her semi-autobiographical novel *The Beth Book* and in her dramatisation of hunger as a distinctly Irish trope, marks her out as a writer of somewhat mixed cultural heritage. Her first novel was not an instant success and failed to find a publisher – partly, I would argue, because of both its focus on self-destructive womanhood and its having been written by a woman whose ideas and lifestyle were highly unorthodox. These same challenges also meant that *Ideala* remained out of print for decades, and, like the other women whose cultural hybridity I note, Grand's marginality accounts, to an extent, for her exclusion from the novelistic canon.

Ideala details the awakening of a feminist consciousness in its eponymous heroine, as a consequence of her unhappy marriage to a violent and unfaithful man. Ideala falls in love with the superintendent of a hospital specialising in nervous disorders, but is convinced not to elope with him by her confidant Lord Dawne. Dawne insists that Ideala must set a good example for other women, and she eventually takes his advice, buries her passions, and chooses to travel and work for the emancipation of all women. Ideala is preoccupied with food, consumption and the moral implications of both starvation and corpulence, stating with disdain that men 'are so easily managed. All you have to do is feed them and flatter them' (Grand 2008: 16). For Ideala, the overweight body encodes an inability to control all appetites, transgressing and eroding gender and class boundaries ideologically embedded in Christianity and internalised by women. In the text, unruly appetites are closely linked to masculinity, and to institutions like the Church, which Ideala accuses of providing refuge for gluttony and hypocrisy. She describes a priest whose indulgence in 'earthly pleasures' made one 'suspect that he had not even yet exhausted them all himself' (2008: 26). By highlighting the male body as a repository of sin and corruption, and the representatives of masculine authority as more concerned with earthly than spiritual pleasures, Grand directly responds to and questions the dualism that genders knowledge and culture as male. However, she also grounds her heroine's critique in the assumption that all bodily desires are sinful. Ideala thus imagines sexual corruption as a gustatory act, describing how

> [t]here are moments when I think that even their reverence for the purity of women is a sham. For why do they keep us pure? Is it not to make each morsel more delicious for themselves, that sense and sentiment may be satisfied together, and their own pleasure made more complete? [. . .] When the history of this age is written, moral cowardice and self-indulgence will be found to have been the most striking characteristics of the people. (Grand 2008: 20)

Grand aligns morality with the ability to resist indulgence, both sexual and gastronomic, configuring consumption as a metaphor for sexual devourment. Through 'morsel' and 'delicious', Grand evokes male cannibalistic fantasies, critiquing the exploitation of the female body as an object of men's carnal, gluttonous and destructive desires.

Grand reclaimed the satisfaction of hunger as essential to 'feminist' purposes and regarded a well-regulated appetite as healthy. As Ann Heilmann observes, Grand's re-envisioning of food as a necessary tool for women's work served as a direct reaction to the New Woman's reputation of 'rapacious and unsexing appetites' (2004: 34) in the periodical press. However, there were limits to what could be considered sustaining, and Grand was careful to draw a distinction between necessary consumption and masculine Epicureanism.[17] Grand derides the corrupt hungers that drive patriarchy, attacking and dismantling men's claim to intellectual superiority, yet she also reveals her 'qualified acceptance of the Victorian aesthetic of the ideal woman' (Silver 2002: 82), who sustains herself morally and spiritually on a meagre diet, like many of the women of the mid-Victorian novels pre-dating *Ideala*.

In her short story 'The Undefinable: A Fantasia' (1908), Grand would mock the male aesthete figure through his gluttony, his indigestion aligned with his inability to recognise female genius. Unlike *Ideala*, this later text satirises masculine greed through a significantly less instructive and caustic tone, suggestive of a comedic, rather than dramatic, critique. In *Ideala*, over-indulgence is explored through an evaluation of late-nineteenth-century literary Aestheticism which 'stimulates' but 'doesn't nourish', 'excites you pleasurably' but is a 'false guide [. . .] He robs you, and leaves you hungry, thirsty, and alone' (Grand 2008: 63). A clear distinction is made between healthy and nourishing education and that which is merely sensuous. Grand would make the same distinction between the frivolous and degenerate novels fed to her heroine Evadne in *The Heavenly Twins* – Tobias Smollett's *The Adventures of Roderick Random* (1748), Henry Fielding's *Tom Jones, a Foundling* (1749) and later 'French' books (Grand 2007: I, 267) – and the biological knowledge with which she would seek to educate and protect herself from venereal disease. In *Ideala* the heroine personifies Aestheticism and Naturalism as masculine through reference to the male possessive, and suggests that by relying upon male-dominated forms of expression and education for intellectual satiety, women only risk further hunger. Interestingly, however, it is the traditionally male form of lyric poetry through which Ideala first seeks creative expression, and it is a historically masculine literary mode through which Grand chooses to first publish. Despite her criticisms of the masculine literary tradition, Grand's text sets out to emulate the formal, if not always thematic, limitations of the novel – a form that necessitates Ideala's absorption into the religious and moral fabric of a society that views her body as a commodity and a vessel of sin, and limits her sphere of influence.

Ideala's deliberate food refusal, her hyperactivity and her seemingly increased energy recall Gull and Lasègue's observations about anorexic women, and reflect Grand's use of anorexia nervosa to depict her heroine's self-harm. Ideala starves for a complicated mixture of largely unconscious reasons that reveal her internalisation of both the Christian aesthetic of self-sacrifice and the paradigm of duality that subordinates her body to her spirit. Despite its centrality in a novel that is principally concerned with liberating one woman's body from a restrictive marriage, little detail about Ideala's appearance is given. This is principally because she is viewed through the eyes of Lord Dawne, whose admiration manifests in a subjective projection of illicit desires on to Ideala's body. Grand's deployment of the first-person male narrator serves to complicate her proto-feminist potential, since we can only view Ideala through the phallocentric conservatism and possessive voyeurism informing Dawne's narration (Youngkin 2008: xx–xxi). Thus, the novel charts Ideala's attempt to 'win her story away from a male narrator who would write her into the marriage plot regardless of her desires' (Mangum 2001: 89).

A similar strategy would be adopted by Grand in her most successful novel, *The Heavenly Twins*, in which a doubly troubling symbol of masculine institutional power (the doctor-husband) narrates the final section.[18] Grand supplemented her male narrator's contribution, entitled 'The Impressions of Doctor Galbraith', with an ironic editorial note. It satirised the doctor figure and was highly critical of his observations, undermining the male narrator's authoritative medical discourse (Heilmann 2002), a technique that *Ideala*, written five years earlier, does not attempt. *Ideala* is structured around a triumvirate of relationships with men: Ideala's husband, Lord Dawne and Lorrimer, the man she falls in love with. All three men read Ideala differently and problematically: her husband misunderstands her unworldly nature and responds with violence; Dawne idealises a version of Ideala constructed from his own romantic illusions; and Lorrimer fails to understand the moral scruples preventing their union. While the structure and narration of the novel problematises the notion of masculine narrative authority, Grand depicts only the fruitlessness of Ideala's endeavours to 'win her story' from the men who misread her body and its desires.

About Ideala, Dawne muses, 'I was going to catalogue her charms, but it seems indelicate to describe a woman, point by point, like a horse that is for sale' (Grand 2008: 22). Dawne's comment would appear reworked seven years later in Ménie Muriel Dowie's *Gallia*, in which the heroine appraises her potential reproductive partner 'as a dealer might notice the points in a horse' (1995: 2). Dowie reverses the male gaze, subverting the workings of the Victorian marriage market and exposing the economy of sexual exchange far more radically than in Grand's first novel. Dawne describes how he 'used to see [Ideala] in one particular frock [. . .], tight-fitting and perfect, yet with no detail evident. It was like an expression of herself, that dress, so quiet to all seeming, and yet so rich in material, so complex in design' (Grand 2008: 22). Dawne's admiration centres on his exoticisation and fetishisation of Ideala's garments, making the 'ultimate enigma' out of the body underneath. Although his comments address the shape of Ideala's body, the reader is never given explicit detail as to what, precisely, that body looks like – like the feminised Gerald Ethridge in *Anna Lombard*, it escapes description entirely. Ideala is 'very absent' (2008: 10) and 'more like a picture than anything' (2008: 13); she is detached, vague and unreal. Her body represents a negative presence, only perceptible by the trace or impression it leaves on material objects. Just as she can only be described through the impression she leaves on Dawne, Ideala's corporeality is called into question by the text's recurrent dynamic of bodily presence and absence, of appetite and starvation.

Ideala's first act of self-starvation appears in the novel at the moment at which she also first articulates anorexic logic, showing dualism to be a crucial tenet of her personal philosophy. She tells Lorrimer, 'I wish I could get behind that horrid veil of flesh that hides you from me. I want to see your soul' (2008: 99). However, Ideala's understanding of the soul as superordinate to – yet also deep and hidden within – the body depends ironically on the corporeality she so ardently rejects. While her comments highlight her acceptance of problematic assumptions about women, she later notes that in Lorrimer 'the highest and most spiritual aspirations warred in him with the most carnal impulses' (2008: 92). She recognises in her ideal lover the competing impulses of body and soul, yet fails to accept this as it manifests within herself. Unlike the idealised Victorian woman, who was derided as soulless yet expected to aspire to the sublimation of body to spirit, Ideala views the male intellectual as capable of negotiating this tension and internalises her own perceived inability to do so.

After declaring her desire to see past Lorrimer's flesh, Ideala commits her first conscious act of food refusal; we are told that she 'could not go through the ordeal of who should pay for lunch again.

She preferred to starve. The *camaraderie* between them was mental enough to be manlike already, but only as long as there was no question of material outlay' (2008: 99). Ideala's equality with Lorrimer is thus fundamentally tied to her denial of the flesh that, once acknowledged, would threaten her transcendence to the masculine intellectual realm. The very materiality of Ideala's body must be abnegated for her to function as an intellectual capable of masculine achievement rather than as an object 'to be looked at, denuded, unveiled' (Brooks 1993: 97).

Grand points to the impossibility of reconciling the two identities that Ideala endeavours to inhabit; she can be neither fully angel nor demon, neither disembodied nor fleshly. The irreconcilability of these conflicting female typologies is insurmountable, resulting in a breakdown in her friendship with Lorrimer, after which she is described as

> cold and faint. The long fast and fatigue were beginning to tell upon her. She was nervous, too; the silence was oppressive, but she could not break it. She felt some inexplicable change in her relations with Lorrimer which made it impossible to speak. (Grand 2008: 113)

Ideala is no longer able to converse as an equal, because her body is subject to cultural constructions designating it as carnal and potentially threatening to bourgeois notions of propriety. She is silenced by the distinction between herself as woman (fleshly and desiring) and Lorrimer as man (knowledgeable and philosophical) and must forgo the pleasures of his company. Such a distinction expects of Ideala angelic and saintly ethereality while claiming, concurrently, that she is incapable of demonstrating such traits. Ideala's hunger is a form of speech, a dialogue through which her body is 'enmeshed in social codes that precede [. . .] and outlast [. . .] its consciousness' (Ellman 1993: 3). Consequently, she becomes increasingly unseen throughout the text, resisting definition as bodily through anorexic acts that both conceal and give voice to her pain.

Lorrimer chastises Ideala, telling her, 'you have had no lunch today again. You will kill yourself if you go on like that' (Grand 2008: 113). His response to her attempts at bodily transcendence are negatively encoded through patronising language; he misunderstands her motives and views her actions as indicative of childish attention-seeking. Like Gull and Lasègue, who viewed self-starvation in part as the product of feminine disobedience, the men in Ideala's life recognise her symptoms yet fail to understand the psychological drives upon which they are predicated. Ideala becomes painfully aware of a change in her camaraderie with Lorrimer, the effect of which she describes when 'at last the twenty-four hours' fasting, fatigue and mental suffering overcame her' (2008: 115).

Following the deterioration of Ideala's intellectual friendship, we are told how she 'grew paler and thinner, and more nervous' (2008: 24), that she was 'drawn and haggard', 'devoured by anxiety', and that 'she neither ate nor slept' (2008: 126). In attempting to resist definition as 'the bodies, sexualities, loves, and flesh' (Heywood 1996: 28) with which the Western philosophical tradition equates women, Ideala's self-starvation merely reaffirms this classification, since it is the disappearance of her body that repeatedly provokes narrative commentary. In deploying the starving body as a recurrent thematic motif, Grand completes the process of signification of the body's 'passage into writing, its becoming a literary body, and generally also a narrative body' (Brooks 1993: 3) in that the inscription of the sign here depends on and produces the story of Ideala's battle against her appetite for romantic and sexual fulfilment. The very process of denying her corporeality thus marks the passage into literature of Ideala's body as the inscription of its own story, a story about self-harm that, by its publication, both explodes the public and private spheres and upholds their divisory principles.

Like the ideal of Christian self-sacrifice that reinforces Ideala's self-renunciation, Dawne's narration of her thin form also enforces religiously framed understandings of the pained body. Dawne's sensual reaction to Ideala's starving body is intensified by his attempt to situate her suffering within well-established discourses of Christian martyrdom, explored in Chapter 1. Upon finding her alone one evening, he describes how

> she sank down on the floor with a low moan beside a chair, and hid her face on her arm. Presently she looked up, and I saw she held something in her hand. It was a gold crucifix, and she fixed her eyes on it. The lamplight fell on her face, and I could see that it was drawn and haggard [. . .] was it a religious difficulty? A weary while she remained in the same attitude, gazing at the crucifix; but evidently there was no pity for her pain, and no relief. (Grand 2008: 126)

Despite having declared that Ideala is 'in a state of don't know' (2008: 23) about religion, Dawne repeatedly interprets her pain as that of a struggling saint. In an act of authoritative dismissal, he imposes his own religious views, imagining her body through Christian frames of reference. He watches her from a hidden position, silently invading her privacy with his proprietary and penetrative stare, betraying his desire to sexually penetrate her thin body. Dawne's impressions foreground Ideala's interaction with the crucifix in a tone that conveys his voyeuristic arousal by her thin form.

Throughout the Bible as well as later secular accounts of the Christian martyrs, violent acts of martyrdom are almost always depicted as transformative and transcendental processes for the subject. Saint Stephen is described as having 'the face of an angel' at his martyrdom (Acts 6: 15); in the book of Matthew the martyrs are offered 'the crown of life' (2: 10), whilst the martyrs 'shall be fulfilled' (6: 11) and shown 'great admiration' in the book of Revelation (17: 6). Similarly, once crucified, Christ's spirit leaves his body in an act of heavenly transfiguration, and the centurion cries that 'truly this man was the son of God' (Mark 5: 39). Ideala does not seek forgiveness, nor is she at peace or subject to saintly, transcendental harmony. Rather, Grand depicts Ideala's submissive acceptance of the religious and social convention of prayer as a gesture of defeatism contrary to biblical depictions of serenity. Dawne's voyeurism also complicates Grand's use of Christian imagery, because his eroticisation is encircled by competing desires for the masculine protection but also sexual appropriation of her starving body.

Dawne's act of watching replicates the historical practices of medical and religious men seeking to validate ascetic food refusal through observation of starving women. In Europe, from the sixteenth century onwards, starvation had been linked to miraculous acts, and women who claimed to survive on little or no food were venerated as saints or prophets.[19] During the medieval period 'fasting was fundamental to the model of female holiness' (Brumberg 2000: 43–4) and prayer became the only sustenance required by the most pious of women. The Reformation had drastically changed the value of female fasting, and during the post-medieval period cases of *anorexia mirabilis* had to be verified to prove that they were not the work of Satan. Verification usually took the form of enticement to food, with priests and doctors presenting an array of delicate consumables to the fasting girl in an attempt to demonstrate her weakness, and to dissociate her from holy or satanic possession.[20] During the nineteenth century, the new scientific attachment to empiricism meant that women who claimed to be nourished only by God had to be rigorously tested.[21] The combined patriarchal apparatus of Christianity and medicine pursued knowledge of the female body and through it the 'truth' of these miracles through intense and prolonged observation of those concerned (Vandereycken and Van Deth 1994: 47–73).[22]

In common with the fasting girls who claimed that their hunger was taken away by God, in almost all accounts of Christian martyrdom, the role of the gaze constituted a sexual objectification of the body by an external audience.[23] In *Ideala* it is the observational influence of Dawne that persuades the heroine to renounce her love for Lorrimer and their plan to elope. Dawne evokes the rhetoric of martyrdom and asceticism, asking:

> Can you not become mistress of yourself again, and enter on a larger life which shall be full of love – not the narrow, selfish passion you are cherishing for one, but that pure and holy love which only the best [. . .] can feel for all? If you could but get the fumes of this evil feeling out of yourself, you would see [. . .] It is a physical condition caused by contact, and kept up by your own perverse pleasure in it – nothing more. Everyone grows out of it in time, and anyone with proper self-control could conquer it. (Grand 2008: 161)

Dawne describes Ideala's feelings for Lorrimer as an infectious miasma, rendering her physical desires degenerate and poisonous. Characterising Ideala's love as an evil force possessing her body, Dawne encourages her to surpass that body by resisting the physicality of passion and self-indulgence. Deploying the rhetoric of corporeal transcendence, of anorexic logic, Dawne further legitimises Ideala's self-starvation by privileging self-sacrifice as a noble and desirable alternative to temptation. Eventually it is through this line of argument that Ideala agrees to break with Lorrimer, and is ready to embark on a successful career as a New Woman philanthropist.

At the end of the novel Dawne notes that Ideala has physically grown, yet he is still able to view her only as a collection of fetishised garments, describing how

> She wore a long robe, exquisitely draped, which was loose, but yet clung to her, and fell in rich folds about her with a grace which satisfied. I cannot describe the fashion of this robe, or the form, but I have seen one like it somewhere – it must have been in a picture, or on a statue of a grand heroic woman or a saint; and it suggested something womanly and strong, but not to be defined. (Grand 2008: 165)

Dawne borrows from iconography the parameters of Ideala's form, refusing to see her as she is but seeing her instead as a saintly martyr whose appearance has 'satisfied' him. Like Cross's Evelyn and Gerald, who imagine Eurydice and Anna respectively as female martyrs, Dawne imposes his fantasy of medieval heroism on the object of his desires. As the subject of the Western patriarchal and epistemophilic perspective, Dawne demonstrates his compulsive inspection of Ideala's body to verify the 'truth' of her as an object of desire, or, as he is ultimately forced to do, to 'make that object into the ultimate enigma'.

Ideala is preoccupied with travel, modernity and the potential for dramatic collisions between the human body and the machine, discussed in my introduction. These collisions are at times literal, but they are also symbolic of the mechanisms of Victorian society by which the body became increasingly dependent on, and subject to, automation. These mechanisms were often depicted in literary Naturalism, in which 'the coupling of bodies and machines is [. . .] a coupling of private and public spaces [. . .] most powerfully literalized in the machinal systems of public transport' (Seltzer 1998: 31).[24] In 'The New Aspect of the Woman Question' Grand confirmed the disapproval of Naturalism referenced in Ideala's criticism of modern literature, yet she was often accused of being a naturalist author. Indeed, one critic for the *Saturday Review* described *Ideala* as 'a modest essay in Naturalism, using that word in the French sense' ('Review of Sarah Grand's *Ideala*', 1888). Despite her condemnation of Decadence, Aestheticism and Naturalism, Grand's first novel betrays the anxieties concerning the 'coupling of bodies and machines' symptomatic of the 'morally corrupt' literature she publicly abhorred. As in a number of naturalist works, the site of much human carnage in *Ideala* is the railway station or train carriage, and Grand uses images of trains and train wrecks throughout.

After separating from Lorrimer, Ideala asks Dawne, 'have you felt the fascination of the trains? [. . .] now and then comes one that is just a flash and a roar, and I [. . .] quiver with excitement, feeling as if I might be swept away' (Grand 2008: 122–5). Through the imagery of railway accidents Grand's heroine articulates the self-destructive impulse driving her food refusal – for her body to disappear into nothingness, to be 'swept away' by the force of that which symbolises the phallic pinnacle of advancement and enterprise.[25] After her husband's mistress dies of scarlet fever in her arms, a traumatised Ideala misses her train and becomes trapped at the station. She is taken in by the porter, who regales her with the story of an accident in which workers 'toiled fearfully amongst the wreck of trains, searching for the mangled and mutilated, the dying and the dead, while the air was filled with horrid shrieks and groans'

(2008: 111). The story mirrors the deathbed scene in the previous pages, in which Ideala listens to the story of her husband's cruelty and philandering as the wasted body of his mistress lies ravaged by fever. Later, Dawne asks Ideala, 'what have they done to you? You're a perfect wreck!' to which she responds that 'wrecks are so interesting' (2008: 123). Whilst both the wreck of Ideala's marriage and her romantic aspirations – emblematised by her wrecked, thin body – remain unarticulated, she entertains her friends with the story of the train wreck, with the images of bodily traumas that replicate yet conceal her own.

Grand's repeated use of the railway as both traumatic locus and symbolic reference suggests an understanding of the ways in which bodily trauma is bound up with both modernity and intellectual progression. As Ideala seeks entrance to masculine pursuits such as education and travel that transgress the normative boundaries of her class and gender, she is beset by traumatic experience. Significantly, these traumas take place at, or lead to, the railway station; her relationship with Lorrimer is enabled by a train journey, and the heroine is viewed as a train wreck. These constructs imply Grand's understanding and exploitation of the embryonic Victorian wound culture, in which 'private desire and public fantasy cross' at the site of mechanisation. Grand locates the train as a central metaphor for her heroine's journey towards self-starvation and eventually self-awareness through self-sacrifice, and the wreck as the pain that must be endured to become fully self-determined. Such discourses evoke the Christian rhetoric of asceticism that, like classical models, privileges the mind and soul over the body, and exemplifies the anorexic logic of Western culture, philosophy and religion.

Trauma breaches the borders between inside and outside, putting them into communication; it 'violently opens passageways between systems that were once discrete, making unforeseen connections that distress or confound' (Luckhurst 2008: 3). Grand's preoccupation with the railway accident – the scene of Victorian mass trauma – works to put into communication the once-discrete categories of masculinity and femininity, public and private. Grand imagines her heroine's wasting body as a product of a society desperate to advance, yet retaining the gendered double standards that restrict women's development. In symbolically aligning Ideala's self-harm with the mass spectacle of modernity's violent collapse, Grand's work opens passageways between the masculine systems of culture, knowledge, economics and politics, and the feminine world in which women are denied access to these systems.

Although *Ideala* offers an alternative to unhappy marriage, proposing fulfilment through altruistic 'feminist' projects, it also suggests that this can only be achieved through bodily sacrifice. Upon seeing Ideala for the first time following her travel abroad as part of her work for women, Lord Dawne exclaims, 'my first impression was that she had grown!' (Grand 2008: 165). Ideala's self-starvation thus appears to have been cured. However, she continues to subscribe to the philosophy of self-sacrifice that enabled and sustained her self-harming behaviour in the earlier sections of the novel. Her body may have temporarily recovered, but her continued desire to sacrifice her time, health and happiness in the service of others betrays her recourse to forms of patriarchal logic privileging women's self-abnegation and abhoring the self-government of the female body. While Grand asserts her heroine's status as a champion of women's rights and an example to all, she does so by establishing a troublingly self-destructive paradigm for the transformation from unhappily married woman to New Woman. This paradigm would be repeated to dramatic effect in her two subsequent novels, *The Heavenly Twins* and *The Beth Book*.

Sickness and Sacrifice: *The Heavenly Twins* and *The Beth Book*

The Heavenly Twins was Grand's most popular and also most controversial novel, largely because it dealt with issues that shocked the sensibilities of the average Victorian reader. Set amidst the campaigns for the repeal of the Contagious Diseases Acts which were 'predicated on the idea that the (fallen) female body pollutes society' (Ledger 1997: 115), Grand makes the case for a reversal of such laws. Grand's story engages with degeneration and eugenics, presenting and critiquing the limited options available to women exposed to venereal disease within their marriages. Through the intertwining narratives of three female characters, Evadne Frayling, Edith Beale and Angelica Ilverthorpe, Grand demonstrates the destructive consequences of any attempt to protect women from Victorian sexual double standards.[26] However, as in *Ideala*, her criticisms of patriarchy and the resultant march towards self-sacrifice enforced by its laws are complicated by her idealisation of the starving woman.

While Edith is the most central of the text's heroines (about whose tragic death from syphilis the other narrative strands interlock), it is Evadne around whom the plot gathers. Just as Edith represents the Old Woman, Evadne is at first Grand's prototypical

New Woman – she has educated herself in medicine and science, contradicts the misogynistic opinions of her father, and engages herself in debates surrounding the Woman Question. Having just married the sexually profligate Colonel Colquhoun, Evadne discovers that he possesses a questionable sexual reputation. She refuses to live with him, resulting in her disownment by her parents, who fail to see Colquhoun's indiscretions in a particularly negative light. Evadne, however, is horrified at the thought of sexual contact with a man who might be tainted by the diseases about which she has informed herself. Eventually, Evadne agrees to live with her new husband, but under the condition that her body remains her own property and that the marriage continues unconsummated. Grand demonstrates the extent to which this strategy fails, as Evadne becomes frail and emaciated by the inertia of frustrated sexual passions and unfulfilled maternal drives. Despite the implication of futility embedded in this resistive strategy, Grand's narrative manifests a contradictory position on self-starvation, since it favours Evadne's thin and atrophied body over the corpulent bodies that also appear. Once a healthy young girl, Evadne, like Ideala, becomes increasingly thin as her marriage progresses, and, as in *Ideala*, Grand favours the small body, denigrating its converse through depictions of male excess.

Evadne is described as having a 'slender figure' (Grand 2007: I, 99) and Grand directly contrasts this with her mother, the archetypal Cow Woman whom she laments in 'The New Aspect of the Woman Question'. Grand's narrator describes Mrs Frayling as 'fair, plump, sweet, yielding, commonplace, prolific' (I, 57), and her plumpness and yielding nature correspond to her lack of control over both her body and her marital destiny. Furthermore, Grand censures the corpulent body through her scathing portrayal of morally corrupt characters such as Colquhoun and the 'round' (I, 232) and 'liberally fed' (I, 245) Guthrie Brimstones. Major Brimstone's 'hands were another offence' since 'they were fat and podgy, with short pointed fingers, indicative of animalism and ill-nature' (I, 248). Drawing on physiognomy, Evadne reads the grotesquery of Brimstone's body as an indicator of moral weakness.[27] As in Grand's previous novel, the overweight body is associated with an inability to control the most basic of animal drives, and as the contrastingly pure character in this scene, the heroine's morality is defined and communicated by her thinness.

Evadne's husband's habits of self-indulgence are well documented, and she articulates the problem with embarking on a sexual relationship with Colquhoun through the imagery of food. Describing Colquhoun's as 'a mind too shallow to contain any sort of mental sustenance for the sharing' (I, 266), Evadne explains, 'my taste is cultivated to so fine an extent, I require something extremely well-flavoured for the dish which is to be the *pièce de résistance* of my life-feast', and 'my appetite is delicate, it requires to be tempted' (I, 109). Grand directly connects consumption to copulation, anticipating Freud's claim that anorexia nervosa was prompted by repressed sexuality (2001b: 15–112). At the beginning of her marriage Evadne's appetite is healthy, yet not excessive, and Grand uses 'delicate' and 'tempted' to suggest that although Evadne envisions married life as a 'feast', greed will not feature. Rather than accepting her husband's voracious desires, Evadne indicates that she must be tempted to participate in sexual intercourse, enticed by the purity of the marriage union that justifies the act. By the close of the text Evadne's husband has become as intemperate and fat as expected, and such juxtaposition emphasises Evadne's own shrivelled form. Evadne's constant repression of her need for both affection and sexual contact leaves her body over-exerted by restraint, and she declines in health and size. She is described as 'shrinking in every inch of her sensitive frame' (I, 145) while her body is 'not as robust as her brain' (I, 132), and she is 'fragile' (II, 268) and 'thin [. . .], pale and weak' (II, 296).

As in Grand's first novel, the most pervasive observation of Evadne's thin body emanates from the perspective of a male narrator. The final volume of the novel is narrated by Doctor Galbraith, who is at first an admirer of the married Mrs Colquhoun but later becomes her second husband. Galbraith's dual characterisation as doting husband and doctor specialising in hysteria echoes Lorrimer in *Ideala* and the husband figure in Charlotte Perkins Gilman's 'The Yellow Wallpaper', published a year previously (Heilmann 2002). Both Gilman's heroine and Grand's Evadne are subject to the gaze of the doctor-husband, whose attempts to regulate and control their respective 'illnesses' require complete submission of the body to male care and observation. Unlike Grand, Gilman narrates the female hysteric through the character's own perspective, detailing the mental and physical devastation of the rest cure, but also the potential for liberation through female defiance as the heroine gets 'out at last!' (Gilman 1993: 117). With the heroine having been locked in a room by her husband, her hysteria finds expression in the shifting wallpaper that, in turn, encodes female creativity and signals mental disintegration. The text ends when the husband unlocks the door only to faint at what he finds, an ambiguous denouement that can be read, amongst other interpretations, as a suicide.

After a failed suicide attempt, Evadne becomes increasingly restricted by a plot twist that, as Naomi Hetherington observes, 'elides medical intervention with marriage and motherhood' (2012: 158) through her second marriage and the birth of her child. In *The Heavenly Twins* Evadne rejects both discourse and resistance, choosing to uphold the promise she made to her first husband to avoid public activity. At the end of the text she asks Galbraith to 'let me live on the surface of life, as most women do' (II, 384), thus Grand points to a lack of alternatives to accepting the commodification and domestication of the female body, a fate that Gilman's text refuses to accept entirely. Gilman's short story is contemporary with Grand's novel, yet it offers a less straightforwardly pessimistic depiction of hysteria and self-harm, and their emancipatory – albeit also violent – potential. The contrast between these texts suggests a link between different bodies of narrative and their diverse strategies for fictionalising female self-damage. Gilman's story, as an experimental form of writing dramatising the psychological interiority of women's experience through narrative ambiguity, says with fewer words what Grand's cannot say at all. As an example of a melodramatic marriage plot, *The Heavenly Twins* fails to resist a predictable and idealised realist conclusion. It sees its female characters overcome unhappiness through self-sacrifice, or punish themselves for self-indulgence, and resolves the problems of non-normative femininity through marriage.

As is the heroine in 'The Yellow Wallpaper', Grand's Evadne is assessed by her doctor-husband through observation that invariably reads her bodily weakness as hysterical frailty. As in the clinical observations of Gull and Lasègue, the anorectic is given as little control as possible over her body, and is not trusted with her own recovery. Galbraith's process of watching leads him to comment frequently on Evadne's thin form, which is 'to the last degree of emaciation' (II, 277), while her 'figure was fragile to a fault' (II, 258). Galbraith romanticises Evadne's figure, which is 'slender [and] silhouetted with dark distinctness against the sloping evening sky' (II, 280). As in *Ideala*, the heroine is subject to the proprietary gaze of the male narrator, yet in *The Heavenly Twins* it is not only the starving body that incites this desire. Evadne's relationship with food is a complex mixture of self-starvation and the deliberate self-induction of illness. At various points in the text Evadne deliberately risks infection or sickness, enjoying the resultant rest and attention her convalescences provide, and Galbraith describes several episodes in which Evadne 'bear[s] up bravely' (II, 282). During these periods Evadne is described in highly complimentary terms, and she is also at her most desirable. Galbraith notes that

> [e]very breath of cold air was cutting her lungs like a knife, but she looked up at me when I took her hand, and smiled. I never knew anyone so patient and uncomplaining. [. . .] She was always the same all through her illness, gentle, uncomplaining, grateful for every little trifle that was done for her, and tranquillity itself. My impression was that she enjoyed being ill. (Grand 2007: II, 283–5)

Strikingly, it is not only Evadne's clear enjoyment of her illness but Galbraith's idealisation of her weakness and passivity that is denoted by the positively encoded language.

Following her unhappy marriage to Colquhoun, Evadne is able to become an angel in her own house only once she is physically ailing. She is docile, submissive and subject to the care and desires of the watching doctor, a combination not experienced in her first marriage. As Bailin has argued, the 'transposition of social pathologies into bodily ailment serves to reclaim these characters in crisis by initiating them into the consoling community of the sickroom' (1994: 5). Evadne only achieves tranquillity during a bout of sickness, a sense of human connection that is possible only with her doctor. On a number of occasions Evadne expresses her physical suffering as 'a relief' (II, 284 and 303), and she actively pursues situations in which she is likely to become ill. She volunteers as a nurse during an outbreak of fever at a military base, during which she restlessly nurses the dying with no concern for her own safety (II, 303–4). Although Galbraith protests about the danger in which she places herself, his desire is nevertheless piqued by her bravery, since

> when she found herself really suffering, she pulled herself together, and bore the trial with heroic calm [. . .] she never uttered a complaint; and she had the strength of mind to ignore annoyances which few people in perfect health could have borne with fortitude. Certainly her attitude then had excited sympathy, and respect as well. It was as admirable as it was unexpected. (Grand 2007: II, 301)

As Evadne's body becomes increasingly weak and subject to both deliberate infection and self-starvation, her mental faculties, we are told, improve. She is described as having 'strength of mind' and 'fortitude', echoing earlier comments that her body is 'not as robust as her brain' (I, 132). By depicting illness and physical weakness as mentally restorative, Grand draws on anorexic logic through refutation of the body as of primary importance to her heroine. Much like Ideala, who attempts to assert her intellectualism through starvation, Evadne's hunger and deliberate self-infection allows her to spiritually ascend. Through illness and thinness, Evadne asserts her existence as 'only a thinking thing, that is, a mind, a soul, or an intellect', as opposed to the 'framework of limbs that is called a human body' (Descartes 2008: 20). This ethos culminates in the text in her suicide attempt whilst pregnant; Evadne fails to recognise this as a sin, but rather sees it as a means by which to save her unborn child from exposure to the potential corruptions of the female body. By attempting to efface her own body through death, and the body of her unborn child (whom she believes to be a girl), Evadne enacts the ultimate act of self-destruction, attempting to free herself from both the gustatory and sexual dangers of corporeality. In Evadne's final attempt to resist bodiliness, her private body is made public spectacle, sensationally exploding the artificial boundary between the two spheres, but ultimately sustaining the logic that designates them as gendered and separate.

It is not only Grand's central heroine who subscribes to anorexic logic in *The Heavenly Twins*, but also her other New Woman character, Angelica. Unlike Evadne, who withers and shrinks under the pressures of an unhappy marriage, Angelica is healthy, spirited and well fed throughout the text. Strikingly similar to the heroine in Grand's *Babs the Impossible*, Angelica is 'on a much larger scale' (I, 179) than her brother, and is 'the taller, stronger, and wickeder' (I, 162) of the titular twins. Angelica's aunt Fulda expresses the conflict between the flesh and the soul as she 'gazed down into [Angelica's] face earnestly; as if she would penetrate the veil of flesh that baffled her when she tried to see clearly the soul of which Angelica occasionally gave her some glimpse' (II, 184). Her comments rework Ideala's impulse to see behind Lorrimer's 'horrid veil of flesh', and the repetition of this phrase attests to Grand's entrenchment in the doctrine of dualism. Although Fulda's comments are treated with irony by the narrator, in that Angelica is shown to be a creature of immense feeling, Grand, however satirically, deploys a system of logic that she elsewhere validates wholeheartedly. The opposite of an anorexic heroine, Angelica does, however, share the 'qualified acceptance of the Victorian aesthetic of slenderness' (Silver 2002: 82), demonstrated by her attitude towards the ascetic body of Israfil the Tenor in the second volume of the novel.

After having asked the elderly Mr Kilroy to marry her, Angelica struggles to find an outlet for her artistic abilities and embarks on an episode of cross-dressing disguised as her twin brother. Angelica befriends the angelically named Israfil, a male chorister whose house she frequents late at night and whose company she enjoys as a consequence of her newly acquired status as 'the Boy'. Israfil is

> tall and striking in appearance; clean shaven, with delicate features, dark dreamy grey eyes, and a tumbled mop of golden hair [. . .] his clothes hung upon him loosely, as if he had grown thinner since they were made; his face was pale too, and pinched in appearance, and his movements were languid, giving him altogether the air of a man just recovering from a serious illness. (Grand 2007: II, 43)

Israfil's feminine qualities are emphasised: his features are 'delicate', his long hair is golden, and his body is pale, weak and lethargic. In a move echoing Galbraith's appraisal of Evadne's ill body as exemplary of the ideal Victorian woman, Grand's narrator endorses the sick and thin body, attaching to it symptoms connoting illness and beauty in equal measure.[28] It is not merely Israfil's beautiful face or voice that inspires the approval of all those he meets, but also his physical sufferings. It is through bodily weakness that Grand communicates his inner strength and goodness, while his acts of self-denial reflect his ascetic tendencies. Israfil's long illness and eventual death are exacerbated by both charity and self-starvation, because 'the malady had been rendered hopeless from the first by his weakness for want of food' and 'he gave too much away' (II, 214). After his death, Angelica realises that Israfil has sacrificed his own food to appease her ferocious nightly appetite, a fact that shames Angelica into more appropriately womanly behaviour and curbs her ravenous appetites.

Israfil's thin body and languorous movements produce the effect of his having emerged triumphant from a battle within, and he is a Christ-like figure, trialled and tortured, spiritually victorious yet doomed to a self-sacrificial death. Israfil is shown to appreciate Angelica's beauty when he sees her dressed as herself while at church, yet his lack of sexual interest in her is underscored by his appreciation of her spirituality, her angelic good looks and feminine obedience. His vocation as a chorister, a form of employment well suited to a man so physically unrobust, further suggests a sense of gender ambiguity, since employment in the masculine world of work is impossible.

Grand's feminisation of a male character through the vocation of singing draws upon a long tradition of gender androgyny associated with male performers (Scholz 2001). The Dean of Morningquest tells Israfil 'you are an opera singer' (II, 47) and a rumour is spread in the village that his mother had been too (II, 49). In Simon Richter's work on the body of the eunuch in classical aesthetics, the feminised bodies of the castrati operatic singers are aligned with the crucified body of Jesus Christ. Richter notes the similarities in the cross-shaped space signalling the absence of genitalia above the buttocks of the eunuch in classical artworks, and the images of crucifixion found in medieval paintings. 'The crucifixion and the pieta insist in their representation on the ponderous presence of the body' (1992: 58), thus Richter argues that the body of Christ reflects an iconographic retelling of 'castration' – of the body in pain, curiously present yet absent in ways similarly represented by the operatic figure of the eunuch. Israfil's feminisation is achieved, partly, through parallels between his own experience and that of Christ, a figure that my first chapter has argued was ambiguously gendered in nineteenth-century culture.

Israfil's saintly qualities correspond to his profession as a chorister in the Cathedral choir, but also to the value the Victorians placed on the beauty of death. As Elisabeth Bronfen has shown, the dying body in Victorian art and fiction became a popular Romantic trope, demonstrating the period's pervasive and highly complex attitudes towards art, femininity and mourning.[29] Grand conflates these concepts when the narrator describes the Tenor as 'haggard and drawn' with 'great black circles round his sunken eyes' yet with an 'expression of strength and sweetness [. . .] he never looked more beautiful than then' (II, 207). Although Bronfen largely examines the dying female body as an object of poetic admiration, she notes the idealisation of the same feminine traits attributed by Grand to the dying chorister. Like the androgynous Christ, Israfil represents the epitome of Victorian values of self-sacrifice and self-denial. It is precisely his lack of embodiment, the separation of gender, sexuality and flesh from his soul through which Israfil achieves what the starving heroines of Grand's fiction cannot – he transcends his human form and gains access to the spiritual world whilst alive, and in death.

For Grand's Israfil, illness, starvation and eventually death are rendered beautiful by virtue of the femininity associated with each. Grand's feminisation and deification of Israfil, as well as her idealisation of his hunger and condemnation of Angelica's greed, further demonstrates her approval of both the Victorian thin ideal and anorexic logic. Grand inverts the traditional novelistic figure of the starving heroine by having her male character starve parallel to her hungry and satisfied New Woman heroine. While ostensibly promoting the healthy, hungry New Woman type, this inversion reflects poorly on Angelica, who is trained by Israfil's death into conduct more befitting her class and gender. Although he is technically male, Israfil, like Evadne, is beatified by his weak and thin form, his feminine frailty and his bravery in the face of self-sacrifice. In narrating the starving male body within a paradigm of womanly beauty and submission, Grand only furthers the ideologies through which Evadne must be taught to renounce intellectual and political selfhood, and by which Ideala must deny her immoderate appetites. Grand also mobilised similar logic in the third of her Morninquest novels, to which I now turn.

Published four years after *The Heavenly Twins*, Grand's *The Beth Book* is a semi-autobiographical account of a woman of genius whose abilities develop parallel to her self-starvation. Beth Caldwell begins, like Angelica Ilverthorpe, as a healthy, hungry child of the kind Grand wrote about in her 1894 essay. Beth's relationship with food is central to the text from the outset, and although this relationship is different to those explored in her two previous novels, it is arguably in *The Beth Book* that Grand's valorisation of the starving female body reaches its climax. As Abigail Dennis has proposed, *The Beth Book* 'constitutes an allegorical diegesis on the subjection of *fin-de-siècle* female appetites' (2007: 19). Like Dennis, I read the heroine's management of her appetite as concomitant with Victorian notions of romantic reward for feminine self-sacrifice, but I also suggest that it is not only sacrifice but the passive aggression of anorexic logic through which Beth's 'happy ending' is achieved. As in her earlier novels, Grand sanctions the thin body and critiques its overweight counterpart through characters reflecting her views on consumption and masculine greed. Thus, Beth's thin Aunt Victoria is the morally superior, self-sacrificing angel, and her obese Uncle James her spurious and corrupted equivalent. Beth is a hungry child who is 'greedy for pudding' (Grand 1980: 103) yet associates food with unpleasant feelings. In the novel there are 'many circumstances which [are] recalled by the taste of food' yet 'all these associations of ideas [were] disagreeable. [Beth] had not a single pleasant one in connection with food' (1980: 17–18).

Beth grows up learning to quiet the desires of her body, as she is taught to silence her growing intellect and unquenchable appetite for adventure. Like the mothers of Grand's Evadne Frayling and Caird's Viola Dendraith, Mrs Caldwell is unhappily married and projects her ideology of self-sacrifice on to her daughter, who is encouraged to digest the restrictions of femininity while simultaneously denying her own hunger. As in Grand's other novels, the Cartesian body/soul paradigm surfaces as the narrator refers to Beth's body as a 'case of clay' from which her 'pure spirit' might be 'released' (1980: 283). The difficulty of women's position as at once examples of angelic, domestic disinterestedness, yet incapable of circumventing their fleshly desires or biological imperatives, is embodied by Beth's characterisation as a woman of genius. Though Beth develops into a woman of power, influence and magnetism, Grand resolves her novel by placing her in a normative, submissive relationship with Alfred Brock – a man for whom she sacrifices her body.

Like Ideala and Evadne, Beth's starving body becomes a site of male eroticisation and exchange, when her portrait is shown to Brock by the artist Gresham Powell. Entitled 'A Study in Starvation', the portrait is painted without Beth's knowledge, at the most vulnerable and desperate stage of her self-denial, when she is forced to sell her hair to buy food. Powell is described as being 'moved by her suffering and gentleness' (1980: 514), and it is Beth's beauty and pain that inspire first his observation, and then his portrait. Like the heroines in Grand's earlier novels, Beth's thin body is subject to the proprietary male gaze. Grand critiques the images of her heroines as viewed through the masculine frameworks that designate them as 'to be looked at, denuded [and] unveiled' (Brooks 1993: 97). She suggests her disapproval of Powell's painting of Beth by having him appraise his subject coldly and dispassionately. Powell only sees Beth's 'interesting face' (1980: 13) and 'pretty hair' (1980: 514), yet the reader is party to her emaciated form and the self-denial that leads her to offer up a part of her body in a synecdoche of masculine consumption. Many of the martyred women depicted in the Pre-Raphaelite art discussed in Chapter 1 were painted with abundant and flowing locks that suggested their sexuality and desirability (Ofek 2009: 30). Beth, however, resists both objectification and classification by cutting her hair off. In an act that is revolutionary by way of its refusal of the identities offered to women in Victorian culture, yet submissive in its commitment to self-sacrifice, Beth attempts to transcend the boundaries of the artist's portrait, yet, to a certain extent, only strengthens its frame.

Although *The Beth Book* has a lot in common with its predecessors, there are points at which it departs from *Ideala* and *The Heavenly Twins*, both in its treatment of self-starvation and in its dramatisation of female self-sacrifice. Unlike Ideala and Evadne,

Beth's privations are not deliberate refusals of her bodiliness, but are for the benefit of those around her. Just as she has been taught by her mother to revoke her claim to her inheritance so that her brother can be educated, Beth eats less so that her family might eat more.[30] As a result, she becomes 'torpid from excessive self-denial' (1980: 214) but her hunger for food is continually referenced. Unlike Ideala and Evadne, whose respective hyperactivity reflects observations about anorexia made by Victorian doctors, Beth is rendered languorous by her starvation. In a reversal of Angelica's consumption of Israfil's food in *The Heavenly Twins*, Beth nurses a sick Alfred Brock, spending all she has on food for his treatment. Beth explains that she 'used to be so hungry sometimes that she hurried past the provision shops when she had to go out, lest she should not be able to resist the temptation to go in and buy food for herself' (1980: 506).

Beth is constantly tempted, because her need to abnegate the desires of her flesh lies not in the pursuit of masculine achievement or spirituality, but in the survival of those she feels she must protect. The self-sacrifice she endures aligns Beth, more than either Ideala or Evadne, with Victorian ideals of passivity, domesticity and maternal care. Unlike the other heroines, Beth emerges from her self-starvation with the promise of sexual and emotional fulfilment in her relationship with Brock, the man for whom she has almost died of hunger. Although her body is starved, the ending of Grand's novel – which sees Brock advancing to meet an emaciated Beth on horseback in the pose of a Romance hero – hints at the potential realisation of Beth's appetites: sexual, maternal and gustatory. Grand's most hungry yet most self-starving heroine is rewarded for her choice to feed Brock whilst denying herself, and this betrays the complex mixture of subversion and traditionalism at the heart of the text and, indeed, Grand's trilogy. Beth's movement from appetite to a denial of bodily desires marks her transition both to adulthood and to the role of domestic Angel, a position that neither of Grand's other starving heroines manages to fulfil adequately. Ideala becomes a political activist, abandoning her hopes for motherhood, and Evadne becomes a mother, only to be atrophied by entrenchment within the domestic sphere, wasting her once-ferocious intellect and eschewing life's pleasures. The ending of *The Beth Book* posits that only a perfect balance between public activity and anorexic self-sacrifice can truly fulfil the New Woman heroine, reflecting Grand's radicalism but also her conservatism and subscription to anorexic logic.

In all three texts that comprise the Morningquest trilogy, New Woman self-starvation is portrayed both as an unfortunate result of phallocentric ideology and as a potentially useful strategy to transcend the limits of Victorian femininity. However, it is through the application of such a strategy that Grand's heroines reinforce patriarchal epistemophilia, since women's bodies figure as objects 'to be looked at, denuded, unveiled'. As rewritings of the marriage plot, all three texts reinforce the importance of womanly self-sacrifice, and assimilate the heroine into a largely domestic world in which she is free to undertake biologically ascribed roles. If, as Brooks suggests, the signs made on the body signify its passage into narrative, then the stories told by these female bodies are troublingly counterproductive in the context of Grand's 'feminist' aims. The sensational New Woman social purity novel aspired to depict the fatal consequences of the separate sphere ideology and gender double standards that underpinned Victorian society. In doing so, writers like Grand attempted a breakdown of the boundaries between public and private, through graphic depictions of starving female bodies. However, these representations were shrouded in a discourse equally damaging to women because they relied too heavily upon classical constructions of gender that viewed the female body as fleshly and desiring, yet also lauded it as the ultimate vessel of purity.

The wound culture of the *fin de siècle* provided the conditions within which previously covert, private bodies entered into cultural discourse, bodies that in Grand's work are painfully emaciated and displayed for the reading public. However, novels like Grand's adopted conventionally masculine forms that may have shaped and ultimately limited their ability to narrate the starving body outside the paradigm of anorexic logic or male-oriented visual economies such as medicine, psychology, art and literature. In choosing to display her starving heroines via literary Realism, Grand ironically left herself no space in which to subvert ideologies that understood the female body as an object for masculine eroticisation and consumption. The bodies of her heroines are eventually consumed by the formal limitations of the realist novel, requiring either their assimilation into the society of which they are a part, or their complete destruction. In the subsequent two chapters, I show how the traditionally masculine narrative form of lyric poetry, as well as emergent new forms of writing such as the short story, provided a new canvas upon which New Woman writers could paint images of self-sacrificing bodies in ways that challenged those as represented by Grand's novels. I also demonstrate a direct correlation between the increasingly experimental and non-traditional forms of New Woman writing that emerged between 1880 and 1900, and the progressively violent images of self-harm contained within. However, the poems and short stories explored in my final two chapters did not always represent an extreme thematic or ideological departure from novels like Grand's, despite their formal radicalism.

Notes

1. See Whelan 2009, Silver 2002 and Haley 1978 on the rise of dieting culture. See William Banting's *Letter on Corpulence* (1863) for an example of diet advice aimed at men.
2. See 'The Wife's Tragedy' (1854) in the Prologue (Patmore 2013). Also see Sutherland 2015: 1–15 and 134–58, in which the 'lady' is discussed in relation to Ruskin's essay.
3. See 'A Letter' (1867: 502) in *The Englishwoman's Domestic Magazine*. See Beetham and Boardman 2001 for additional examples.
4. See Christ and Jordan 1995, Braziel and Le Besco 2001, Silver 2002, Swafford 2007 and Cranton 2009.
5. The term 'apepsia hysterica' was abandoned in 1873. Gull eventually came to disagree with the association between hysteria and self-starvation.
6. The diagnosis of Victorian anorexic patients was limited to women. Gull concedes that he has 'occasionally seen it in males' (Acland 1894: 306) but effectively genders the disorder as female.
7. The drive for thinness (which neither Gull nor Lasègue discusses) is noted by Jean-Martin Charcot and Pierre Janet, who were both nineteenth-century (French) physicians. See Vandereycken and Van Deth 1990.
8. For the Irish, hunger is an ancient and deeply meaningful trope that cannot be fully examined within the remit of this project. See Ellman 1993: 30–57, Beresford 1994 and Vernon 2009: 8–17 for discussion of hunger in the context of Irish nationalism. See van Wingerden 1999: 90–2 and Smith 2010: 28–9 and 59 for discussion of the starving suffragettes.
9. Victorian doctors noted that anorexia manifested in adolescent males, but their work failed to investigate cases outside the remit of their experience with middle-class women, and my discussion is limited to recorded cases. See Langley 2006 and Morgan 2008.
10. See Ellman 1993, Showalter 1993 and Bartley 2012.
11. See Bruch 1979 and Chernin 1986 for discussion of Freud's emphasis on the sexual component of anorexia.
12. Authors like Malet and Lee have been reclaimed as New Women by contemporary literary scholars, who convincingly argue that their work corresponds to that of authors like Grand, Caird and Schreiner. However, Grand was a self-proclaimed New Woman (despite remaining ambivalent about the term's popular usage), while Malet and Lee would not have seen themselves as such.
13. See Gilbert and Gubar 1984 and Michie 1987.

14. See Auerbach 1982, Bailin 1994, Gilbert 2005 and Talairach-Vielmas 2013.
15. Mid-Victorian women's fiction included overt acts of food refusal prefiguring those deployed by New Woman writers. See Charlotte Brontë's *Shirley* (1849); Shirley Keeldar is consumed by desire, yet her behaviour in relation to food is at times aggressive and masculine.
16. Not all three-volume novels written by New Woman writers were realist. The late-Victorian authors Lucas Malet and George Egerton both wrote novels that dealt with shocking subject matter like Grand's. However, their novels were experimental and formally closer to Modernism.
17. Grand may also have critiqued masculine Epicureanism as a criticism of the reverence shown by Decadent and/or aesthete figures such as Walter Pater and Oscar Wilde, for the philosophies of Epicurus.
18. *The Heavenly Twins* sold 20,000 copies in its first print run in 1893, and was reprinted six times during the nineteenth century.
19. Brumberg gives the examples of Saint Catherine of Siena (1347–80), who ate only herbs and who made herself vomit after consuming any other food (2000: 33–5); also see Gutierrez 2003.
20. See Hammond 2010 for further.
21. See Showalter 1993 and Vandereycken and Van Deth 1994, who discuss the fasting girls in both medieval and Victorian medicine.
22. See Stacey 2002 for a detailed account of a Victorian fasting girl subject to tests and observations.
23. See Vandereycken and Van Deth 1994.
24. Wounded bodies were fictionalised in the work of Zola, Baudelaire, Daudet, Vallès and Huysmans, and also the Decadent writers of the British *fin de siècle*. See Seltzer 1998: 1–3 for further discussion.
25. See Harrington 1999 on the railway as a symbol of British colonial (masculine) power.
26. Edith is the wife of Lot in the Old Testament who is turned to salt upon looking back at the destruction of Sodom. In Greek mythology Evadne is the wife of Capaneus who killed herself on the funeral pyre of her dead husband. Angelica literally means 'of the angels' and is ironic, as is her designation as a 'heavenly twin'.
27. See Pearl 2010 for discussion of physiognomy in relation to Victorian culture.
28. See Byrne 2010 for an analysis of the ways in which the wasting body was valorised in Victorian literary and visual culture.
29. See Bronfen 1992 and Byrne 2010 for discussion.
30. This plot device is often used by New Woman writers; in *The Wing of Azrael*, Viola is forced to sacrifice her education because her brothers take priority. Ironically, Viola's brothers are the reason for her family's financial collapse, so her sacrifice is pointless.

Chapter 3

Deconstructing the Drunkard's Path: Drunken Bodies in New Woman Fiction

Drinking as Self-Harm

Like the diagnostic criteria for anorexia nervosa, the study of alcoholism and addiction evolved out of late-nineteenth-century psychological and social research, at a time when drinking had been largely depoliticised (Zieger 2008: 11). The disease of addiction was widely circulated as a discourse from the 1890s, at a time of unprecedented commercial expansion in Britain, allowing medical and social commentators to parallel mass production and consumption with substance misuse or dependence. Thanks to an 'explicit analogy between the excesses of the addict and the everyday experience of the consumer' (Margolis 2002: 21), addiction became intelligible to those struggling to contain their excessive desires, and those who treated them.[1] As I have argued, modernity represented and facilitated the coupling of the human body with the machine, and the potential for atrocity inherent in the interface of these previously disparate forms. The relationship between modernity, consumerism and addiction in machine culture was complicated by the pathologisation of the 'living dead subject' (Seltzer 1998: 90), whose individuality and agency were under constant threat from their own reproducibility as both consumer and commodity. The relationship between addiction and consumerism is complex precisely because 'self-production in machine-culture is tied to both compulsive repetition and compulsive sexual violence' (Seltzer 1998: 91). As part of a socio-economic system rooted in repetition and in (sexual) violence, excessive drinking featured as one of a collection of self-damaging practices in New Woman writing, at a critical juncture at which notions of selfhood, free will and self-determination were in flux.

Unlike self-starvation, alcohol abuse occupies an unsteady, transitory and at times contradictory space on the spectrum of behaviours with which *Self-Harm in New Woman Writing* is concerned. It is, to

a certain extent, a culturally acceptable form of self-harm function-
ing variously as a rite of passage, a celebration or an understandable
response to grief or trauma in our society.[2] Because of its cultural
acceptability, excessive drinking is rarely conceived of as self-harm
outside of the clinical environment. As Eve Kosofsky Sedgwick points
out, it is possible to become addicted to addiction and difficult to
draw a line between 'healthy free will' (1994: 131–2) and unhealthy
excess. According to leading medical researchers, the current model
of self-harm is 'too narrow in its scope', because 'self-harming tendencies find expression in many different ways, ranging from the highly
dramatic, to the virtually invisible' (Turp 2002: 9).[3] Psychologists and
cultural critics recognise that alcoholism operates as part of a range of
self-harming activities often adopted by those who injure themselves
in more visual or painful ways (Aldridge et al. 2011, Sutton 2007,
Haw et al. 2005, Favazza 2011). Indeed, current National Health
Service advice lists 'deliberate misuse of alcohol' ('NHS Choices: Your
Health, Your Choices'), along with anorexia, excessive exercising,
poisoning, and cutting or burning the skin, as examples of self-harm.

For the purpose of this chapter, it is useful to consider excessive
drinking as a pathology, as a practice deployed by the 'living dead
subject' escaping the repetitive mundanity of a machine culture in
which the body is imbibed by both capitalism and patriarchy. I take
as my point of departure the notion that habitual consumption of
alcohol might be understood as self-harm, and that self-harmful
drinking is tied implicitly to the socio-economic arrangements of Victorian machine culture. In light of women's position as subordinate
to the mechanisms of the late-Victorian economy, I argue that New
Woman writing about inebriation depicts the self-destructive drives
of female experience under patriarchy. However, I also show that
New Woman writing dealt with the figure of the female 'alcoholic'
very differently from the texts in which she had featured previously.[4]

In the texts by and about the New Woman examined in this chapter, the iconography and organising structures of Christianity examined in Chapter 1 emerge as both a central cause and symbolic locus
of women's excessive consumption of alcohol. I examine the fictionalisation of female drunkenness at a point in history when old conceptions of madness and excess began to give way to new theories of
disease and addiction, and experimental literatures began to compete
with more traditional forms of writing. I explore the ways in which
these uneasy transitions are highlighted and complicated by representations of excessive drinking associated with pseudo-religious images,
and I directly link drinking to a subversive proto-feminist dialectic of
the body in New Woman fiction. I suggest that the differences in the

treatment of the female inebriate in the Victorian novel and in the New Woman short story highlight the growing potential for representing violent female self-harm in shorter narrative forms at the *fin de siècle*. In doing so, I position the female drunk as a problematic emblem of modernity, feminist agitation and wound culture, a figure through which conflicting notions of the body and the self are enacted in New Woman writing.

Drunkenness in Victorian Britain

Unlike drug use – increasingly criminalised in nineteenth-century Britain – alcohol and the spaces in which it was consumed were subject to forms of governance and regulation, separating them from later-emerging narratives of addiction (Harrison 1994). Alcohol was relatively inexpensive, and since clean water was at a premium, it was widely consumed as a sanitary alternative amongst the poor. Outbreaks of cholera had made water supplies unsafe in a number of Victorian cities and among the poorer classes it became widely accepted that alcohol could prevent the disease (Gilbert 2008: 51). As a result, it was common for most working-class Victorians to regularly consume lower concentrations of alcohol in beer. Since the concept of alcoholism as a disease would not become medically or culturally entrenched until the twentieth century, excessive drinking was subject to ethical rather than clinical debate, as part of a wider discourse about the perceived moral failings of a Victorian society increasingly estranged from conventional religion.[5] Indeed, alcohol itself would not be classified as a drug in Britain until the mid-twentieth century, and its socio-economic impact was largely downplayed by the mid-Victorian establishment (Huggins 2015).[6]

Towards the end of the nineteenth century, developments in psychology and neurology paved the way for new theories of addiction that continue to underpin twenty-first-century treatment.[7] Indeed, the *fin de siècle* witnessed wide-reaching socio-cultural developments that shifted the way in which alcohol was perceived and the way in which the drunk (and in particular the female drunk) was figured as both a social problem and a fictional construct. The distinction between genteel beer drinking and the degenerate consumption of spirits had been schematised by the popular British artist William Hogarth in both *Gin Lane* and *Beer Street* (1751) during the previous century. Furthermore, as Kevin Swafford reminds us, 'in almost all of the major realist representations of the working class in the nineteenth century, there is at least one working-class character "sodden with drink"' (2007: 57). Thus, at least textually, the habitual drunkard was not regularly seen as a middle-class character, and even less frequently as a story's heroine.[8]

Late-Victorian fictional representations of alcohol consumption responded to deep class anxieties that discursively imagined the poor as both pitiable and disgusting, as worthy of sympathy but ultimately as other than the middle-class readership. Whether dulling the pangs of hunger or escaping the twin realities of grinding poverty and hard labour, the body of the working-class drunk featured prominently in a variety of popular novels throughout the century, eliciting both compassion and revulsion. Esther in Gaskell's *Mary Barton* (1848), Mr Dolls in Dickens's *Our Mutual Friend* (1865), and Mr Dagley and Mr Raffles in Eliot's *Middlemarch* all demonstrate the expediency of the working-class 'alcoholic' stock character. The expansion of the Victorian middle class, as well as the overpopulation of urban centres and the poverty and criminality that accompanied it, led to the predominant perception of drunkenness as a social evil tied specifically to class. In 'The Bitter Cry of Outcast London' (1883), Andrew Mearns laments that 'the misery and sin caused by drink in these districts have often been told, but the horrors can never be set forth either by pen or artist's pencil' (2002: 30). Though designed to elicit sympathy by shocking his readership, commentary like Mearns's explicitly associated alcohol with the visceral and visual problem of the inherently corrupt poor. In demonstrating the depths of wretchedness and sin into which the drinkers, brothel-keepers, prostitutes and child workers of the slums had slipped, Mearns – like William Booth in 'In Darkest England and the Way Out' (1890) – drew attention to the susceptibility of the poor body to self-destructive practices.

It was not that aristocrats and the upwardly mobile did not get drunk, but that their intoxication could be kept private behind the closed doors of the home or the theatre, the restaurant or the gentleman's club. The public nature of working-class intoxication made it the focus of both middle-class disapprobation and philanthropy, and movements for both temperance and teetotalism became popular strategies for elevating the conditions of the poor (Breton 2013). Teetotalism was widespread during the 1830s and 1840s, and was tied to political movements such as Chartism. Although socialist in its conception, it became unavoidably part of the wider project of delineating and enforcing class hierarchies that othered the working-class body as fundamentally deviant. Deploying an Arnoldian rhetoric that sought the rehabilitation of the workforce through exposure to middle-class culture and morality, temperance attempted to govern manners and behaviour.[9] Christianity was a central component of the temperance agenda, and its importance was underscored by both the prominence of its religious leaders and its use of hymns and Christian tracts.[10] It drew on biblical references to the immorality of drunkenness found in 1 Corinthians (6: 9–10, 5: 11), Ephesians (5: 18–20), Proverbs (31: 4, 23: 20–1) and Isaiah (5: 11, 28: 1–29), and equated excessive drinking with original sin (Nott 1831). Temperance and teetotalism offered a challenge to the formulaic teleology of the 'drunkard's path' in which increasing dependence on alcohol lead in linear fashion to degeneration and eventually death. They focused instead on the possibilities of recovery, disputing the assured decline and death reinforced by the scientific naturalism that asserted the hereditism (and thus certainty) of the drinker's fate. Foregrounding the potential for self-salvation, both teetotalism and temperance challenged prevailing notions of the irredeemability of the drunk rooted in the same science that posited the New Woman as an example of female degeneracy.

The excessive corporeality of the drunken working-class body was frequently fictionalised in the slum narratives of the late nineteenth century. These texts are a particularly rich site for examination of attitudes towards gender, class and alcohol; they exhibited paternalistic rejections of the paradigm of alcohol as social deviance, as well as naturalist depictions that demonised the poor. In Arthur Morrison's *A Child of the Jago* (1897) abstinence from, or even moderation in, drinking is treated with the utmost suspicion, a fact confirmed by the unpopular Mrs Perrott, a threat to the reciprocal fabric of her community because she 'had not entirely fallen in with Jago ways; she had soon grown sluttish and dirty, but she was never drunk [. . .]' (2012: 22). Unlike the working classes, who to a certain extent reflected and internalised bourgeois morality, the slum-dwellers of nineteenth-century fiction often inverted such codes by celebrating degeneration and vice. In *A Child of the Jago* and, for example, George Gissing's *The Netherworld* (1889), drunkenness is depicted as a transmissible family trait, a predetermined and inescapable tendency bestowed upon the children of degenerates.

Unlike the men and women of Morrison's Jago or Gissing's Netherworld, the middle-class drunkard was not so frequently or uncomplicatedly represented. Where narratives of middle-class or aristocratic inebriation did appear, they were often heavily codified. For instance, Thomas L. Reed proposes that the 'transforming draught' (2006: 38) that metamorphoses the respectable Jekyll into the murderous Hyde in Robert Louis Stevenson's *Strange Case of Dr Jekyll and Mr Hyde* (1886) shows that middle-class drunkenness was hiding in plain sight in Victorian fiction. The suggestion that the middle classes could be vulnerable to the degeneracy of their poorer counterparts challenged paternalistic and hierarchical notions that the poor could be influenced by the inherent morality of their social superiors. For example, the drinking, drug addiction and sexual degradation of the hero of Oscar Wilde's *The Picture of Dorian Gray* (1890/1891) remains largely unconfirmed because of Dorian's aristocratic grace and excellent manners. Dorian's contemporaries hear 'the most evil things against him' (2008: 108), yet the text resists articulating these evils fully. Dorian frequents 'the sordid room of the little ill-famed tavern' (2008: 109), yet the main clue as to his misuse of assorted substances is his painting, which betrays the 'hideous lines that seared the wrinkling forehead', the 'coarse bloated hands' and 'misshapen body and failing limbs' (2008: 109) of an addict.

By the end of the nineteenth century excessive drinking amongst the upper and middle classes continued to be represented in indistinct, indefinite and metaphorical ways. However, as in the case of Wilde's novel, it was also imagined in ways which challenged prevailing notions of degeneration as physically decipherable and thus merely an affliction of the poor, ugly, uneducated or overworked. The readings of New Woman fiction offered by this chapter demonstrate the extent to which women writers confronted prevalent scientific theories about the female body and its hereditary and degenerative afflictions, as well as the bourgeois religious ideologies that defined and constructed it. They also reveal a direct challenge to the Cartesian dualism that had, for centuries, been a staple tenet of Christianity, and that the heroines discussed in Chapter 2 both undermine and reinforce. Unlike the starving heroines of the New Woman novel who practise the art of self-elision, the female drunk instead asserts her corporeality through excessive consumption. This chapter shows how the drunken heroine of New Woman fiction demands to be seen (and heard) through acts of bodily display that contest the strict gender dictates governing separate sphere ideology. It also demonstrates that texts that displayed the female drunken body as subject to self-harming impulses failed to recognise that they operated within an epistemophilic tradition that limited the potential for self-harm as an effective resistive strategy.

The Victorian Woman Drinker

The inability to control alcoholic consumption was characterised by Victorian medical science using a variety of complex and unstable terms, drawn from research carried out in European medical and psychiatric establishments. In France, Philippe Pinel, Jean-Étienne Dominique Esquirol and Jean-Martin Charcot had attempted to frame the condition using several theoretical models, all of which stemmed from the basic assumption that excessive drinking was a form of mania. Mania described a mind disturbed by 'mental exaltation, [. . .] excitation, hyperactivity, [and] symptoms such as visions and delusions' (Clouston 1887: 138–60).[11] Unlike the popular Victorian diagnosis of melancholia, which referred to patients who were merely depressed, mania was concomitant with lunacy, and was applied to those unable to control their impulses, to account for a range of psychological disorders now recognised as distinct illnesses.[12] The clinical terminology used to describe alcoholic mania included monomania, lunacy, dipsomania, oenomania and moral insanity (Valverde 1998: 43), all of which were deployed in relation to alcohol abusers in complicated and contradictory ways. During the nineteenth century 'alcoholism' could be found in medical dictionaries as 'dipsomania', yet Victorian definitions tended to focus on the long-term physiological effects of heavy drinking rather than the cause of the disorder (Valverde 1998: 43). Such classifications were based on the essential belief that the inability to control one's desires constituted a malady of the will that was the fundamental effect of excessive alcohol consumption and that this resulted from hereditary psychological deviance.

Nordau's *Degeneration* condemned the New Woman, viewing her intellectual development as dangerous to her health, yet also deployed the imagery of drunkenness in its wider evaluation of degeneracy. Nordau based his assertions on the work of the nineteenth-century psychiatrist Bénédict Augustin Morel, who cited poisoning of the bodily system by alcohol as a cause of degeneration (Mosse 1993: xxi). Explaining that 'things as they are totter and plunge, as they are suffered to reel and fall' (1993: 5–6), Nordau summons the language of intoxication, pre-empting his later commentary on the 'fin-de-siècle disposition' (1993: 15), since

[a] race that is regularly addicted, even without excess, to narcotics and stimulants in any form (such as fermented alcoholic drinks, opium, hashish, arsenic) [. . .] begets degenerate descendants who, if they remain exposed to the same influences, rapidly descend to the lowest degree of degeneracy, to idiocy, to dwarfishness. (Nordau 1993: 34)

Nordau's understanding of substance misuse as a formative factor in, and product of, emerging modernity anticipates twentieth-century medicine and psychiatry, as well as contemporary literary criticism by Seltzer and Sedgwick. However, Nordau's focus on the genetic inheritance of alcohol dependence as a feature of national decline limited his understanding of the complex social issues surrounding excessive consumption that were recognised, in part, by New Woman writers.

Limiting theories of degeneration were applied not only to the body of the drinker, but to any body that failed to conform to Victorian social expectations or moral dictates. This was particularly true of women, whose multifarious deviances from normative patterns of behaviour became discursively intertwined regardless of their lack of connection. Nineteenth-century attitudes towards the female inebriate can be seen as the ultimate example of the anorexic logic of Victorian middle-class values. Unlike the anorectic discussed in Chapter 2, whose small size attested to her lack of autonomous needs and ability to control her body, the drunken woman represented the opposite. If anorexia enacted 'the process that Western logic inscribes', the 'horror of the female flesh that is often the unconscious of discourse' (Heywood 1996: 8), then the drunk female body was the physical manifestation of that horror, the breakdown of womanly virtue and all consumptive restriction. This breakdown was rendered both socially and morally unacceptable by way of bourgeois religion, which – as Chapter 1 has shown – discouraged the desires typified by the fall of humankind through Eve's consumption of fruit in the Garden of Eden.

All the texts explored in this chapter represent the female inebriate with reference to the ideologies, organising structures and imagery of Christianity. I have already explored the Christian act of Eucharistic consumption, the sharing and absorption of Christ's body and blood into one's own. In this chapter I argue that this process is replicated by female drinkers reacting against, or attempting to internalise, Christ's self-sacrificial example. By drinking excessively these women recreate, yet also invert, the sacramental process whereby the sacrifice of Christ's body and blood for humankind is remembered through the symbolic consumption of his martyrdom through bread and wine.[13] In their acts of bodily consumption, women subjected to the demands of Victorian religious and moral laws symbolically reproduce the Eucharist in their internalisation and over-consumption of patriarchy. However, they also challenge notions of Christian bodily self-sacrifice as exemplified by Christ, asserting their right to embodiment at a time when the female body was supposed to be desexualised, incorporeal and undesiring.

As the supposed exponents of the domestic ideal and carriers of a future generation of strong and healthy Englishmen, drunk women were viewed by Victorian society as doubly transgressive. The working-class housewife who drank neglected her family; her self-directed desires needed to be subdued in order for patriarchy to prevail. Indeed, the middle-class woman whose boredom of decorous life or unfulfilled ambitions drove her to drink failed to set the happy example required by her husband and master. Women of all classes who drank committed the grave sin of having independent needs, since the fulfilment of these needs might herald demands for further freedoms that could threaten the status quo. Like the pseudo-religious domestic Angel, and the anorexic logic that required women's disembodiment, discourses surrounding female drunkenness privileged bodily containment. Ideals of female passivity, submission and docility could not be reconciled with the figure of the female inebriate, who epitomised every charge levelled at women who failed to live up to the requirements of feminine perfection. Her self-indulgence and neglect of familial duties made her a demon in her own house, unlike male drinkers, whose actions could be excused equally by gentlemanly over-indulgence or the demands of excessive physical work.[14]

Like the New Woman, the drunken wife represented a threat to masculinity and to capitalism. She could 'substantially handicap her sober husband's efforts to rise; she would waste his money, exhaust him emotionally, and fail to make the kind of home that he needed' (Nelson 2007: 16). Furthermore, a causal relationship between unwomanly conduct and men's drunkenness was established by commentators eager to enforce an ideal of womanly self-discipline. In *Some Habits and Customs of the Working Classes* (1867), Thomas Wright remarks that

> drunkenness is in many cases, doubtless, the result of innate depravity, and a confirmed drunkard is rarely to be reclaimed by home comforts, which to his degraded mind offer no charm; but at the same time there can be no doubt in the mind of any person who is acquainted with the manners and habits of the working classes, that thousands of working men are driven by lazy, slovenly, mismanaging wives, to courses which ultimately result in their becoming drunkards amid disreputable members of society. (Wright 1867: 190)

In presenting a poorly regulated household as an underlying factor in man's descent into depravity, Wright justifies men's use of alcohol as a natural response to female mismanagement. In an 1888 lecture, Glasgow medical examiner James B. Russell cites that 'every year the deaths of from 60 to 70 children under five years of age are [. . .] due to accident or negligence', explaining that 'half of that number are overlain by drunken mothers [. . .] or poisoned with whisky' (1888: 15). The death of children at the hands of drunken fathers is not addressed, and Russell's omission exemplifies Victorian expectations that women should nurture and safeguard children, whilst men are exonerated of parental accountability.

Russell's account engaged with an already well-established rhetoric of the twin horrors of poverty and female drunkenness at work in mid-century accounts of a similar nature. For example, in an anonymously penned 1851 exposé, a 'Medical Gentleman' recounts that

> shoeless and shivering in the raw damp of a chilly November night, might have been seen a few Saturdays ago, a woman, with one child in her arms and two little ones tugging at her gown – drunk, almost unable to stand – who, a few minutes before entering the dram-shop, had pawned her shawl for fourpence, in order to get a glass of the accursed liquor, the love of which had reduced her to the appalling condition in which we saw her. She was a bloated and besotted looking wretch. Her dress consisted of only a few rags, and her red skeleton-like legs were bare to the thigh [. . .] her bosom was nearly bare [. . .] (*An Enquiry into Destitution* 1851: 43)

Despite apparent sympathy, the woman is described as a bloated wretch – a symbol of female vice, criminality and degradation. While her drunkenness disgusts the Medical Gentleman and is suggested by her bloated body and inability to stand, the voyeurism inherent in his consideration of the drunken female body is made explicit by his attention to the detail of her bare thigh and barely covered bosom. His compassion is complicated by the eroticism of his stare, a gaze bound up with both disgust of and desire for the corrupted female form. Like the suffering female martyrs and the anorexic bodies discussed in my first two chapters, women's intoxicated bodies were subject to a masculine field of vision which situated them as objects of narrative desire. However, unlike the virginal and devout saints, and the thin bodies of ethereal, childlike and desexualised anorexic heroines, it is the corporeality of the female drunk – her inability to defer or negate her bodiliness – that makes her the 'ultimate enigma' (Brooks 1993: 70), an 'other', who, in Lacanian terms, affirms masculine subjectivity.

Drunkenness and Sexuality

Victorian women's consumption of alcohol was discursively equated with their powerlessness to control other bodily drives, and the figure of the female alcoholic was culturally interposed with that of the fallen woman. The term 'fallen' was applied variously to the prostitute, the adulteress and the seductress, and was more generally deployed as an epithet for any woman who, like the New Woman, failed to comply with strict regulations governing female morality.[15] Amanda Anderson observes that the instability of the expressions that were applied to women of compromised character are testament to 'cultural anxieties about the very possibility of deliberative moral action' (1993: 2). Anderson's point makes sense of the use of the same terminology to describe female drinkers. If the fallen woman occupied a liminal space between linguistic uncertainty and moral ambiguity, as a symbol of the loss of will and self-regulating identity, then it follows that fallenness itself had more to do with the Victorian establishment's loss of control than with a state of specifically sexual criminality. The tendency to equate alcohol consumption with sexual licentiousness and prostitution is not surprising given that political, legal, philanthropic and social responses to both social evils retained near-parallel trajectories throughout the nineteenth century.

Like drunkenness, prostitution inspired debates and laws that dichotomised it as a terrible sin committed by the sexually deviant, and a response to poverty by victims of social neglect – a disease of the female will. 'Fallen' was used in relation to drunkards who were 'delinquent lower-class women' (Anderson 1993: 2), and this is evidenced by a number of nineteenth-century journalistic and fictional artefacts. In *The Maiden Tribute of Modern Babylon* (1885), W. T. Stead refers repeatedly to the use of alcohol as part of a routine of seduction by which teenage girls are 'snared, trapped and outraged' (Stead 1885: 15) by men who render their victims 'dazed with the drink' (1885: 19) before delivering them to the highest bidder. Prime targets for seduction are 'daughters of drunken parents' (1885: 25) who are 'poor, dissolute, and indifferent to everything but drink' (1885: 33).[16] In Deborah Logan's work on Victorian fallenness, the connection between sobriety and propriety is key to understanding the ways in which delinquent women were ostracised and blamed, regardless of their actual crimes. Logan confirms that 'scholarship of women's responses to cultural powerlessness reveals their tendency to internalize oppression through such addictive and suicidal behaviours' (1998: 144) as habitual drinking. Such internalisations manifested not only in the work of investigators like Stead, but in the popular fiction and social-problem novels of the nineteenth century that featured women drinkers.

In Thackeray's *Vanity Fair*, Becky Sharp consumes excessive quantities of alcohol as she falls from social grace and her dissolution is both drunken and sexual. In Charles Dickens's *Hard Times*, a more explicit condemnation of the female drunk appears. Mrs Blackpool is 'something', an 'it' (2006: 67), a 'disabled, drunken creature' (2006: 68) entirely dehumanised by her use of alcohol. Dickens's narrator uses emotive, animalistic language in his description of the female drunk, who – unlike his ethereal, thin and angelic heroines – is hideously corporeal:

> with one begrimed hand on the floor, while the other was so purposeless in trying to push away her tangled hair from her face, that it only blinded her the more with the dirt upon it. A creature so foul to look at, in her tatters, stains and splashes, but so much fouler than that in her moral infamy, that it was a shameful thing to even see her. (Dickens 2006: 68)

Paying particular attention to the filth that both encases and is diffused by Mrs Blackpool, the narrator details the collapse of her womanly and domestic faculties. She is unable to stand or to clean herself or her surroundings, and as such she is figured as a demon who haunts the domestic space of which society expects her to be the angel. Her involvement in prostitution to fund her drinking is not articulated in the novel, yet the reader is led to assume that this is a possibility, given the allegation of Mrs Blackpool's 'moral infamy' (2006: 68).

Just six years before the publication of *Hard Times*, Elizabeth Gaskell had also included the drunken woman in her social-problem novel *Mary Barton*. Unlike Thackeray and Dickens, Gaskell's treatment of the 'alcoholic' was highly sympathetic. Like the New Woman writers whose work I examine, Gaskell attempted to account, socially and politically, for the various evils that forced women into self-destructive activities. Gaskell represents the drunken prostitute Esther, her repentance, and her attempts to save others from her own fate with great compassion. However, Esther dies at the end of *Mary Barton*, her body sickened by hunger, disease and alcohol. It is inassimilable into a novel that requires the fallen woman's punishment to satisfy its realist structure. Gaskell 'allows the drunken-prostitute stereotype to prevail by not explaining a fact of which she was clearly aware': that alcoholism, like prostitution, 'was generally more a matter of economics than of sensuous self-indulgence or inherent moral depravity' (Logan 1998: 13). In failing to reinstate Esther into the Barton family or society, Gaskell demonstrates the extent to which the female body, corrupted by excessive consumptionary desires, remained an infectious, dangerous and therefore intolerable entity in Victorian fictional works.

Written a few years after *Mary Barton*, George Eliot's short story 'Janet's Repentance', from *Scenes of Clerical Life* (1857), features a wife who drinks to escape the physical brutalities of her marriage, and who is neither sexually ruined nor irretrievably shamed. Janet Dempster's drinking is predominantly met with pity because her equally drunk but exceptionally vicious husband treats her so appallingly. When, following a particularly violent episode, she is forced out of her home, Janet is welcomed by the women of her community with tenderness and understanding. Her use of the short story meant that Eliot could not develop her plot in the level of detail permitted and required by the novel, and her references to Janet's inebriation are resultantly vague. Unlike that of the inhuman Mrs Blackpool or the sexually irredeemable Esther, Janet's drinking is neither demonstrative nor public, and is never described in grotesque physical detail. Janet's drunken body is not dirty, sexually compromised or publicly readable, an inconsistency that New Woman short-story writers would address in their own fictional offerings four decades later.

In proposing a redemptive trajectory for the female drunk, Eliot allows a social reintegration that can only succeed by virtue of her heroine's middle-class status, and her adherence to codes that confine and regulate her body within the domestic sphere. Janet must first confess her sin, then repent and find salvation through a Christian faith that designates her body as a symbol of fleshly corruption. The text does not allow redemption for women who fail to adhere to these codes, since it also details the parallel 'fall' of Mr Tryan's former lover Lucy. Lucy is found dead 'with paint on her cheeks' (2009b: 259) – killed off by an idealised, realist plot offering redemption only to women whose class status, sexual purity and domesticity allow them the potential for salvation. Janet's internalisation of middle-class values allows her to prevail, particularly her confession and absolution by a representative of Christianity. Mr Tryan offers forgiveness for Janet's sins, yet he is punished in the text for his immoral past with a slow and painful death. Lucy's and Tryan's respective punishments highlight Eliot's subscription to both penance and sacrifice, as well as to the realist mode.

As I have shown in Chapter 1, New Woman fiction continued to deploy Christian ideologies despite attempting to disrupt a social order deeply rooted in bourgeois religion. In this chapter I detail how New Woman short stories about women who drink reflect and respond to texts like 'Janet's Repentance' in ways that challenge the hegemonic structures within which Janet aspires to bodily containment. Yet, ultimately, these 'new' stories of female drunken self-harm generate fresh ideological and structural boundaries of their own. Although the mid-Victorian novelistic tradition offered a range of narrative equivalence between the body of the female drunk and the sexually, socially or maternally unfit body, it was not only compromised bodies that were so connected. The body of any woman who transgressed the Victorian ideology of separate spheres was subject to fictional and discursive alignment with fallenness, disease and sterility.

Alcohol, the New Woman and the Odd Woman

The perceived spread of female drunkenness in Victorian Britain was rhetorically associated with women's increased freedoms at the turn of the nineteenth century. In 'Life and Labour of the People in London' (1886–1903), Charles Booth alleges that the blame is 'to be laid mainly to the account of the female sex [as] one of the unexpected results of the emancipation of women', explaining that

> on the one hand she has become more independent of man, industrially and financially, and on the other more of a comrade than before, and in neither capacity does she feel any shame at entering a public house [. . .] 'One drunken woman in a street will set all the women in it drinking' [. . .] (Booth 1886–1903)

Booth's comments demonstrate the extent to which discourses of shame permeated perceptions of women's bodily desires, their potential for polluting others with those desires, and their interactions with men, despite women's experience of new social freedoms. Anxieties about female drunkenness and anxieties about the New Woman writer were often expressed through similar rhetorical formulae. Although the middle-class woman was not widely recognised as capable of habitual drunkenness, her fictional counterpart was entirely susceptible to the demons of drink in writing by and about the New Woman. Like the woman drinker, the New Woman was accused of neglecting her duties and her family, of attacking and infecting the sacred primacy of the home, and of eschewing her responsibilities to produce and raise healthy English children.

The late nineteenth century saw a huge surplus of women who were unmarried and financially unsupported, and who simply could not adhere to society's expectations. The surplus was calculated at 104 females for every 100 males (Nelson 2007: 5) and was largely due to the loss of men to Victorian conflicts abroad, and to the mass emigration required by the expansion of the Empire into new territories.

While poorer women had opportunities to work, Odd Women were a middle-class problem, since their training and education made them unfit for the sorts of professions to which women were beginning to be admitted. Middle-class women were only given access to a basic education that focused on preparing them for marriage. Skills such as housekeeping, reading and music were emphasised, while academic or practical skills were not encouraged (Sutherland 2015, Hamilton 2007, Burstyn 1980). Despite difficult conditions for many women who faced uncertain futures without the means to earn their living, the figure of the New Woman, who demanded both the education and the legislation necessary for independence, was much maligned by a society that treated with incredulity her claims to intellectual equality.

Victorian fiction explored the contradictory expectations of bourgeois religion and morality that designated women as born to embody the characteristics of the saintly martyrs, the Virgin Mary and Jesus Christ, despite a lack of opportunity to inhabit marital or maternal positions. Charlotte Yonge's *The Clever Woman of the Family* and later George Gissing's *The Odd Women* both dramatised the problem of surplus women, demonstrating the hypocrisy of a society that demanded women's domesticity but could not offer it to all. As my introduction has shown, women who rejected the roles ascribed to them by biology and religion were criticised and pitied by both the medico-scientific establishment and the general public. For instance, concerned about the surplus, prevalent medical thinking 'offered an emphatic warning that girls were reaching breaking point on account of intellectual work' (Richardson 2008: 40). As Elaine Showalter notes, the New Woman's claims to previously male-oriented pursuits such as work and education were figured in the language of 'insurrection and apocalypse' and women were warned that 'such ambitions would lead to' the kind of 'sickness, freakishness, sterility and racial degeneration' (1991: 39) also caused by habitual alcohol consumption.

Just like the prostitute, whose capacity for breeding was purportedly sacrificed to financial and sexual desires, or the drunk woman, whose reproductive potential and maternal aptitude were stalled by her excessive consumptions, the New Woman was figured as deliberately ill and threateningly infertile. In refusing to make the generation and maintenance of children her central goals, the New Woman also countermanded Christian instruction about the role of women as teachers, care givers and spiritual guides for both their husbands and any potential offspring. While the childless, unmarried woman was pitied, she was also encouraged to fulfil her biological and religious destiny by extending her maternal qualities to the wider community as a governess or nurse (Hughes 2001). The New Woman's perceived self-interest, and her refusal to adopt the passive roles ascribed by a society undergirded by Christianity, made her innately disruptive. Unlike the Odd Woman, who garnered sympathy for her life of repression and financial insecurity, and was commiserated with for her unsolicited state of childlessness, the New Woman was like the drunk woman, utterly transgressive and useless to a society that privileged obedience and self-sacrifice.

The Narrative Striptease in the New Woman Novel: Gissing's *The Odd Women*

The female inebriate appears in George Moore's *fin-de-siècle* novel *A Mummer's Wife* (1885), in which a middle-class landlady elopes with her tenant, works as an actress in a travelling company, and, after the death of her child, becomes increasingly intoxicated. Moore's naturalist text was accused of being an 'immoral publication' (Moore 1885: 5), and Mudie's circulating library refused to stock it. However, its remarkably thorough depiction of a bored housewife's descent into alcohol dependency and prostitution was protected from absolute censorship because of the heroine's precarious class status.[17] Although middle class, Kate Ede is poor, and when she leaves her husband and elopes with Dick Lennox, the manager of an *opéra bouffe* company, she becomes part of a morally loose, bohemian milieu. Kate's constant intoxication is the sole subject of the final third of the novel, and represents the most detailed and explicit account of a Victorian female 'alcoholic' outside of the social-problem genre. While Moore situates drunkenness as an inevitable consequence of women's reliance on men and the lottery of middle-class marriage, he also constructs excessive drinking as an activity undertaken only when the regulatory trappings of bourgeois respectability have been shed.

Eight years after the publication of *A Mummer's Wife*, George Gissing also featured the drunken woman in his 'New Woman' novel *The Odd Women*. While he resisted narrating the drunkard's path with the precision evinced by Moore, Gissing challenged the notion that the middle-class woman was protected from intemperance by either her class status or her sexual purity. While Gissing was not a New Woman writer, an examination of his New Woman novel presents an opportunity to underscore the connection between female drunkenness and the Woman Question, bringing into frame the New Woman's adoption of female drunkenness as a plot feature. Gissing's account of the female inebriate is far less detailed but in some ways more subversive than Moore's in its depiction of middle-class intoxication. It is a useful counterpoint to the short stories of George Egerton and Mary Angela Dickens, since it represents the only known account of a drunken female heroine in a New Woman novel written by a man. Gissing's representation of female self-harm through excessive drinking contrasts with those of his New Woman rivals. Both Egerton and Dickens, as I will later show, foreground the body of the suffering heroine, calling into question the tactics of quiet and appropriately feminine self-harm deployed by Gissing's female drunk, and directly addressing the impossibility of women's (somatic or narrative) silence on such matters.

The Odd Women is concerned with the education and training of Odd Women and the role to be played by the New Woman, and is highly compassionate towards the female inebriate as a victim of the surplus. Gissing was ostensibly a supporter of sexual equality, and his own unsuccessful experience of marriage to the 'alcoholic' former prostitute Nell Harrison made him more sympathetic towards the woman drinker than many of his contemporaries.[18] Gissing's grim, naturalist depiction of the middle-class Madden sisters, left penniless after the death of their father, contrasts with the romanticised poverty of many of the heroines in the New Woman novels that had already been published. Unlike Grand's Ideala, Evadne, Edith and Angelica, Caird's Viola and Hadria, Ella Hepworth Dixon's Mary Earle, or even Grant Allen's Herminia Barton, Gissing's Madden sisters live in neither relative luxury nor genteel poverty but are genuinely destitute. In the case of Virginia Madden, such poverty is emphasised by her decision to forgo food rather than be without the alcohol she secretly consumes.

At the outset of the novel, Virginia's drunken self-harm is ambiguously presented – her visit to a bar at Charing Cross station is narrated as opportunistic. However, Virginia's knowledge of the bar is intimated by the ease with which she locates it, and the restorative effect of alcohol on symptoms of withdrawal suggest habituation. Upon entering the bar, 'beads of perspiration were on her face, which had turned to a ghostly pallor', yet after her dram, 'colour flowed to her cheeks [. . .] she hastily wiped her lips, and walked away with firm step' (Gissing 2008b: 23). Mirroring the 'sensation of absolute relief' (Moore 1893: 358) described when Kate Ede counters withdrawal with gin in a trip to the public house in *A Mummer's Wife*, Virginia also embarks on the drunkard's path, a teleology beginning with occasional drinking and ending in moral and physical disgrace. Such a course parallels Virginia's rejection of her religious studies, which are supplanted by the reading of novels required by her job as a companion.

Virginia symbolically and literally shifts both from the intellectual literary climate of her childhood and from her engagement with ecclesiastical history. She immerses herself in the new economy of mass publication driven by a growing demand for sensational literature. Her descent into heavy drinking is mirrored by her dismissal of religion in favour of significantly less wholesome and improving texts. She 'lost all power of giving her mind to anything but feebler fiction' and, 'ashamed at first to indulge this taste' (Gissing 2008b: 18), Virginia eventually succumbs to the pleasures afforded by less transcendental consumptions. Just as she voraciously consumes novels, Virginia drinks with fervour to internalise and subvert Christian self-sacrifice, to deny her body through lack of food and exhaustive reading, but also to satiate her need for self-obliteration. Her adoption of drinking once she has abandoned the study of divinity suggests Virginia's transmutation of engagement with her faith to a bodily act that replicates and reverses the transubstantiation of Christ's body. As the Eucharist performs the literalisation of body and blood, Virginia's absorption of alcohol attempts (unsuccessfully) to reverse the sacrament by transforming her into something 'other than the bodies, sexualities, loves, and flesh' (Heywood 1996: 28) with which she is equated in Western philosophy and religion.

Virginia's 'dangerous indulgence' (Gissing 2008b: 28) requires her to sacrifice food, leading her to commit regular acts of self-neglect. Perhaps more perilous, though, is the grave social danger implied by Virginia's drinking, since it represents a fall from womanly grace and thus both marriageability and masculine pity. When Virginia's brother-in-law Mr Widdowson finds her intoxicated, he

> was for a moment in perplexity. If the evidence of his eyes could be trusted, Miss Madden's indisposition pointed to a cause so strange that it seemed incredible [. . .] His pity was mingled with disgust [. . .] He would have thought it utterly impossible for Miss Madden to disgrace herself in this vulgar way, and the appalling discovery affected his view of Monica [. . .] If the elder woman could fall into this degradation, might there not be possibilities in Monica's character such as he had refused to contemplate. (Gissing 2008b: 266–7)

As an unmarried Odd Woman she might inspire pity, but Virginia's consumptions compromise her morality, suggesting an inability to perform the saint-like endurance of the nineteenth-century domestic ideal. To the male spectator, it seems almost impossible that a middle-class woman of reduced circumstances yet genteel birth could succumb to selfish and ungodly desires of the flesh. Widdowson is disgusted by the vulgarity and disgrace of Virginia's drunkenness, as her body betrays the signs of her transgression. Like the anonymous Medical Gentleman, whose pity and disgust are mingled with arousal, Widdowson's gaze is underwritten by sexual desire and eugenic panic. Terrified by any potential hereditary taint, Widdowson reads Virginia's body through his own fears of contamination, since he is married to Virginia's sister Monica. Virginia's 'fall' and 'degradation' are moral and implicitly sexual, since Widdowson imagines her self-disgrace in the language of biblical fall in much the same way that Dickens's narrator describes the 'foul' Mrs Blackpool. However, unlike in *Hard Times*, the comments of Gissing's male observer are undermined by the narrative. So too is the critique of the female inebriate, since it is through Widdowson that Gissing satirises both degeneration and eugenics, and, unlike Becky Sharp, Mrs Blackpool, Esther and Kate Ede, Virginia retains her sexual purity.

Despite its predominantly compassionate characterisation of the drunken woman, Gissing's novel interrogates Virginia's inability to effect feminine disinterestedness and physical abstinence, suggesting that her consumption of alcohol is unacceptable only because of its visuality. Virginia is a walking symbol of Victorian wound culture, yet, since this symbolic wound is hidden from view, Virginia's body is offensive only if she exits the domestic space. As the locus of narrative desire in this text, the female body is slowly revealed to be the site of self-harming drives, in a narrative striptease that sees Gissing incrementally (and only partially) reveal the drunken body. As that which is to be 'denuded [and] unveiled' (Brooks 1993: 97), Virginia's secret is the corporeal secret at the heart of the narrative, decoded at first through fragmentary and elusive, then eventually obvious, signs. Gissing at first avoids narrating Virginia's body, preferring to subtly suggest – to allude to, rather than clearly depict – her self-harmful consumptions. Although Gissing's avoidance of naturalist hyper-sensuality may account for this (Liggins 2006: x–xi), Virginia embodies the 'horror of the flesh' that is the 'unconscious of discourse' and thus her drinking cannot be straightforwardly articulated without endangering potential reader sympathy or provoking the kind of censure experienced by Moore in 1885.

Virginia's drinking is an 'indisposition' of 'so strange a cause' (Gissing 2008b: 267), a 'secret vice' (2008b: 327) and one of life's 'temptations' (2008b: 267); its lack of narrative embodiment exemplifies what Deirdre David calls Gissing's 'flat, unembroidered, and almost clinical style' (1984: 122). As Virginia's body increasingly reflects the damage she inflicts upon it by heavy drinking, it garners more detailed description. A 'disagreeable redness tinged [Virginia's] eyelids' and her mouth 'was growing coarse and lax, the under lip hanging a little' (2008b: 318–19). Her dress alters to accommodate her indulgence; it is 'conducive to bodily ease' (2008b: 333) but socially unacceptable and demonstrative of the 'foul associations' (2008b: 334) bestirred by her increasing use of gin. Focusing on Virginia's deflated face and lax, unwomanly dress, Gissing's narrator operates in the linguistic world of manners rather than that of the visceral. In contrast to the quasi-religious figure of the self-sacrificing domestic Angel, Virginia's poor manners and coarse expression betray her bodily fall, although Gissing restores her to grace at the end of the text when her drinking comes under control through her institutionalisation. Once installed in a clinic for recovering inebriates, Virginia is removed from public view, yet can be safely watched over and regulated by her (male) doctors.

Gissing's almost affectionate treatment of Virginia's struggle with alcohol exemplifies one of the many ambiguities at the heart of his text, and its complicated attitude towards women's position in nineteenth-century society. Gissing's Naturalism is illustrated by his inability to suggest a wholly viable or successful course for any of his female characters. Monica dies from complications during childbirth; Virginia asks to be institutionalised; Alice's project for opening a school is subsumed by maternal duties; Mary Barfoot's desire for her cousin remains unexpressed; Rhoda Nunn's opportunity for romantic love is replaced by a future in which marriage and self-actualisation are irreconcilable; and three of the Madden sisters die early in the novel. In its rendering of the female drunk, Gissing's text sympathises with a woman driven to alcohol by both her poverty and her inability to prove useful to a society that privileges youth and beauty. Conversely, as the New Woman character, Rhoda Nunn's act of 'self-harm' (the ascetic refusal of her romantic desires) is treated with less compassion, since unlike the womanly (if useless) Virginia Madden, Rhoda is frighteningly masculine and aggressively self-sufficient.

The text's ambivalence towards female political expression is signified by the narrator's veiled critique of Rhoda's unfeminine physicality and invulnerability. While the once-beautiful but drunken Virginia 'had been comely [. . .] her countenance still had a grace, a sweetness' (2008b: 14), of the comparatively beautiful Rhoda the narrator muses, 'Whether or not she could be called a comely woman, might have furnished matter for male discussion' (2008b: 25). By the end of the novel the drunken woman holds the hope of reabsorption into a female community whose domestic attentions provide potential for recovery, while the suggestion is that Rhoda's subversive politics will ensure her a fate far less comfortable. Unlike Virginia, whose social transgressions are largely hidden from view both in and by the text, Rhoda's demands for autonomy make her an object of vulgar public display. As she is one of the novel's most vehement supporters of mechanisation – the repetitive work carried out on the mass type-writers of the workplace she supervises – Rhoda's activities typify the new 'relations of private bodies and private persons to public spaces' (Seltzer 1998: 21). Wearing her psychological damage like a 'badge [. . .] of identity' (Seltzer 1998: 2), Rhoda's consideration of, then resistance to, marriage and domestication establishes her irreconcilability with a system that requires the type of containment practised on Virginia.

Gissing's text represents female 'alcoholic' self-harm as a womanly response to social and economic pressures, whilst the woman who transgresses the domestic sphere as a reaction to the same conditions is subject to far less generosity. It satirises the self-interested New Woman, suggesting that participation in the public sphere is far less desirable for women than strategies of quiet, private self-harm. Gissing's novel reverses the tactic of display deployed by New Woman writers in that the body of his self-harming heroine is encouraged to self-conceal. This concealment is rendered possible by a novel that, despite its literary Naturalism, fails to fully narrate the self-harming female body. *The Odd Women* demonstrates its formal limitations by positioning the female body as the secret to be known and mastered, and by rehabilitating the woman who adheres to idealised social codes, and punishing the woman who does not. Contrastingly, New Woman short stories featuring drunken self-harmers subvert patriarchal strategies of containment, asserting women's right to embodiment in a complex and ultimately fruitless attempt to challenge the epistemophilic gaze of the male-oriented novelistic tradition and its teleologies of irrefutable fall.

Drunkenness and Fallenness in George Egerton's Short Stories

At the vanguard of proto-modernist literary experimentation, George Egerton was arguably the New Woman writer most concerned with representing the female body, its drives and its desires as part of her highly experimental fiction. Born Mary Chavelita Dunne in 1859, Egerton adopted the masculine pseudonym George in the tradition of the mid-Victorian women writers who had preceded her, whose work her own reproduced, expanded and dismantled. Egerton's work reveals a deep concern with the ways in which the female body

operated as a Victorian cultural topos, and the potential for both liberation and condemnation in the sexual freedoms and social taboos
about which she wrote. However, she was highly critical of the New
Woman figure, and disagreed entirely with the demand for women's
suffrage, championing sexual rather than civil freedoms for women,
and in particular women's right to 'free unions' with men.

In 1893 Egerton's first collection of short stories, entitled *Keynotes*,
was published by John Lane of the Bodley Head publishing house.
Marketed as being within the Decadent school, with a subtly provocative cover illustration by Aubrey Beardsley, the collection garnered as
much commercial success as it did mainstream criticism (Patterson
2013). Her second volume, *Discords*, published the following year,
was accused of 'hysterical frankness' in the *Athenaeum* ('The Year in
Review', 1894: 118) and was, according to W. T. Stead, suggestive of
the 'unpleasant side [. . .] of the modern woman' (1894: 68). Egerton's
work dealt with female sexuality and depicted independent and provocative female protagonists whose decisions contravened Victorian
moral, religious and social norms. In an 1894 letter to Lane, Egerton
articulated her dissatisfaction with Victorian novelistic practice, discussing George Moore's recently published *Esther Waters*:

> There is [. . .] a marvellous reticence in it, a magnificent self-control and
> if genius be patience – genius. It is simply wonderful in the patient labour
> of its detail. To me, it is wearisome to read, because it is like life itself.
> Life is too much with me as it is – one common everyday event succeeds
> the other in it, and one plods and plods through as one plods through
> the round of one's days. It is only when one has finished it that one
> realises how all the mass of detail has gone to form, as the patient setting
> of stones in a mosaic form, a grand whole. (De Vere White 1958: 36)

Despite Moore's own fight against the 'worthless, the false, and the
commonplace' (1885: 16) in novels, and his attempt to pioneer a
more realistic form of Realism, Egerton's ironic tone implies criticism of Moore's 'genius' and her impatience with the detailed reading
required by his novel. Indeed, Egerton's own stories were structurally
– if not always thematically – a far cry from *Esther Waters*, refusing to
represent 'a grand whole', evading the finite, and in doing so raising
uncomfortable questions about gender, sexuality and the management
of women's bodies. Egerton's stories are unorthodox, and formally
much closer to twentieth-century Modernism than the Victorian staple of the realist novel. Rather than a traditional plot and characters,
many of her stories focus on psychological interiority, presenting snap-
shots of female sexual and intellectual development set in a restrictive

masculine society. Kate Krueger Henderson calls this device 'the attempt to render and communicate perceptual moments' through 'suggestions of atmosphere and mood' (2001: 188). Focusing on psychological landscapes, Egerton 'subordinates plot, fragments form and intensifies affective responses', allowing her to present shockingly seditious material, through literary techniques such as vague and ambiguous language, and elusive metaphors.

Egerton's stories depict violent images of female self-harm that would have been impossible to broach in the novel form, and her refusal to conclude her stories with a resolution that reinforced nineteenth-century moral and religious values made them vulnerable to attack from the Victorian mainstream, particularly after the 1895 Wilde trial (Standlee 2010, Ledger 2006). Unlike authors like Sarah Grand, who had advocated a higher standard of sexual purity in her fiction, Egerton's interest in female sexuality had no such claim to didacticism. Her exploration of the internal landscapes of the female psyche and her representations of damaged and eroticised female bodies made her writing particularly ripe for accusations of immorality. Accused by one reviewer for the *Athenaeum* of being 'revolting studies of drink and lust and murder' that should 'never have been printed' ('Review of *Discords* by George Egerton', 1895: 375), Egerton's stories are preoccupied with self-damaging acts, and drunkenness and self-mutilation feature frequently. This chapter addresses alcohol misuse in *Discords*; however, I revisit Egerton's writing in Chapter 4 with reference to self-mutilation in both *Discords* and her later collection *Symphonies* (1897).

Egerton's use of the trope of female drunkenness critiques Victorian patriarchy, and her increasingly violent imagery demonstrates her strategic use of the short story. In deploying excessive alcohol consumption on the spectrum of progressively damaging practices enacted by her heroines, Egerton makes the damaged female body the narrative centre of her texts. Despite the brevity required by the short story, her use of it to dramatise self-harm demonstrates that the bodies of damaged women, and the bodies of narrative that contained them, were elements in a relationship in which, paradoxically, the shorter form allowed the narrative space to express what nine hundred pages could not. Like the anorexic body, around which a surplus of signifiers accumulates in the New Woman social purity novel, the damaged female body takes centre stage in Egerton's stories. However, unlike the starving bodies of Grand's heroines who are simultaneously depicted and erased through a form of narrative disembodiment, the lack of textual profusion in Egerton's work dramatises the self-harmer in a way that could not have been directly described. Narrative form must thus be considered as content, in its reflection of dominant discourse and the impossibility of this discourse to contain and enforce social hegemony (Lanser 2009: 497–9).

Egerton's use of the female drunk figure in *Discords* begins in the aptly titled 'Gone Under', which recounts a brief friendship between a young, unmarried girl and a fallen woman as they travel by boat to England. Like Gaskell's Esther and Eliot's Lucy, Egerton's female antagonist, Edith Grey, has been sexually ruined by a wealthy man who has promised marriage, but by the close of the story she is both dependent on alcohol and working as a prostitute. Edith is mistress to a married man, who has seduced her and sent her abroad to give birth to his illegitimate child. She is forced to return to him in England after being told that her child has been stillborn, and her affair with her lover's cousin is discovered. Alone and desperate, Edith is subject to the disapproval of almost all on board, and 'Gone Under' functions as a critique both of the Victorian medical system (Edith alleges her baby has been murdered) and of the damage done by women to their own sex, as an outcome of moral double standards. Egerton's text directly challenges Eliot's 'Janet's Repentance' in which the female inebriate is supported by a community of women who sympathise with her condition. 'Gone Under' suggests that this outcome is highly unlikely, since women tend to internalise the strict moral codes that limit their own freedoms and apply them rigorously to those who fail to do the same.[19]

Unlike Gissing's Virginia Madden, whose condition must be slowly decoded, or Eliot's Janet Dempster, whose intoxication is covertly expressed, 'Gone Under' immediately highlights Edith's excessive drinking through overt physiognomic codes. These same codes also indicate Edith's sensuality, because her body is both damaged by self-harming impulses and erotically charged. She wears an inappropriately ornamental red dress, 'her lips are crimson', and although she is described as young, 'there are fine lines about her eyes' which are 'circled with heavy indigo stains' (Egerton 2006: 102). The redness of her lips and dress and the darkness of the circles around her eyes attest to Edith's sexuality, suggesting late nights and little sleep in her role as a mistress. However, equally decipherable are the bodily effects of alcohol abuse, evident in the fine lines and dark circles, and later in Edith's public displays of drunkenness.

Edith's position as a kept woman is designated by her appearance in newly bought yet unsuitably showy garments, which connote a financial investment in her appearance quite different to the taste and simplicity required in a wife's dress. Similarly, Edith's physical features contribute to her readability and, like Grand, Egerton relies on her reader's knowledge of, and investment in, physiognomy. We are told of Edith's beauty, that 'the mouth cannot lie – the pout of wine red lips, the soft receding chin, and the strange indefinable expression that lurks about them rather fits a priestess of passion' (2006: 104). These words are uttered by Egerton's girl-narrator, who befriends Edith yet fails to see her beyond Victorian cultural stereotypes. The girl imagines Edith as a priestess, orienting her passionate nature towards pagan – and by implication sensual – rather than Judeo-Christian religion. Despite Edith's beauty, the girl is, like the Medical Gentleman, both 'attracted to her, and yet repelled' (2006: 102); the girl is made uncomfortable by Edith's difference yet is fascinated by her as an object of masculine desire and feminine disapproval.

The girl-narrator fails to disassociate Edith from images of angelic and fallen women, or from the biblical and classical figures found in popular art and literature. Thus, Edith's 'head and forehead and drooping white lids have the delicacy of a Madonna by Ary Scheffer' (2006: 104). Egerton draws on Scheffer's *The Heavenly and Earthly Love* (1850), which features two female images: one, the Madonna pointing instructively at heaven, the other a female nude, her breasts bare, draped in a crimson garment. The nude figure stares knowingly at the Virgin and yet her line of sight stretches beyond her saintly counterpart towards more worldly concerns; her hair is ruffled and her cheeks are flushed, while her interlocutor shows only a trace of colour. The juxtaposition of the figures in Scheffer's painting is replicated by the narrator's framing of Edith, who inhabits both female typologies – the spiritual and the carnal, the Madonna and the priestess of passion. Egerton disrupts the dualism that denies Edith the right to straddle both categories, undermining the anorexic logic that would make her either transcendentally angelic or dangerously fleshly.

Later in the text, the girl-narrator describes how 'something in the crouching figure, with the rippling waves of hair falling about her in a glory of colour, recalls to her the beautiful story of tender pity for such another' (2006: 110). The visualisation of the scene of Mary Magdalene crouched at the feet of Christ – a sexually ruined woman forgiven through the favour of the Son of God – justifies the narrator's pity for the fallen woman through appropriate biblical mythoi. Later the narrator exclaims that 'I would paint her as Helen' (2006: 104), reading Edith's body within an established classical archetype of beautiful yet sexually transgressive femininity.[20] By referencing Scheffer's painting, Mary Magdalene and Helen of Troy, Egerton's narrator highlights the competing feminine identities at play in a reading of the drunken female body. Like the Mater

Dolorosa in the poems of Baudelaire and Swinburne, Edith combines both facets of the Victorian angel/whore dichotomy and mind/body dualism, through which the female body is designated corporeal and thus tainted, yet expected to transcend its fleshliness. Just like the medieval martyrs in Pre-Raphaelite paintings and the masochistic Madonna of Decadent poetry, Edith is both angelic and sensual.

In contrast to the heroines of Grand's novels who try to transcend their bodies, or the martyrs whose bodies were subordinate to their souls, Edith's acts of drunken self-harm assert her corporeality and violently disrupt a male-controlled aesthetic of female self-sacrifice. In avowing Edith's right to corporeality, Egerton undermines the Western philosophical tradition by depicting one woman's refusal to deny or be shamed by her body in line with masculine ideologies. However, Edith's strategy to disrupt patriarchal somatic control not only results in her self-destruction but also, at times, plays into the same problematic dynamic of eroticised display found in Victorian literature and art. While Edith's recourse to alcohol strategically resists the slavery of her decorative existence, at times Egerton's characterisation of her heroine's excessive consumption of alcohol reinforces Edith's ornamental function both in her position as a mistress and in the narrative. For example, Edith is found

> moaning in the lower berth; the bed-clothes had fallen into a confused heap upon the floor, and she was uncovered, shivering with cold, her hair streaming out like amber drift-weed at every lurch; a trickle of blood ran from one of her white wrists. A diminutive pair of boots, an empty champagne bottle, fragments of glass and china, and an upturned tray slid noisily to and fro on the floor; an unopened bottle is propped with towels in the basin. (Egerton 2006: 103)

The signs of Edith's heavy drinking are self-evident, and she is a pitiable yet highly sensual figure, her self-harming drives evident in her unsuccessful attempt at suicide, and the excessive drinking by which it has been driven. Edith's body is positioned by Egerton's narrator as both tragic and erotic, as a spectacle worthy of compassion, but also as a beautiful and tragic *objet d'art*.

The scene of Edith's exposure recreates the 'fall' of certain tragic heroines of nineteenth-century art and literature. In particular, it reimagines the death of Ophelia in Shakespeare's *Hamlet* (1603) as depicted in John Everett Millais's oil on canvas entitled *Ophelia* (1852). In Millais's image, Ophelia is partly submerged in water, her auburn hair mirroring the surrounding reeds and bracken in both colour and texture. Millais pays particular attention to the dying figure, her arms parted in a supplicant gesture as she takes her final breath; she is represented as neither dead nor alive. Ophelia's final inhalation is depicted as subtly orgasmic, and presents an eroticised rendering of her last moments, suggestive of necrophilia since Shakespeare's play sees Ophelia drowned off stage. Although Ophelia is not necessarily fallen by nineteenth-century standards, her death is closely connected to her excessive passion and unmanageable desires. Thus, Ophelia is imagined as sexually compromised in a variety of Pre-Raphaelite works that (similarly) depict her in a boat or in the water with reed-like hair, and in a state of physical collapse. These include Arthur Hughes's 1871 painting entitled *Ophelia (And He Will Not Come Again)* and John William Waterhouse's series of paintings of the same subject in 1889, 1894 and 1910.

Edith's wet, shivering and partially naked body, like that of the drowned Ophelia, contributes to an aesthetic that reads female sexuality through codes valuing neatness, order and restraint; they also eroticise, and ultimately devalue, bodies that do not adhere to these codes. Egerton was not alone in her use of Pre-Raphaelitism as inspiration for her fallen woman characters, since it 'became an integral part of most Victorian novels, conveying contemporary anxieties over various socio-political issues' (Andres 2005: xv). Discussing the *fin-de-siècle* novelist Lucas Malet, Catherine Delyfer advises that women writers 'use, critique and subvert visual works' in order to challenge 'readers' representations and the pictures' meanings, as well as to create interstitial spaces of expressive literary freedom' (2011: 4). While Egerton's work frequently engages with mid-Victorian artworks to disrupt linear narrative and corrode 'accepted representations of social roles' (Delyfer 2011: 5), she also, at times, reinforces those roles. Deeply suspicious of Aestheticism, yet preoccupied with Pre-Raphaelitism, Egerton's formal and political divergence from her literary predecessors seems oddly in conflict with her retention of nineteenth-century artistic conventions.

About Edith's drinking, the girl-narrator asks, 'Why do you? It shows so plainly, and people notice it, and it spoils you – you are so beautiful, it's such a pity!' (Egerton 2006: 106). Her comments convey sympathy for the drunken, fallen woman, yet they are framed by a veiled but deeply ingrained Victorian idealisation of beauty that is problematic in a story that critiques this fantasy. Egerton undermines the nineteenth-century belief in physiognomy by exposing the naivety of a narrator who cannot understand how the drunken woman could be at once both beautiful and bodily corrupt. However, while exposing the injunctive system of somatic indicators by which the Victorian body is read, Egerton continually deploys these signs in her display of the damaged female body as a metaphorical tool. The narrator's question is rearranged and redeployed a few paragraphs later as the words of Edith's married lover, who 'said [the baby] would spoil me' (2006: 107). Tellingly, the same phrase is used by the kindly girl-narrator and, later, by the man whose cruelty and abandonment have been the cause of his victim's drinking. The repetition suggests disapproval of a society in which the potential reconciliation of the fallen woman by way of female community is doomed to failure, as is maternity, which cannot be allowed since it might undermine her aesthetic and bodily functions as a sexual commodity.

Towards the end of the text Edith is working as a prostitute, having adhered to the drunkard's path and the Victorian seduction narrative respectively. Upon recognising Edith, 'a stifled cry of horror burst through the girl's lips [. . .] Phthisis and drink have run riot together; have wasted her frame, hollowed her cheeks, puffed her eyelids, dried the dreadful purple lips and soddened the soul within' (2006: 113). Egerton portrays Edith's journey from genteel vice to prostitution, depicting the self-harming, drunken body of her fallen female character as central to her negative appraisal of the bourgeois morality that forces women into self-destruction. However, she also defines Edith through a system of signs encoding the corporeal with aesthetic properties in line with the limiting and male-oriented discourses found in Victorian art, literature and culture. She simultaneously suggests that natural motherhood is a vital vocation for the Victorian woman, just as in Eliot's 'Janet's Repentance' and Gissing's *The Odd Women*, a point she would reiterate in her most shocking story 'Wedlock'.

In 'Wedlock' Egerton tells the tale of a wife and mother, whose episodes of intoxication are witnessed by both male construction workers on the street outside her house and the New Woman lodger living inside it. Egerton's drunken heroine is Mrs Jones, a lower-middle-class mother of an illegitimate child, married to a cruel husband whose three children she cares for while forced to neglect her own. In the first section Mrs Jones 'fumbles stupidly' at her door, while she is heard 'mumbling unintelligibly' (Egerton 2006: 116) by two workmen who are transfixed by the grotesque spectacle of her inebriety. Though often drunk, Mrs Jones is not physically unattractive, and much like Edith Grey is 'attractive and repellent' (2006: 120) and beautiful 'in a singular way' (2006: 120). The text describes the woman drinker in terms of both her physical beauty and bodily disorder as

> [t]he woman reeling and stumbling up the lane [who] feels her way to the back-yard door of the next house, and, rocking on her feet, tries

to find the pocket of her gown. She is much under thirty, with a finely developed figure. Her gown is torn from the gathers at the back and trails down showing her striped petticoat; her jacket is of good material, trimmed with silk, but it is dusty and lime-marked. Her face is flushed and dirty; her light golden-brown fringe stands out straight over her white forehead; her bonnet is awry on the back of her head; her watch dangles from the end of a heavy gold chain, and the buttons of her jersey bodice gape open. (Egerton 2006: 115–16)

Mrs Jones's intemperance is defined in terms of her inability to maintain the orderliness required by middle-class standards. Her face and hair are dirty and her bonnet is askew; her dress is torn so that her petticoat is displayed, suggesting a sense of sexual availability that – along with her intoxication – justifies the vocality of the men's comments and the intrusive nature of their stares. Narrative gathers around the drunken body, which is read through the materiality of dress, the textures, colours, fabrics and ornaments of which Mrs Jones is composed. As in *Ideala*, attention is given to the detail of dress; however, unlike in Grand's novel, the description of Mrs Jones's clothing emphasises, rather than detracts from, the presence of flesh beneath. By depicting the transgressive female body through material and commercial objects, Egerton stresses the 'process that Western logic inscribes', the 'horror of the female flesh that is often the unconscious of discourse' (Heywood 1996: 8), framing the workmen's disgust and desire through the dualism that required women to transcend the corporeal, yet denied that they could be capable of doing so.

Blaming "eredity, wot comes down from parents to children', and making the case that 'she canrn't 'elp it no more nor the colour of 'er 'air' (2006: 117), one of the workmen suggests a cause of Mrs Jones's condition. Theories of inheritance are, however, downplayed by the narrative which, once having moved inside the house, begins to reveal the complexity of Mrs Jones's self-destruction. Tricked into marrying a man who had promised to undertake the care of her daughter, Mrs Jones finds herself trapped in a brutal marriage to a violent husband who sends her child away. Mrs Jones's drinking is thus located not in her female physiology, nor in hereditary degeneracy, but in her mistreatment at the hands of her husband and more generally by a system that has denied her maternal and legal rights.

Eventually, the illegitimate Susie dies from an illness that Mr Jones has kept secret from his wife, denying her the motherly right to nurse her sick child and to say goodbye, and the story ends as Mrs Jones murders her husband's children in retaliation before committing suicide. Egerton draws on Greek mythological tropes including Medea's murder of Jason's children, as well as the myth of Clytemnestra and Iphigenia – just as Mona Caird had done in *The Daughters of Danaus*. While Caird imagines Hadria Fullerton as Iphigenia, Egerton casts Mrs Jones as her mother Clytemnestra, who murdered her own husband in retaliation for the sacrifice of their daughter. In her version of Thomas Hardy's climactic scene of child murder in *Jude the Obscure* (1895), Egerton has her female character murder the children for whom she feels she cannot continue to care. Unlike the innocent Father Time, who kills his siblings and himself because they are 'too menny' (Hardy 2009: 298), Egerton's child killer is monstrous because a Christian society has determined it her biological duty to care for children. Despite this, a causal relationship is established between a denial of maternal rights and murderous revenge, and such a relationship is depicted as both inevitable and potentially justifiable. Egerton suggests that childlessness and enforced motherhood are equally unnatural and dangerous roles to be occupied by women. In doing so, she proposes that until marriage and motherhood become free and biologically, rather than socially, determined professions, violence – especially self-directed and against those with less power – is likely to ensue.

Egerton's greatest condemnation is reserved for those in observational positions within 'Wedlock' who, as in the case of the Medical Gentleman, Gissing's Widdowson, and even the girl-narrator in 'Gone Under', attempt to read the body of the female drinker through bourgeois moral and religious conventions. Mrs Jones's body is observed by her female lodger, a woman writer whose detached appraisal is negatively encoded in the text. Finding her landlady drunk and beaten, the New Woman character 'supports her into the bedroom and on to the unmade bed [. . .] A look of weary disgust crosses her face as she sees the litter on the table' (2006: 118), demonstrating the extent to which her censure originates in Victorian values of order and containment. After a violent altercation during which Mr Jones assaults his wife and throws her on to the street, the lodger notes that Mrs Jones

> has on a clean pink cotton gown and her hair is nicely done and her skin looks very pink and white; but her eyes are swollen, and there is a bruise on the one temple and a bad scratch on her cheek [. . .] The other woman observes her closely as she does most things – as material. It is not that her sympathies are less keen since she took to writing, but that the habit of analysis is always uppermost. (Egerton 2006: 120)

Assessing her as merely 'material', the woman writer commodifies Mrs Jones, subjecting her to a gaze that undermines her humanity and positions her as an object. Like the girl-narrator in 'Gone Under', the male narrators of Grand's novels, and the medico-scientific establishment, the woman writer performs the masculine scopic function in Egerton's 'Wedlock'. She is a problematic figure in a narrative that criticises looking, yet communicates its disapproval by displaying the damaged female body as an exhibition of atrocity for its readership.

If Mrs Jones is the embodiment of excessive and unwomanly corporeality – fleshly, consuming, desiring – then the woman writer is the converse, equally a manifestation of the anorexic logic of patriarchy, of an internalised disavowal of the body and an overemphasis of the mind, much like some of Grand's heroines. The woman writer is described as 'barren', 'nervous', 'overwrought', 'dry', 'arid', 'feverish', 'worn', 'frail' (2006: 188) and hollowed out. An example of what Heywood calls 'an attempt to enter the magic inner circle of culture' (1996: 28), the woman writer is equally an incarnation of the Western philosophy that reads women through reductive binaries that limit their opportunities and devalue their experiences. The abundance of signifiers collecting around the frail and maternally unproductive body of the fictional New Woman writer do as much to challenge a 'horror of the flesh' as Egerton's satirical representation of the way the 'alcoholic' body is read and devalued by patriarchy. Centralising drunkenness as self-harm within her short stories, Egerton refused to erode it from the narrative in the way the starving body had been excised in the novels of some of her New Woman contemporaries.

Egerton's strategy of corporeal spectacle exploited the late-century wound culture, in which looking at the body and its assorted violations challenged the ideology restricting women's participation in the public sphere. The damaged, drunken, female body is never allowed to survive in Egerton's stories, which, despite their focus on psychological interiority rather than descriptive detail, represent 'the commutability of word counts and body counts' (Seltzer 1998: 40), the opening of the private body in public, as a site of social (and narrative) debate. The late-nineteenth-century process of writing was bound up with anxieties about modernity and corporeality in machine culture; these anxieties are embodied in 'Wedlock' by the woman writer, whose attempts at cultural production are interspaced with, challenged by and aroused by the spectacle of Mrs Jones's drunken body. From the perspective of both the male and the female observer, sympathy for the drunken woman is limited since, although she is subject to the restrictive tyranny of marriage, she is also unsuccessful in her attempts at both domesticity and motherhood.

The parallel narrative of the analytical, and judgemental, woman writer indicates an ambivalence towards the emergent 'feminism' of the late nineteenth century. Her depiction of the damaging effect of enforced motherhood expounds Egerton's views on women's right to marital and maternal freedoms but not the entire catalogue of demands for equality. In 'Wedlock' Egerton once again points out that 'true' motherhood and honest maternal feeling (exemplified by Mrs Jones and the absent Susie) must be encouraged, or the consequences might be both self-destructive and homicidal. It is Mrs Jones's inability to channel properly her maternal skills that seals her fate, and the woman writer's childlessness which makes her powerless to sympathise fully with Mrs Jones. In *A Literature of Their Own* (1977), Elaine Showalter argues that Egerton's central female characters fail to direct their repressed rage at men, instead effecting an 'avoidance of these central confrontations' (2007: 214) by attacking weaker characters. I would suggest that the central confrontations in these stories are those fought within the heroines; their rage becomes inwardly focused through acts of drunkenness and self-harm that help to sustain their (albeit limited) survival in a society that (ironically) requires them to swallow their pain.

Mary Angela Dickens's Drunken Female Parishioner

Mary Angela Dickens was well known in her lifetime, firstly as the eldest granddaughter of the author Charles Dickens, and latterly as a writer of children's fiction. Dickens was the daughter of Charles Dickens Junior and Elisabeth Matilda Moule Dickens and was named after her aunt, Mary Dickens. In addition to her children's collections, Dickens published a number of novels and essays, and her short stories appeared in *All the Year Round* (the periodical inherited by her father from her grandfather), as well as in other nineteenth-century periodicals.[21] Like Victoria Cross, Dickens was not publicly involved in the gender debates of the late nineteenth century, and while Caird, Grand and Egerton had published essays and reviews that made clear their positions on most key areas of debate, Dickens did not. Despite writing about New Woman-ish heroines, fictionalising women's issues in most of her texts, and interviewing the controversial woman writer Lucas Malet in 1889 (Lundberg 2003: 192–4), she appears not to have concerned herself with women's political agitation until well into the twentieth century, when she became a vocal opponent of women's suffrage. Published materials do not indicate that Dickens campaigned in any way for women's rights, nor does her biographical work about her memories of her grandfather hint at such interests.[22]

Although Dickens's writing appears in a number of twentieth-century collections of women's short stories, her novels remain largely out of print, and little attention has been paid to the ways in which her work engages with nineteenth-century gender debates. Perhaps this is in part due to her lineage, and in part because her novels betray a tendency towards sentimentalism at odds with the aesthetic of better-known New Woman authors. Dickens's heroines are often forced to take drastic action in response to dire situations – fraud, bankruptcy and suicide in *A Valiant Ignorance* (1894) and secrets, madness and murder in *Against the Tide* (1898) are just two examples of the sensationalist plot features found in her novels. Although the writing of New Woman novelists Sarah Grand and Mona Caird came under fire for their melodramatic rewritings of the conventional marriage plot, their respective works could not be accused of the type of sentimentalism found in Dickens's longer writings.

It is in Dickens's short stories that serious criticisms of bourgeois masculine ideologies begin to appear, and her stories about women reveal a decidedly 'feminist' subtext at odds with her (albeit limited) public persona and the Dickensian traditionalism of most of her novels. In writing about the female body, Dickens traverses a space between tradition and revolt that aligns her work with the New Woman writers of her day, despite her reservations about women's political freedoms.[23] Dickens's literary output slowed considerably after the turn of the century and it appears that she stopped writing fiction after the publication of her final novel *Sanctuary* (1916). Her texts offer a significant snapshot of *fin-de-siècle* concerns about the female body from a writer who was unavoidably part of the old order of Victorian social and literary values, and simultaneously part of the challenge to it.

In her 1896 collection *Some Women's Ways*, Dickens depicts a cross section of female types, from the shameless flirt in 'Kitty's Victim' to the beautiful yet lonely society woman in 'Another Freak', and the domineering New Woman in 'An Unprincipled Woman'. All of Dickens's women are subject to bodily regulation in line with phallocentric imperatives, despite their unruly behaviour or combative tendencies. Where these women do defy convention or subvert bourgeois morality, they are left unhappy and alone, and their respective problems are resolved only by marriage or the assertion of moral superiority at great personal cost. These plot resolutions are framed by nineteenth-century religious dictates that viewed marriage or self-abnegation as the only two possible routes to happiness for women. However, more so than in her novels, or in the novels of some of her New Woman contemporaries, the women in

Dickens's short stories subvert assumptions about female moral and intellectual inferiority and rally against their positions as objects of exchange. Dickens's use of the short story allowed her enough ambiguity to explore more complex and less melodramatic characterisations of women under pressure, in a way that she avoided in her longer works.

The female drunk appears in two stories from *Some Women's Ways*, both of which take place in ecclesiastical settings. 'An Unprincipled Woman' features the New Woman Magdalene Cotgreave, ironically named to suggest her sullied public persona. Contrary to her perceived lack of principle, Magdalene is in fact highly honourable, and when she detects that the Reverend Paul Marvin has stolen parish funds, she intervenes and demands an explanation. Marvin expounds a sad tale of financial ruin precipitated by his drunken mother who 'is a confirmed dipsomaniac' and 'not a desirable appendage' given that 'comfortable and private asylums for elderly ladies thus afflicted are by no means unimportant expenditure' (Dickens 1896: 167). Despite his embezzlement, Marvin is given a second chance by Mrs Cotgreave, who pays his debts and keeps his secret on the condition that he leave the Church. Dickens questions the suitability of men for clerical positions purely on the basis of gender, as well as the power and responsibility for spiritual guidance placed in the hands of those to whom power is its own reward. She undermines the primacy of religion as a purely positive social force, yet also restores Christianity's healing powers through the unwavering yet practical faith of her New Woman heroine.

In the second of her tales of priestly affairs, entitled 'So as by Fire', Dickens depicts the female inebriate in far more detail, but draws on a similar rhetoric of male clerical incompetence. Upon his arrival in the village of Abbot's Cordon, the Reverend Maurice Drury immediately finds himself rehabilitating the aptly named drunken schoolmistress, Mrs Neale. While the vicar's support and attention fortifies Mrs Neale, helping her to temporarily live a sober and useful life, Drury begins to fall in love with his lost sheep, despite his engagement to another woman. From his first encounter with Mrs Neale, Drury is attracted to her suffering body for reasons both physical and, at least ostensibly, spiritual. A beautiful martyr to narrow social codes, Mrs Neale destroys herself with alcohol because of her tragic past. Her husband's fraud, conviction and consequent suicide, as well as her loneliness and the absence of compassion from her neighbours, drives Mrs Neale to drink excessively.

While disgusting to the villagers of Abbot's Cordon, Mrs Neale is beatified by Drury who imagines her as a suffering saint – angelic, dignified yet deeply tormented by spiritual unrest. Drury frames the drunken woman through the anorexic logic of Cartesian dualism, explaining, 'I have never seen a face which gave me stronger feeling that behind it was a soul needing help' (Dickens 1896: 289). Like Galbraith in *Ideala*, Drury separates Mrs Neale's body and soul, suggesting her beautiful face is a mask and her body might be transcended and her soul revealed. Drury's authority in such matters is undermined immediately by the text, since, despite his efforts to help Mrs Neale, it is Drury's own soul that hangs in the balance. While Abbot's Cordon views Mrs Neale as a sinner, it is precisely the fallenness of her face and form that Drury finds sexually appealing. He describes her as 'a tall woman, very pale, and with striking eyes' (1896: 289) and as 'tall and finely proportioned' (1896: 295), as statuesque despite her constant intoxication. Drury explains that

[s]he had a beautiful head admirably set upon her shoulders. Her features had evidently once been very handsome; and marred as they were by the expression of bitterness and defiance which lurked in every line, there was still an almost painful beauty about them. (Dickens 1896: 295)

His desire for the penitent sinner is located in his need to reform her; he imagines her, in turn, as both saint and sinner, and his failure to rehabilitate her is the consequence of his inability to see past these basic constructions. Increasingly unable to disentangle his priestly duties from his sexual desire, Drury's eyes are 'vaguely troubled' (1896: 294) yet repeatedly drawn to the scenes of Mrs Neale's bodily struggles. As the spectator to a sacrifice, Drury's need to observe the suffering of his female parishioner is, like Galbraith's secret observations of Ideala, deeply problematic. As the narrator is quick to point out, 'the ease which had come to him with Mrs Neale was not his priestly ease [. . .] in her presence, he evince[d] no access of priestly dignity or patronage' (1896: 304–5), and the only assistance he can offer her is a sexual union through marriage.

Drury's concern for the body of the female inebriate takes the form of scopic paternalism, as he asks her not to 'think of me as forcing myself upon you' while 'a slight touch of intense appeal crept into his voice' (1896: 314). When he cannot cure her of her excessive drinking and is faced with uncontrollable desire, Drury proposes marriage to Mrs Neale to better observe and control her from the authoritative position of a husband. His attempts to regulate and reform the female drunk are tied inherently to his need to master her disorderly body in line with codes of Christian virtue and womanly submission. When Mrs Neale relapses, coming to choir practice drunk and dishevelled, her descent from feminine grace is imagined both as a biblical fall and as disease:

> from head to foot she was weighed down by the degrading physical consequences of her fall. But, infinitely more degrading, crushing her to the earth, there was upon her the cloud of shame; shame which spoke in every line of her figure, in every line of her hard, sullen face, and in the set, defiant stare of her eyes. (Dickens 1896: 314)

Here Dickens's language contrasts with earlier descriptions of Mrs Neale, emphasising physical degeneration, infection and bodily distortion. Mrs Neale's saintliness is disputed here because her inebriety has brought her down to earth from the position of dignity and beauty she occupies as a repentant and abstaining sinner. Like Ideala's irreligious love for Lorrimer – imagined by Grand's male narrator as infectious vapour – Mrs Neale's shame is a miasmic cloud that encapsulates her body and symbolises her fall. Yet, despite its mist-like properties, Mrs Neale's shame is simultaneously heavy and crushing. Her defiance, which is mentioned on a number of occasions, is characteristic of the story's central tenet: that Mrs Neale is a martyr to the weakness of men and society, and as such will not be saved by a religion managed by either. Mrs Neale recreates the sacramental process, consuming alcohol in a reversal of the Eucharist that both internalises society's criticism of her consumptive desires and also challenges Christ's example of self-sacrifice. Her body, which fails to operate as a vessel of Christian purity and as a potential container for children, reverses the transubstantiation through which symbols of Christ's body are personified. In Mrs Neale's case, her body becomes a sign, her metaphorical wounds a 'badge of identity', transformed by the consumption of alcohol that marks the passage of the Christian symbol of wine into blood.

The image of Mrs Neale as fallen through both Drury's descriptions and her sense of her own 'disgraceful and contaminating presence' (1896: 335) implies a sense of sexual compromise that Dickens's narrator makes clear is not the case. As a Victorian woman drinker, Mrs Neale's consumptionary desires are rhetorically aligned with prostitution within the text and by the central characters. However, this notion is undermined by her pride, beauty and defiance, by 'something about Mrs Neale which even degradation, as it seemed, could not destroy' (1896: 326). The narration of Mrs Neale's defiance imaginatively entangles her with Victorian artworks depicting two of the most famous of all fallen women: Eve and Mary Magdalene. Mrs Neale's shame, sensuality and defiant stare recall Frederick Sandys's 1862 painting *Mary Magdalene*, in which the central female figure looks over her shoulder, her eyes dropped, yet her face insolent in its expression. Mary Magdalene is also depicted in Dante Gabriel Rossetti's drawing *Mary Magdalene at the Door of Simon the Pharisee* (1858) in both her 'carnal loveliness' (Waldman 2008: 152) and bodily allure as a fallen yet desirable woman, still capable of heavenly ascendance. Although she turns away from the world of the body represented by the mass of humanity in the background of the image, the accompanying poem suggests a degree of sexual ambiguity (Bullen 1998: 74–6).[24]

Dickens has her narrator frame the female drunk using archetypal images of feminine fall found in popular Victorian art, in much the same way as Egerton's female narrator in 'Gone Under'. While Egerton attempts to undermine women's reliance on male-oriented modes of interpretation, Dickens posits these interpretations as the product of a religious discourse that should be challenged when shown to be corrupt. When Mrs Neale refuses Drury's proposal it is because she understands that it is only within herself that she can find the strength to survive. While she tells Drury 'you have saved – one woman' (Dickens 1896: 340), the reader is left in no doubt that it is Mrs Neale who has saved herself: from habitual drunkenness, from marriage to a weak man, and from ruining the life of another woman. Dickens suggests that the female drunk represents the body of women who fail to adhere to the expectations of a gendered Christian tradition, and that only innate female strength will restore women to the society that demands their sacrifice. Though Drury attempts to help Mrs Neale, it is from a position of masculine desire and observation that problematises his efforts, and reveals that masculine intervention is implicitly tied to mastery and control. Unlike Virginia Madden or Egerton's heroines, Mrs Neale masters herself, refusing to be defined by patriarchal dictates requiring her shame and submission, and eventually finding her place in society. In many ways, Dickens's character has much in common with the reintegrated Janet Dempster; however, Dickens goes much further than Eliot by allowing her self-harming heroine to restore her own body within normative boundaries of femininity. This self-restoration, subversive as it is in one sense, still sees Dickens's female drunkard adhering to bourgeois moral and religious expectations as she aspires to the hegemonic ordering of her disruptive body.

In the texts produced by and about the New Woman that fictionalise the female drunk, a variety of strategies emerge in representing self-harming female bodies. In Gissing's novel, the New Woman is subject to criticism because of her demands for admission to the public space, and her attempts to widen women's access to the male-oriented economic world. At the same time, the appropriately feminine domestic woman is sympathetically rendered as an unfortunate casualty of the Victorian marriage market, and her consumption of alcohol is forgiven whilst it can be kept behind closed doors. Though the drunken female body in Gissing is subject to a slow process of narrative revelation, it never features as a spectacle of atrocity like the bodies of women drinkers in the short stories of Gissing's New Woman contemporaries. I would argue that this is because the novel format could not permit detailed description of middle-class drunken women without shocking its readers, and because it required clear and coherent resolutions to its plot.[25] George Egerton's drunken women are displayed in public places, their bodies observed by characters within the narrative and displayed by the narrative for the reader. Egerton's strategy of exhibiting the suffering bodies of her heroines addresses what Gissing's novel does not – the eroticisation of the female body by the very masculine field of vision that leaves them with no option but to self-destruct.

While the drunken female body in *The Odd Women* is unattractive and repeatedly hidden by a narrative that requires it to be kept private, the very public body of the drunk in Egerton's stories is curiously both beautiful and repulsive, grotesque yet also sexually alluring. However, in drawing attention to the twin evils of epistemophilia and self-damage, Egerton herself participates in wound culture, presenting 'spectacles of public sex and public violence', critiquing, yet resorting to, a display of female bodies corresponding to limiting dichotomies of femininity embedded in Christian ideology and iconography. Mary Angela Dickens's story dramatises the intemperate woman as a figure of feminine self-assertion who drinks to escape the cruelties of a male-oriented society. Nevertheless, Mrs Neale's attempt to restore her broken body to the hegemonic order suggests that acts of drunken self-harm are, while highly subversive, too risky a strategy for successful female rebellion.

All three writers represent alcohol as a form of escape from the horrifying realities of a limiting world in which financial, social and religious pressures force women to commit self-destructive acts. However, in the short stories of Egerton and Dickens, the body of the female drunk is presented in ways that elide the borders between public and private spaces, disclosing an 'erotics at the crossing point of private fantasy and public space' (Seltzer 1998: 31). In doing so, both writers disrupt the boundaries that excluded women from the public domain, simultaneously offering no viable means of protest other than their own self-harm. In adopting the short-story form, Egerton and Dickens achieve what Moore and Gissing cannot: the detailed display of the drunken, damaged and (usually) middle-class female body. Although the novel format offered Gissing an abundance of pages by which to explore the drunken female body, as in the novels of Sarah Grand that body curiously escapes textual embodiment. However, in the structurally unconstrained mode of the short story, these bodies are painfully embodied; the physical manifestations of feminine trauma are given a textual presence despite the limited space of the artefacts in which they appear. This paradox will be explored further in my final chapter, which examines the most violent manifestation of self-harm in New Woman writing between 1880 and 1900 – self-mutilation in the short-story form.

Notes

1. See Levine 1978.
2. See Wilson 2005 for discussion of culturally acceptable drinking behaviours.
3. See McAllister 2003 and Nock 2008 for discussion of alcoholism as self-harm.
4. I refer to the drunken Victorian woman as an alcoholic, for ease of reference. This terminology emerged at the beginning of the twentieth century, and I acknowledge that the authors examined in this study would not have characterised their heroines using this term.
5. See Edwards 1990 on the emergence of alcoholism as a disease.
6. It was only when drinking reached levels that interfered with economic output – owing to absenteeism or poor workmanship – that the working classes were called to account for their intemperance (Shiman 1988: 1–3).
7. See Stiles 2007 for discussion of Victorian neurology in relation to addiction.
8. Drunken characters who were not working class did, however, feature in both Anne Brontë's *The Tenant of Wildfell Hall* (1848) and Ellen Wood's *Danesbury House* (1860).
9. In *Culture and Anarchy* (1869), Matthew Arnold argued that exposure to middle-class culture could elevate the conditions of the poor.
10. See Nicholls 2009 and Harrison 1994: 225–6.
11. See Berrios 1996 for further examples.
12. These include schizophrenia, bipolar disorder and a range of obsessive-compulsive disorders.

13. In the Catholic tradition the process of transubstantiation allows the bread and wine to 'become' the body and blood of Christ, while most other denominations believe that the bread and wine merely represent Christ's body and blood.

14. The Matrimonial Causes Act of 1857 specified alcoholism along with drug use and adultery as grounds for divorce, but it was only upper-middle-class husbands who could afford to do so, and women could not divorce men on the same grounds (Helsinger et al. 1983: 21–38).

15. See Logan 1998, Walkowitz 1992, Watt 1984 and Auerbach 1980 for discussion.

16. The moral outcry caused by Stead's report led to the Criminal Law Amendment Act of 1885, which raised the age of sexual consent for women from thirteen to sixteen years.

17. Despite Mudie's refusal to stock his novel, Moore's depiction of his heroine's fall did remain publishable. Contrastingly, Émile Zola's *L'Assommoire* (1877), which depicted female alcoholism in a more tangential and slightly less explicit fashion, was subject to censorship in France, and was not made available in an English translation until 1893.

18. See Huguet and James 2013 for discussion of Gissing's involvement with the Woman Question, and Liggins 2006 and Nelson 2007 on Nell Harrison.

19. See Hager 2006 for extensive discussion of constructions of female community in *Keynotes* and *Discords*.

20. See Fluhr 2001, in which Egerton's reference to Helen of Troy is noted.

21. Dickens published in *The Strand Magazine* in February 1897 and July 1897.

22. See Dickens 1897b.

23. Dickens would later accuse the 'shrieking sisterhood' ('Women and Votes') of weakening the nation, at a meeting of the Women's National Anti-Suffrage League in Gloucester in 1908 at which she was a guest speaker.

24. Mary Magdalene is conflated with Eve in Rossetti's painting *Mary Magdalene* (1877), in which the beautiful fallen woman – as in Rossetti's *Proserpine* (1874) – holds a spherical object, replicating the fall of Eve in the Garden of Eden (Genesis 3: 1–24). In these images, the fallen woman is painted as sensuous and desiring, with a vacant look of challenge.

25. Circulating libraries provided access to novels for a mostly middle-class readership, and access could be controlled and restricted dependent on bourgeois tastes and morality. Conversely, circulation of the kinds of periodicals that published short stories was less restricted. Periodicals required new stories to satisfy the demands of a more diverse readership, and they provided women writers with a format for publishing that did not rely on the approval of the bourgeoisie for success.

Chapter 4

Damaging the Body Politic: Self-Mutilation as Spectacle

While self-starvation and excessive drinking manifested in the triple-decker novels of the mid-Victorian period and the New Woman novels and short stories of the *fin de siècle*, deliberately self-injurious acts were a less easily recognisable thematic concern. As New Woman writing increasingly departed from publication in male-favoured forms, and pursued shorter narrative structures, it also began to adopt more violent imagery. In this chapter I posit a clear link between the escalating use of self-mutilation as a theme, and the New Woman's adoption of newer modes of expression such as poetry and short stories. I also explore the continued deployment of both classical Western philosophies of the body and the Christian ideologies discussed in previous chapters. I suggest that the same logic of bodily denial that reifies both the anorexic experience and the 'alcoholic' response to trauma can also be traced through the increasing resistance to larger bodies of text that marked the New Woman's growing presence in the hitherto male-dominated publication environment of the *fin de siècle*.

Unlike the comparatively passive-aggressive acts of self-starvation and excessive drinking, self-mutilation constituted a means by which to rip apart both the fictional female body and the bodies of narrative within which it had been traditionally represented. If the experience of reading is bound up with the desire to know and possess the body, if narrative marks the beginning, middle and end of this process of desire, then the New Woman's rejection of traditional forms subverted this practice. The 'public fascination with torn and open bodies and torn and open persons' (Seltzer 1998: 1) upon which the Victorian wound culture was fashioned provided the New Woman with an opportunity to express the previously inexpressible. However, in deploying the imagery of self-mutilation, New Woman writers came close to committing acts of literary self-sabotage, enacting dangerous and self-mutilative strategies on both the bodies of their heroines and their own bodies of narrative.

Victorian Self-Mutilation

As a distinct pathology, self-mutilation received very little medical or psychotherapeutic attention during the early part of the nineteenth century. Although the first case study was published in Britain in 1846, it was not until 1920 that Freud's work on life and death instincts in *Beyond the Pleasure Principle* provided the beginnings of a framework within which to read such behaviour.[1] Alienists had begun to document cases of self-injury including scratching, skin-picking, biting, hair-pulling and swallowing foreign bodies in asylum settings. However, there is no substantive data to suggest that female Victorian self-harmers deliberately, repeatedly mutilated themselves (Chaney 2011a: 280–1) or that these behaviours manifested outside of the Victorian prison or asylum, or in the middle-class contexts in which most New Woman writers operated. In the 1892 edition of *A Dictionary of Psychological Medicine*, self-mutilation warrants a five-page entry in which origins, causes and symptoms are given:

> Many, perhaps most of those self-inflicted tortures have at times had their origin in unduly exaggerated religious fervour, enthusiasm, or fanaticism [. . .] we have in the monastic flagellations of the Christian church instances of self-torture as an expiation for sin [. . .] All the states of mind leading to self-mutilation, self-torture, &c., hitherto considered, are compatible with reputed sanity, although they are to insanity near akin, and generally indicate more or less mental derangement [. . .] In the present day it is found that although instances of self-injury are not unfrequent [*sic*], probably the intention of those inflicting them is more commonly suicidal in character. (Tuke 1976: 1147–8)

Penned by alienist James Adam, the entry posits self-mutilation as intrinsic to Christianity, owing much of its nineteenth-century pathology to the fanaticism once practised as part of cultural rituals. As I have already shown, Western philosophy and Christian practices of asceticism denigrated the body as the corrupt vessel in which the soul resided. Conceptualising self-mutilation as a historically religious practice, Adam's work reinforces the notion that such acts are steeped in religious tradition – and thus acceptable – yet are simultaneously indicative of insanity. Adam's definition exemplifies nineteenth-century psychiatric assumptions about self-mutilation, and more generally about self-harm – that it was overwhelmingly a symptom of suicide. Where Adam concedes that 'wilful self-mutilation' (Tuke 1976: 1148) does occur, he connects it to psychiatric illnesses that induce 'hallucination' or 'delusion' (1149). As I have noted, the medical profession continued to view self-harm as a type of suicide until well into the twentieth century, failing to acknowledge its potential as a psychological survival strategy; at the same time, New Woman writers were fictionalising it as such. The connection to suicide was supported by sensational cases of female self-mutilation that were thought to indicate both suicidal insanity and specifically sexual deviance.

Extreme or violent cases of self-mutilation were either exceptionally rare or not recorded. In recorded cases, women's self-mutilation was diagnosed as hysterical, and it was often connected to other sexual 'perversions'. In the case of Helen Miller – a kleptomaniac incarcerated in New York's Sing Sing prison between 1875 and 1877 – the self-mutilator 'enjoyed the attention of doctors and experienced sexual pleasure from having her wounds probed' (Channing 1878: 369). Armando Favazza (2011: 158) and Marilee Strong (2000: 29–33) both refer to cases of nineteenth-century self-mutilation in their respective studies. However, few of these were recorded in Britain, and cases were publicised in medical journals and not in the mainstream press. The case of Helen Miller was not national news in Britain, but was published in the *American Journal of Psychiatry* which would have been available to British physicians and psychiatrists. Like Krafft-Ebing and Freud, psychiatrists who witnessed self-harming acts failed to dissociate them from eroticism, especially where women were concerned.[2] As with anorexia, self-mutilation was viewed as a deviant resistance to the sexual corruptions of femininity. As I have shown, literary and journalistic accounts offer some of the most significant and varied representations of the practice of self-harm documented at the *fin de siècle*, particularly those detailing violent acts of bodily self-wounding. However, these representations generally serve to complicate rather than to enlighten our understanding of the psychological and medical phenomena that appeared in New Woman writing but would not be properly diagnosed and treated until almost a century later.

In 1880 the national newspapers reported that a man's corpse had been found horribly mutilated in London's East River, setting in motion a lengthy murder inquiry that would end with the revelation that he had committed the act himself ('Extraordinary Case of Self-Mutilation'). Similarly, in 1882, the case of Isaac Brooks – who suffered from paranoid delusions – caught the attention of the public when the release of his alleged attackers was reported in *The Lancet* and then *The Times* in subsequent weeks. Brooks had claimed to have had his genitals mutilated during an attack by two men, leaving him semi-castrated. Following Brooks's death-bed confession that he had committed the act himself, the release of his 'attackers' became national news, and served to strengthen public interest in the seemingly inexplicable practice of self-mutilation (Warrington 1882, Chaney 2011a and 2011b). In *A Bright Red Scream* (1998), Marilee Strong describes how in the same year as the Brooks case a married labourer cut off his testicle after sleeping with a prostitute, and in 1897 a Russian peasant ripped off his own scrotum and handed it to his mother, declaring, 'Take that, I don't want it anymore' (2000: 30). Examples of self-mutilation like these were shocking and, along with accounts of self-injury to avoid military service, provided a sensational tabloid backdrop to the everyday battles that self-mutilators may have actually faced.

Self-mutilation was an important facet of Victorian entertainment that both spectacularised and normalised the wounded body as a subject of middle-class observation (Tromp 2008). The sword-swallowers and human pincushions of the Victorian freak show formed popular displays of self-wounding for entertainment, eliciting little more than temporary and transient public interest (Cranton 2009: 12–14). Across nineteenth-century Europe and America, cases of teenage girls who inserted sharp objects into their skin, seemingly without pain, were also reported (Gould and Pyle 1956: 517). Unlike the fasting medieval saints, or the human oddities of the freak show, these self-mutilators were hystericised, like Helen Miller (Favazza 2011: 158). While the majority of the human pincushions exhibited at freak shows were men (Bending 2000: 190, 208), cases of girls inserting needles into their skin were common enough for European doctors to name them 'needle girls' (Gould and Pyle 1956: 517). Owing to their gender, physicians saw the actions of these self-mutilators as symptoms of feminine madness, or compulsive sexual disorders such as kleptomania and masochism, because medicine had yet to produce a distinct psychological framework within which to imagine them. Despite the media furore created by Isaac Brooks and others, and despite the fact that the public display of, and debate surrounding, the deformed or wounded body was a well-established facet of nineteenth-century entertainment, self-mutilation largely evaded official record. It was not until the twentieth century that research into self-mutilation began to disentangle the practice from suicide, hysteria and religious fanaticism, associations exemplified by *A Dictionary of Psychological Medicine* and case studies such as those of Brooks and Miller.

Theorising Self-Mutilation

Unlike anorexia nervosa and dipsomania, which were widely recognised and researched by Victorian medical professionals, self-mutilation was not a nineteenth-century condition. Although I hesitate to retrospectively apply contemporary terminologies and theoretical frameworks to the *fin-de-siècle* context, it is useful to consider twentieth- and twenty-first-century approaches to self-mutilation, to provide an appropriate language through which to discuss such acts in New Woman fiction, since one did not exist at the time. All theoretical models of self-harm, including those proposed by nineteenth-century figures such as Freud, emphasise the role of traumatic memory, in the 'dramatic repetition' (Turp 2002: 89) of anxieties or abuse. Twenty-first-century psychiatric research has demonstrated a direct correlation between self-mutilation and histories of abuse or neglect, or failures of relationships during childhood.[3] Unable to express the pain caused by psychological trauma, violently attacking the body communicates anxieties that cannot be spoken, mastering physical pain when emotional suffering is uncontrollable (Arnold and Babiker 1997). In this way self-mutilation shares some of the dialogic characteristics of self-starvation and excessive drinking, especially the ways in which it communicates (female) experience.

According to neurologists, self-mutilation triggers the release of hormones that work to counteract pain, anxiety, agitation or depression (Lee et al. 2015, Groschwitz and Plener 2012). Studies suggest self-mutilators have neurological pathways that differ from healthy individuals, and that by deliberately self-wounding a sufferer can force the release of endorphins (Favazza and Simeon 2001: 18). In this way self-mutilators become the architects of their own pain, regulating themselves when all else appears or feels overwhelming, using a similar (if more overtly violent) approach to the anorectic. Despite characteristics common to diagnosed sufferers, the practice of self-mutilation is not easy to categorise, nor are acts of self-wounding physically or psychologically consistent. Contemporary self-wounders use a variety of means by which to harm their bodies, many of which constitute a response to the specific conditions of their trauma.

As well as differences in the types of wounds inflicted and their location, the psychopathology of self-mutilation differs depending on developmental factors. Non-dissociative self-mutilation is usually the consequence of a reversal of dependence during a child's formative years. The child is required to suppress negative emotions for fear of parental alienation, and projects intolerable rage on to the surface of his or her skin (Levenkron 2006: 48). Dissociative self-mutilation is different, in that sufferers become entirely disconnected from themselves and others. The result is mental disintegration requiring distraction in the form of blood and/or pain, which functions as a tool by which to self-soothe (Levenkron 2006: 48). Consistent in all acts of self-mutilation is the importance of the skin as a metaphorical surface and biological communicative tool. The 'success' of the act of self-mutilation depends upon the complicated purpose of the skin, which both connects us to the world and is a private and internal organ of the body. Just as the body functions as both a biological and a cultural signifier, the skin 'cannot be taken for granted as merely organic matter, nor as a passive surface onto which social meaning is straightforwardly inscribed' (Cavanagh et al. 2013: 2). The skin bears numerous, complex pressures from both within and without, and also 'separates us from and connects us to others and to objects in the world' (Cavanagh et al. 2013: 2–3). As Armando Favazza notes, 'we normally live within our skins' unless something interferes with this process, resulting in an 'inability to perceive where the body ends and the outside world begins' (1996: 148).

Freud had argued that trauma facilitated the creation of a 'parasitic double' (2001b: 209), at once both part of and apart from the individual, integral to the internal workings of the psyche but equally its external projection. Freud's recognition of an inability to distinguish between oneself and the external projection of the psyche anticipated twenty-first-century understandings of the self-mutilator's inability to perceive the boundaries between the body and the outside world. Those who are unable to distinguish between the borders of the self and the skin experience depersonalisation, an anomaly of the mechanism by which an individual usually processes self-awareness, characterised by the feeling of watching oneself act, yet having no control over those actions, often due to high levels of stress. Sufferers describe feeling that the world has become vague, dreamlike, or lacking in significance[4] and are unable to recognise fully the limits of their bodies. Like the anorexic logic of mind/body dualism, depersonalisation privileges the mind over the body, resulting in deference of psychological trauma through destruction of the flesh. In the case of self-mutilation, the skin functions as a membrane through which the ego and the body remain connected, and thus must be attacked, which

> may seem paradoxical since skin cutting might be thought to open the portal through which the inner self and outer world might flow into each other. In fact, a very different process occurs. The cutting causes blood to appear and stimulates nerve endings in the skin. When this occurs cutters first are able to verify that they are alive, and then are able to focus attention on their skin border and to perceive the limit of their bodies. (Favazza 1996: 148)

In attempting to address the disconnection of the skin and the self through self-wounding, the dissociative self-mutilator opens up the body, temporarily putting inside and outside into communication.

Didier Anzieu's theory of the skin ego presents a useful way of reading Victorian self-mutilation, since it draws on the nineteenth-century research that had begun to scrutinise the drives that facilitated such behaviour. Victorian doctors had yet to identify or investigate self-mutilation as a psychological process, but Freud's concept of the life and death instincts – developed during the nineteenth century and fully formulated in *Beyond the Pleasure Principle* – provided the basis for Anzieu's later work. Anzieu theorises the disordered relationship between the skin and the psyche as the result of disrupted infantile development, explaining:

> the biological function is performed by what Winnicott calls 'holding', i.e. by the way the mother supports the baby's body. The psychical function develops through the interiorization of this maternal holding [. . .] In extreme cases, inflicting a real envelope of suffering on oneself can be an attempt to restore the skin's containing function not performed by the mother or those in one's early environment. (Anzieu 1989: 98–201)

Deficient physical contact during the pre-Oedipal phase results in a desire to reassert lost communication between the psyche and the dermis through acts of bodily violence. Claiming that self-mutilation constitutes a disruption of the boundaries between 'inner and outer surfaces' (Anzieu 1989: 201), what Winnicott calls the 'continuity of being' (ibid.), self-mutilators author their own suffering, in communication with the maternally neglected 'self' through inscription on the bodily surface.[5] Rather than representing the self, the mutilated body becomes a vessel through which unfulfilled maternal care is avenged, assuaged, and thus entered into narrative to be held to account. Given the frequent fictionalisation of failed maternal relationships and poor maternal examples in New Woman fiction, Anzieu's notion of the skin ego provides a pertinent psychoanalytic framework within which to consider self-mutilation in these texts.

The concept of enacting parental failures on the body makes sense in light of theories of self-harm (as in the case of Freud's work on anorexia) that view attacking the female form as a denial of sexuality stemming from an inability to identify with the maternal body. Estella Welldon contends that adolescent girls who self-harm express 'tremendous dissatisfaction, not only with themselves, but also with their mothers, who provided them with the bodies they are now fighting' (2000: 40). Read through the skin ego, female self-mutilation can be understood as an attack on the body as a site of unsatisfactory maternal but also sexual identification, a resistance to its femaleness (Smith et al. 1998). Unlike the anorectic's desire to transcend or deny the body and its feminine appetites, the self-mutilator (like the dipsomaniac) requires embodiment to communicate with, and between, inner and outer selves. Self-mutilation, like anorexia, is about controlling the body; its health and stability are not the primary goals of those who choose to self-inflict pain. Rather, suffering is a strategy by which to cope with trauma: to enter it into narrative and negotiate its meaning, through a system of signs and codes that make the body bear witness.

Twenty-first-century psychotherapeutic work has supported Anzieu's conceptualisation of self-mutilation as the flesh put into violent, if temporary, communication with the psyche. Attacking the body is a 'paradoxical gesture in that the apparently destructive act reflects a desire to continue to live and get on with life', therefore self-mutilation functions 'as a way of cutting off from pain by providing a distraction' (Gardner 2001: 25). Conceived in this way, one of the central (and ontologically Victorian) misconceptions surrounding self-mutilation and indeed self-harm can be corrected. Rather than a form of suicide, self-mutilation is a complex coping behaviour that, however maladaptive, represents for sufferers the difference between survival and total self-annihilation.[6] Like self-harm in general, self-mutilation is, statistically speaking, a female condition. The vast majority of diagnosed cases confirm this (Levenkron 2006: 21), and the ratio of self-mutilators to healthy patients is thought to be approximately one in 250 adolescent women (Arnold 1994: 1). Like anorexia, the distinctly (although not exclusively) feminine pathology of self-mutilation can be situated as a response to the subordinate position historically occupied by women. Like their Victorian counterparts who were denied a political voice, contemporary self-mutilators find themselves unable to identify, express or release emotions as others do.

As I have argued, Victorian women were expected to repress feelings of anxiety in line with a model of feminine forbearance typified by the Virgin Mary, Jesus Christ and other martyrs. Middle-class women were required to silence their demands for everything from sexual and economic autonomy to political enfranchisement. At a time when women were agitating to have their voices heard, self-mutilation represents an important metaphor for tensions between attempts to communicate dissatisfaction and the internalised social expectations that required the repression of feminine voices and desires. The enactment of traumatic memory on to the surface of the body is, to a certain extent, fictionalised throughout the New Woman oeuvre. However, depictions of self-mutilation and the psychological structures within which it is actuated are not explicitly expressed within more traditional forms of writing, the production of which was determined by the male-dominated publishing industry. New Woman writers were beginning to narrate these concerns, but they failed to fully articulate them within the literary formats that had hitherto been available, and instead sought new ways to dramatise female traumas.

Many of the fictional self-harmers examined in this chapter demonstrate an inability to perceive the boundaries between their bodies and the cultures that write them into limiting discourses. In a Victorian society that reads itself through the human form as a synecdoche for its body politic, attacking the body functions as a rebellion against the powers that punish deviance from strict religious and moral norms. Self-mutilation is a way of opening up the skin to merge its internal and external functions; to elide the boundaries keeping inner and outer discrete, to enact metaphorically the 'everyday openness of *every* body' (Seltzer 1998: 2), the flaws in the cohesive fabric of a sexually and economically repressive culture. I show in this chapter how New Woman writing was beginning to associate religious and moral self-criticism with both dissociative and non-dissociative forms of self-mutilation. In doing so, I demonstrate not only how New Woman writers inhabited the new literary spaces at the margins of heteronormative culture, but, additionally, how these spaces were also occupied by troubling counter dynamics of defeatism and display.

The Rhetoric of Dissociation in New Woman Writing

As Chapter 2 details, the New Woman novel deployed passive-aggressive tropes of feminine resistance, such as self-starvation and deliberate self-infection. While these tropes were less covert than similar imagery found in mid-Victorian women's writing, they negotiated a tension between the display of female self-damage and its nature as a concealed and private narrative. This chapter examines self-mutilation in the short-story form, which makes the wounded female body its political and erotic locus. I argue that the limited narrative space of the poem and the short story allowed New Woman authors to articulate metaphorically self-harming impulses, and I acknowledge the literary debt owed by writers like George Egerton to some of her New Woman contemporaries. While self-mutilation does not emerge as a trope in the New Woman novels discussed, discourses that highlight the dissociative strategies by which the heroines of the short story are driven first materialise in this earlier writing. Dissociation appears frequently in Grand's Morningquest trilogy: Ideala's acts of social self-harm are described as a 'safety valve by means of which she regained her composure' (Grand 2008: 41); Evadne enjoys illness as a distraction from marital discord (Grand 2007); and of Beth Caldwell we are told 'the trouble of her mind ceased when the physical pain became acute, and therefore she welcomed it as a pleasant distraction' (Grand 1980: 8).

Meanwhile, Mona Caird connects Hadria Fullerton's sufferings to her inability to dissociate herself from her family as 'the incessant rising and quelling of her impulse and her courage [. . .] represented a vast amount of force [. . .] expended in producing wear and tear upon the system' (1894: 78). Hadria disconnects from those around her, distracting herself from emotional pain with self-defeating acts of obedience while a 'superficial apathy was creeping over [her], below which burnt a slow fire of pain' (1894: 335). In adopting a coping mechanism through which to diffuse her rage, Hadria enacts a paradoxical gesture of self-harm *and* self-care in which emotional trauma is masked by a painfully achieved outward serenity. Similarly, in *The Wing of Azrael*, Viola Sedley finds 'a strange desperate pleasure in self-torture' (2010b: 72) when her emotions become overwhelming. Although these are not explicit references to self-mutilation, they suggest a consideration of the mechanisms through which female survival might be assured through self-destructive and dissociative practices, and anticipate twenty-first-century psychiatric models. Descriptions of self-mutilation, however deeply encoded, would have been almost impossible in the realist novel; poetry, however, could offer a less concrete account of self-harm that required no resolutions or particular moral framework. It is to New Woman poetry that I now turn, to demonstrate how the imagery of the mutilated body found its way into a traditionally masculine mode, and laid the groundwork for the short stories that would graphically represent self-mutilation by women.

During the 1880s and 1890s, women writers formulated concerns about the female body and its self-destructive drives in poems that adapted masculine literary convention for proto-feminist purposes. Many such authors were implicated in the New Woman oeuvre and subverted the formal features of the epic, the ode and the ballad to address issues of gender and sexuality that otherwise would have been difficult to broach. For instance, in the work of Olive Custance, despair, death and suicidal impulses are modulated by the use of Homeric and folkloric figures and settings. While scholarship of Custance's work has focused on her use of mythoi to encode homoeroticism (Parker 2015, Pulham 2007, Vanita 1996, Vicinus 1994, Lasner and Stetz 1990), I would extend such claims to include the occlusion of her speaker's suicidal drives. In 'Doubts' from *Opals* (1897), Custance's speaker describes a 'dream of death' (1897: 17, line 9) as 'life strips us naked but leaves us breath' (line 12). The speaker expands, lamenting ' – slow sorrows, are life – in vain | To praise white peace when the wine of pain | Fate's purple wine, is so fiery sweet! | Think you we should be glad to die' (lines 26–9). Similarly, in 'A Mood' Custance's speaker describes the futility of life, since 'In vain my winged songs beat against the bars | Of bitter life [. . .]' (1897: 20, lines 25–6), and in both 'The Changeling' and 'The Vision' from her later collection *The Inn of Dreams* (1911) the melancholic speakers drink from a 'crystal cup' and slip into oblivion. While her speakers are presumably male, and are often (as with the poems' addressees) ambiguously gendered, Custance also tempers her representations of melancholy, death and suicide, using familiar classical and mythical tropes, making her poetry publishable despite its subversive content.

One of Custance's contemporaries was Amy Levy, a young Anglo-Jewish woman living in London, who published poems, short stories, novels and essays confronting issues of gender, class and race from a position at the margins of all three. Levy's concern with what Cynthia Scheinberg describes as intersecting notions of 'minority' and 'otherness' (2002: 190–1) has made her work ripe for rediscovery by contemporary critics in diverse fields of study. Levy has been resurrected variously as the first modern Jewish poetess (Valman 2010, Beckman 2005), an innovative urban novelist

(Goody 2006, Vadillo 2005), a feminist essayist (Francis 1990, Nord 1990, Beckman 2005, L. Hughes 2007) and a conflicted lesbian writer (Donoghue 1997, Hennegan 2000, Reynolds 2000). While Levy's imbrication of such varied textual, cultural and critical categories has made her a panacea for scholars examining both gender and genre, it is her complicated relationship with religion that best exemplifies the double marginality experienced by most of the other writers whose work I examine. Like Caird, Cross, Grand and Egerton, Levy was other – both a part of, and apart from, British, Anglo-Saxon, Christian society. Like Mary Angela Dickens, Levy challenged both her cultural heritage and the literary canon, adopting and undermining Victorian authorial traditions.

Educated for two years at Newnham College, Levy was the first Jewish woman to attend the historically Christian institution of Cambridge University (Hetherington and Valman 2010: 1). Her education was paid for by her father, who had made his fortune in Australia, and whose commercial interests and liberal approach to his faith allowed his daughter an education that most Jewish women could not access (Pullen 2010). Levy's complicated relationship with her faith has been much examined by contemporary literary critics, who have noted both the perceived anti-Semitism in her work – her portrayal of 'Jewish self-hatred' (Beckman 1999: 186, Gilman 1986: 1–2) and Jewish 'vulgarity' (Bernstein 2010: 135–7) – and also her deep connection to Judaism as a source of both inspiration and anxiety (Scheinberg 2002, Divine 2011). Levy's work depicted Jewish life, but also the social structures that limited women's sexual, artistic and economic freedoms in Victorian society, which were based broadly on Judeo-Christian religion and were rooted in restrictive eugenic assumptions about race and gender (Valman 2010). Levy's dissatisfaction with the polarised representations of her own race as mercenary and vulgar, yet also racially weak and culturally disempowered, in many ways also critiqued the Christian faith, a tradition from which Levy drew imagery and rhetoric in her examination of nineteenth-century values.[7] While Levy was neither a Christian nor a particularly committed or devout Jew, she narrativised the frustrations of contemporary life through Christian symbolism that was recognisable to her gentile readership.

Levy's 1881 poem 'Felo de Se' signified her first engagement with the subject that would dominate her writing over the next eight years until her suicide by carbon monoxide poisoning in 1889. The Latin term translates as 'felony on the self', and it was the British law used to prosecute those who attempted suicide during the nineteenth century, and (technically, although not often practically) until suicide was decriminalised in 1961. An example of what Joseph Bristow, quoting Germaine Greer, describes as Levy's 'uncontrolled "misery stream"' (2005: 78), 'Felo de Se' represents unsuitable material by a woman poet, and implicates Levy as an unsuitable Victorian woman, unlikely to be lauded and absorbed into a predominantly male poetic canon. Her use of the verse form allowed Levy to portray taboo subjects as poetic, romantic and abstract concepts, using death 'as a lexicon through which speakers seek to understand their experience' (Francis 1990: 190). By adopting recognisable Romantic imagery of lost love and suicidal tragedy, Levy's verse was made palatable to a general public that would otherwise have disapproved overwhelmingly of such inappropriate subject matter in poetry by a woman. As with Grand's use of the male narrator and the romance plot, Levy's appropriation of the traditionally male form of lyric poetry aimed to establish a feminist discourse within a historically masculine narrative form. Like Grand, Levy's use of a male tradition, to a certain degree, worked to subvert the notion of female inferiority and exclusion implicit in its conventions.

'Felo de Se': The Dissociative Poetry of Amy Levy

Exhibiting dissociative rhetoric similar to that found in the work of contemporaries like Grand and Caird, Levy's use of the male poet-speaker allowed her to explore self-harming impulses.[8] The melancholic male poet was a figure with whom the Victorian public had been enamoured since the general popularity of the Romantics and Alfred, Lord Tennyson's *In Memoriam* (1850). The expression of suicidal impulses through the narrative voice of Levy's 'hungry poet' (Beckman 2000: 59) persona complicated Victorian poetic canons. On the one hand, the public would have been comfortable and familiar with the figure of the suicidal poet. On the other hand, the use of the suicidal 'minor' poet to question the paternalistic strictures placed upon women writers demonstrated a subversion of Romanticism. Such traditions lauded men's authorship as an extension of personal genius, whilst for female writers pessimism was inherently disturbing and contrary to maternal instincts. Admittedly, female suicide had appeared in the work of earlier nineteenth-century women poets (Felicia Hemans, Elizabeth Barrett Browning and Mary Robinson, for example), but, like Custance, these women turned to 'figures of otherness removed in time and culture' (Higonnet 2015: 685) to escape censorship.[9] Levy's decision to voice women's deep unhappiness through a male persona subverted the gendered archetypes of traditional poetry (Scheinberg 2002, Olverson 2010), yet her strategy complicates feminist readings, since her inability to openly depict the struggling female poet suggests a sense of futility concerning women's entrance into what would become the Victorian poetic canon (Bristow 2000: 91).

'Felo de Se' is dedicated 'With Apologies to Mr. Swinburne', and reproduces the alliterative verse that Swinburne had parodied in 'Nephelidia' (1880), through the technique of assonance. 'Felo de Se' is linguistically comparable to Swinburne's 'Anactoria' (1866), a poem dedicated to the lesbian poet Sappho, who addresses her unfaithful lover, announcing:

> My life is bitter with thy love; thine eyes
> Blind me, thy tresses burn me, thy sharp sighs
> Divide my flesh and spirit with soft sound,
> And my blood strengthens, and my veins abound.
> I pray thee sigh not, speak not, draw not breath;
> Let life burn down, and dream it is not death.
> (Swinburne 2000: 47, lines 1–6)

Deploying similar imagery, Levy's narrator laments that he 'was wan and weary with life; my sick soul yearned for death | I was weary of women and war and the sea and the wind's wild breath (New 1993: 366, lines 3–4). Levy reproduces Swinburne's rhyme scheme, her regular rhythm, long lines and light punctuation imitate Swinburne's enjambment to the same weary, emphatic effect, and, like Swinburne, Levy rhymes 'death' with 'breath'. Swinburne eroticises metaphorical acts of blinding, burning and cutting at the hands of Anactoria as behaviours that merely strengthen Sappho's desire. While Levy's male poet takes no sexual pleasure in his suffering, her adoption of Swinburnian imagery suggests an intersectional interest in self-administered pain. Levy's assumption of Swinburne's style and subject matter underscores the importance of her dedicatory offering, given Swinburne's preoccupation with the erotics of religious torture and martyrdom noted in Chapter 1.

In 'A Minor Poet' (1884) Levy would adopt a similar style of narration; her male speaker attempts suicide, finally succeeding on his third effort. He announces that 'The world's a rock, and I will beat no more | A breast of flesh and blood against a rock' (New 1993: 373, lines 71–2). The metaphor of beating his head on a rock suggests the speaker's refusal to enact psychic pain on his body as a coping mechanism; he would thus prefer to end his life than prolong it with futile acts. Conversely, on a number of occasions in 'Felo de Se', Levy's speaker attempts to survive in the wake of traumatic experience; he imagines his torments through the imagery of bodily mutilation and suicide, explaining:

> I cull'd sweet poppies and crush'd them, the blood ran rich
>   and red:–
> And I cast it in crystal chalice and drank of it till I was dead.
> And the mould of the man was mute, pulseless in ev'ry part,
> The long limbs lay on the sand with an eagle eating the heart.
>
> (New 1993: 366, lines 6–9)

The reference to the bloody liquid of crushed poppies works on two levels. The dark red colour signifies dripping blood but also sleep and death, because of the use of poppies in the production of opium during the nineteenth century. It is likely that Levy's readers would have been aware of the origins of opium and the dangers of its use. Self-medication was widespread amongst Victorians of all classes, and the debate surrounding the pharmaceutical use of opium was influenced by the increasing number of opiate suicides during the latter half of the century (Berridge 1978: 444). Suicide by overdose or poisoning was a trope that Levy used more than once in her work, further signifying the centrality of this imagery to her conception of the artistic self-destruction that drives her male poet characters.[10]

Levy's use of red connotes a symbolic identification of poppies with death by suicide, and significantly the death-draught is administered via a chalice, a vessel usually containing the red wine of the Christian sacrament of Holy Communion. Like Custance's folkloric speakers, several of whom die after drinking from a 'crystal cup', Levy's poet drinks poison from the vessel with which the Eucharist is performed, explicitly referencing Christianity. On one level, the chalice is the container of the blood of Christ through Catholic transubstantiation, and can be understood as a further reference to blood. The content of the chalice brings death, and therefore its symbolic use may function as a critique of conventional religion. The chalice also references the Holy Grail, and the poet's resultant death as mirroring the death (and eternal life) of Jesus Christ, following Christ's use of the Grail cup at the Last Supper. The Grail features in Arthurian Romance as an object symbolic of the power and beneficence of God, and the chivalric hero must prove himself worthy to be in its presence through quest or challenge.[11] To read the chalice in 'Felo de Se' as the Holy Grail is to recognise Levy's understanding of the impossibility of female chivalric quest within a male-produced and male-oriented culture. The inability of women to transcend the limitations of the roles designed and perpetuated by a patriarchal society seems at one with Levy's broader critique of religion in 'Felo de Se'. However, the notion that Levy's work attempts to address the limitations of the nineteenth-century publication environment through her own quest for authorship is in part destabilised by her continued deployment of a male speaker in her lyric poetry.

As in Swinburne's 'Anactoria', Levy refers to the circulatory system in 'Felo de Se', citing bloodlessness as a desirable state. Levy's speaker addresses his unfavourable position as a suicidal poet for whom 'the Gods have decreed no rest' (New 1993: 366, line 11), hinting at the peace that might be achieved through suicide. Levy's constant reference to the hands is significant; her speaker

> Could wail with the wailing wind; strike sharply the hands
> in despair,
> Could shriek with shrieking blast, grow frenzied and tear
> the hair;
> Could fight fierce fights with foe, or clutch at a human hand;
> And weary could lie on the soft sweet saffron sand . . .
> I have neither a voice nor hands, nor any friend nor a foe;
> I am I – just a pulse of pain – I am I, that is all I know.
> (New 1993: 367, lines 24–9)

The striking of the hands 'sharply' is highly suggestive of self-mutilation, and the tearing of hair from the speaker's own head depicts directly another form of self-harm. The repetition of references to the hands is notable, and despite the lack of official data on self-mutilation in the period in which Levy wrote, she offers up for wounding the part of the body most favoured by twenty-first-century self-mutilators (Turp 2002: 13). In this stanza the hands have a dual function, as a site of violence and potential salvation. The speaker describes how he could 'fight fierce fights with a foe, or clutch at a human hand', noting the aggressive as well as conciliatory (and possibly penitential) function of the hands.

In 'A Prayer' (1881) Levy's speaker is less clearly gendered, perhaps because the poem deals with loneliness and despair as opposed to suicide. The speaker decries that 'To live – it is my doom – I Lonely as in a tomb, I This cross on me was laid; I My God I know not why; I Here in the dark I lie' (New 1993: 365, lines 13–17). Both the title of the poem and the direct appeal to God suggest the penitent posture of prayer, and the hands as a tool for worship. In both Jewish and Christian tradition, the hands feature in prayer and in ceremonial practice – for example, the washing of hands at a Jewish funeral

(Patai 1983: 103) – and the clasping of hands in prayer had been practised by Jews long before the appearance of Christ in the Gospels (Ausubel 1964: 351). In the Christian tradition the folding or placing hands together in prayer is a gesture of submission, piety, sincerity and repentance. Given the futility of the prayer offered by Levy's speaker and the sense of abandonment by an unresponsive deity, the implication of hands clasped in prayer is both an acknowledgement of and a challenge to tradition. Both Christianity and Judaism required women to submit to men, and to repent of the irreligious thoughts or acts exemplified by the suicidal impulses that feature elsewhere in Levy's poetry.

Since the hands were the means by which New Woman writers such as Levy earned their living, their destruction in 'Felo de Se' is highly symbolic and both draws on and extends a history of such metaphors in New Woman writing. For example, in Mary Cholmondeley's *Red Pottage* (1899) the novelist Hester Gresley rescues her manuscript from a fireplace only to find it has been destroyed and her hands have been horribly burnt. Hester likens the death of her novel to infanticide (1900: 209–13), and her burnt hands offer a distraction from the emotional pain of her loss through physical pain. In Grand's *The Heavenly Twins* Angelica wrings her hands violently, both when admonishing Israfil for rescuing her from drowning (2007: II, 154) and when confessing that her transgression has led to his death from pneumonia (2007: II, 220). In the same year, Ella Hepworth Dixon's *The Story of a Modern Woman* describes the 'red knuckles' (2004: 21) of the 'advanced' Alison Ives, who rescues fallen women, and the shaking hands of Mary Earle, a painter, novelist and journalist who must make her living by her pen (2004: 62). In all three texts the New Woman's hands connote her participation in normally male-dominated arenas, or her transgression of prescribed roles and her resultant punishment. Levy's use of the hands as the site of her speaker's self-mutilative drives highlights the importance of women's cultural production as well as the financial difficulties faced by women writers. Like Levy, many unmarried but educated women struggled to earn enough by their hands, and they often failed to find a place in either the literary or the broader economic world. The hands thus encode the possibilities offered by literary endeavour, as well as the painful internalisation of nonconformity and resultant self-punishment.

Pain and self-punishment are central to 'Felo de Se' and the speaker's feelings reflect contemporary psychiatric models of non-dissociative self-harm. The reference to a 'pulse of pain' and the poem's refrain 'I am held in the Circle of Being and caught in the Circle of Pain' (New 1993: 366, line 3) evoke a sense of entrapment by emotional trauma.

Like Grand's Ideala, Evadne and Beth, and Caird's Viola and Hadria, Levy's poet-speaker seeks distraction from emotional pain through bodily discomfort and punishment. He suggests a number of painful self-harming behaviours that might provide such distraction, but eventually rejects them all and continues to suffer. So too is death by suicide rejected when the speaker states: 'Bitter indeed is Life, and bitter of Life the breath | But give me Life and its ways and its men, if this be Death' (New 1993: 366, lines 14–15). Again, the rejection of death in favour of distraction from emotional pain via physical pain exemplifies Levy's engagement with the rhetoric of self-mutilation long before its emergence as a definitive pathology.

Levy aligns her speaker's cyclical drives with the woman poet's need to produce commercially successful work in order to survive as part of a ceaseless cycle of literary production. This required the sacrifice of energies both physical and intellectual in order to live, but never provided enough remuneration for the cycle to abate. Levy's explicit use of the imagery of suicide and mutilation appears somewhat radical in light of the expectations of Victorian women writers to adhere to the strict moral, religious and social values governing the publication of poetry. However, Levy adopts a male persona to voice such disturbing themes, whilst aligning suicidal impulses with an established and easily recognisable narrative of the traumatised male poet or returning soldier. In 1881, Levy was unable to articulate fully the inner landscape of the drive towards self-destruction, to which she would fall prey in 1889. 'Felo de Se' functioned as a vehicle for expressing such concerns, as a transitional space through which self-harm could appear in print without challenging poetic traditions and while remaining publishable and thus commercial. *Fin-de-siècle* poetry was caught between the High Victorianism that characterised the work of popular poets such as Tennyson and Robert Browning, and the Modernism that would begin to emerge in the early years of the twentieth century. However, what was often viewed by scholars as a confused and uncertain period of poetic production was in fact a time of exciting and potentially freeing transition, during which poets combined the conventions of the past with the possibilities of the future (Bristow 2005: 1–3). Straddling the boundary between the nobility and imperial grandeur of Romanticism and the crass consumerism and implied degeneracy of popular culture, late-nineteenth-century poets operated in a space that was morally prescriptive, yet also conducive to the rejection of tradition exemplified by Modernism.

Like those of Custance, whose Decadent poetry was a vehicle for expressing the instability of sexual identities, Levy's poems address the double marginalisation of the non-white, non-English woman poet through the trope of self-destruction. However, they do so from a complicated position of a woman poet who was viewed as racially inferior by way of her Jewish identity, but whose education had been provided as a consequence of her family's participation within the very colonialism through which she was maligned as other. Levy's work was radical in its approach to self-harm; however, it was not until women writers began to adopt new types of writing, and to reject male-oriented literary production altogether, that the body of the female self-mutilator would be staged boldly in print. One such example of the dramatisation of self-mutilated female bodies is the work of George Egerton, whose short stories heralded a new and controversial expression of the traumatised female psyche in wound culture.

Textual Traumas: George Egerton's Self-Mutilating Mistresses

In a 2001 article, Nicole Fluhr cites George Egerton's now muchquoted comment:

> I realized that in literature everything had been better done by a man than woman could hope to emulate. There was only one small plot left for her to tell: the *terra incognita* of herself, as she knew herself to be, not as a man liked to imagine her. (Gawsworth 1932: 58)

Fluhr views Egerton's words as both an expression of 'exploratory glee' (2001: 244) and an explicit advocation of the revisionist opportunity open to women writers, to refuse representation as alreadyestablished typologies. Egerton's use of the innovative form of the short story provided a space in which the tensions between the 'inner and outer surfaces' of the psyche and the body, the private and the public, could be explored. However, as I began to show in my previous chapter, Egerton's work featured instances of self-destructive behaviour highlighting how her project to represent woman 'not as a man liked to imagine her' was arguably self-sabotaged. Despite her revolutionary use of psychological interiors and images of violence, I suggest that Egerton participated in the mutilation of her own body of work, through representations of the wounded female body precisely 'as man liked to imagine her'.

Egerton's short stories are awash with traumatic imagery. Written long before Freud's work with victims of shell-shock, and the development of any persuasive psychiatric framework through which to read self-mutilation, *Keynotes*, *Discords* and *Symphonies* anticipate both. Egerton's concern with what were to become key symptoms in later psychiatric diagnoses of post-traumatic stress disorder indicates her preoccupation with the bodily manifestations of trauma long before the medical establishment could agree on what they actually were. Her stories feature hallucinations, flashbacks, blackouts and traumatic collisions, what Seltzer calls 'the milling around the point of impact' (1998: 1), the moment at which trauma occurs or is re-enacted and transposed on to the body. In 'Virgin Soil' from *Discords*, an unhappily married daughter returns home to punish the worldly mother who has allowed her child to become a victim of marital ignorance. When they meet, it is described 'as if a bomb had gone off' (Egerton 2006: 130) and Egerton compares the shock of the news with the imagery of an explosion – an event capable of causing physical wounds but one also firmly entrenched in the history of trauma. Twenty-first-century readers of Egerton's story might be tempted to associate the image of bombing with the shell-shock that prompted Freud's work on traumatic neurosis following the First World War, but in 1894 Egerton had no such knowledge. Thus, her use of this imagery indicates her general interest in, and understanding of, war as a source of symbolic reference, one that would be eagerly adopted by Egerton's modernist contemporaries during the twentieth century.[12]

In 'Wedlock', Mrs Jones's murder of her stepchildren and her own suicide are obscured by a narrative aporia, a textual wound – a numbing of memory, signifying an event too disturbing for articulation. Egerton's narrator thus describes how

> upstairs in a back room in the silent house a pale strip of moonlight flickers over a dark streak on the floor, that trickles slowly from the pool at the bedside out under the door, making a second ghastly pool on the top of the stairs – a thick sorghum red [. . .] Downstairs the woman sits in her chair with her arms hanging down. Her hands are crimson as if she had dipped them in dye. (Egerton 2006: 126)

The aftermath, the silent house, the pooling blood on the floor, and the woman's blood-stained hands are the only means by which the event can be processed and narrated, suggesting 'the total absence of recall of the significant event' (Luckhurst 2008: 1). Egerton's narrative of infanticide departs from the novelistic tradition because it does not avoid fictionalising the figure of the parent-murderer. Hardy's *Jude the Obscure* (1895) was serialised a year before *Discords* and featured a child-murderer, a plot device that allowed the author to render the murderer less culpable (Ledger 1997: 185). However, in 'Wedlock' Egerton makes it clear that Mrs Jones is responsible for infanticide, yet, by deploying a detached and dreamlike narration, Egerton resists describing the event itself. The macabre imagery in 'Wedlock' is perhaps Egerton's most graphic depiction of the consequences of women's subjugation by men. However, it is in her short story 'A Psychological Moment at Three Periods' that Egerton undertakes to express the susceptibility of the female body to patriarchal wounding, through shockingly overt references to self-mutilation.

'A Psychological Moment', from *Discords*, features a single female protagonist whose development is traced across childhood, adolescence and adulthood through a series of 'moments'. The heroine is Isabel, who is highly intelligent and possesses intense personal magnetism, but is blackmailed into becoming mistress to the married Mr St Ledger. The blackmail plot hinges on certain ambiguous financial papers, a parody of Nora's act of fraud in Ibsen's *A Doll's House* (1879) with which, as a translator of Ibsen's work, Egerton was highly familiar. The papers are possibly evidence of debts owed by Isabel's family, since we are told that she recognises the name of the receiver and the signature, and her actions appear to protect those she loves. Parallel to the stages at which the reader encounters Isabel are the geographical locations in which she variously resides: as a child and a girl in Ireland and the Netherlands, as prey to an unscrupulous man in London, and as a kept woman in Paris. The social and topographical landscapes she inhabits are also mirrored by her relationship with Christianity, from a deep engagement with Catholicism in Ireland to her rejection of religion in the later sections of the text.

In Ireland Isabel begins a pseudo-masochistic dialogue of self-criticism, according to which she both forgoes pleasure and punishes herself for transgression. After mesmerising her school friends with a collection of cleverly constructed lies, she repents her sin and confesses, despite the inevitability of their reproofs. Isabel 'has promised she would punish herself' yet she is dissatisfied when her confession elicits no more than a few words of criticism from her compatriots, leaving her with 'a sick sense of shame' (Egerton 2006: 69–70). When Isabel decides to confess to one remaining girl, she describes her act as an attempt to 'drain the chalice to the dregs' (2006: 70), imbuing her sacrifice with Eucharistic undertones in similar ways to both Custance's and Levy's poetic speakers. Disappointed by the response to her revelation, Isabel reflects that 'grinding her forehead into rough bark would be a relief', then 'bites her tongue in self-abasement' (2006: 69).

Egerton references religion in 'A Psychological Moment' through both the location of Isabel's first act of self-harm (Catholic Ireland) and her repeated allusions to physical pain as a form of penitential activity.[13] Throughout *Keynotes* and *Discords*, Christianity is treated with suspicion, and is satirised to convey deep criticism of the restrictive power exerted over women by the Church. When enjoying the pleasures of reading, Isabel figures her delight as a sin, and overwrites her desire for education as wickedness for which atonement is required, telling herself:

> shut the book now – now, just when the exciting part begins. No, you may not read to the end of the page – no, not even a line more. If you want to be brave, if you want to be strong, sacrifice; sacrifice, mortify yourself. If you don't want to! No, you are weak, you cannot do that, not even that small thing, for God. (Egerton 2006: 67)

The mortification of the flesh is an institutional expiatory act of penance for the punishment of sins and achievement of sanctity. The practice is most notably performed by the penitential saints of the Roman Catholic Church, and common forms include flagellation in imitation of Christ's suffering and death by crucifixion.[14] Egerton's frequent references to mortification position her heroine within the broader nineteenth-century Christian framework of self-renunciation, as well as what Kucich calls the 'masochistic phenomena' (2002: 79) operating in New Woman writing. As discussed in previous chapters, while the New Woman writer often adopted masochistic imagery, it was usually as part of a literary assault against sexual double standards by social purity writers, or by proto-feminists seeking specifically educational and legal freedoms. Egerton was neither a social purist nor a supporter of institutions like marriage, and her insistence on the naturalness of motherhood as a vocation was at best disappointingly essentialist. While Grand's use of martyrdom as a way to imagine women's self-denial was at times deployed to critique the masculine scopic drive, her valorisation of self-sacrifice was largely in earnest. In contrast, Egerton's use of Christian imagery is, from the outset, insincere and at times contemptuous, denying the potentially positive or redemptive possibilities of connecting with the faith in which she had been raised. However, some ambivalence is evident in Egerton's approval of appropriate maternity, a lionisation of self-renunciation that drew on the example of the Holy Virgin's meek acceptance of her unexpected motherly responsibility.

'A Psychological Moment' subverts the process of mortification by depicting a child's interpretation of penance and applying it to the pursuit of education through literary experience. The tragi-comic effect of the child's punishment for transgressing the boundaries of her sphere is manifested in her gratuitous self-sacrifice, and satirises the systemic education of women into a dialogue of relentlessly inter-nalised condemnation. This same system, one that posits women as 'to be looked at, denuded [and] unveiled' (Brooks 1993: 97), views Isabel's attempt to exert her scrutiny upon the masculine world as a reversal of the gaze that must be punished. Having a self-mutilating child-heroine castigate herself for inverting masculine scopic econo-mies obliquely establishes self-mutilation as a response to restrictive constructions of femininity. This is confirmed by Isabel's appearance in the reading rooms of the British Library. While conducting her search for knowledge, she is interrupted by a meeting with Mr St Ledger, who forces her to become an object to be looked at, denuded, unveiled and, once known, discarded.

As Isabel is increasingly estranged, both spiritually and geo-graphically, from the Catholicism of her childhood, she begins to question the religion that has, until this point, provided the struc-ture within which her self-destructive drives are enacted. Images of atonement and mortification are further developed in the second period of the story, during which Isabel awakens to the futility of her existence. We are told how, upon witnessing the deformed fig-ure of a disabled fairground worker tied by his legs to a tree and forced to operate the rides, Isabel rejects God, asking Him 'is that what I am to find in the world to come – some idiot turning a wheel for the world to dance – ?' (Egerton 2006: 75). Egerton returned to this image in naming her semi-autobiographical novel *The Wheel of God* (1898), in a nod to the cycle of (female) bodily sacrifice here described by her earlier heroine. Isabel's comments function as a prophetic signposting of her future, since she too will be victimised by the relentless pressures of a patriarchal economy in general, and the whim of one despotic man in particular. She screams:

> Oh poor thing! That poor thing! You needn't have made him; God I tell you, you needn't have made him! [. . .] She bruises her poor little clenched fist against the gnarled roots as she emphasises her words, and shakes it up at the silent sky [. . .] (Egerton 2006: 75)

Egerton's heroine questions God, but also the exploitation of the human body subject to unstoppable economic and social forces jus-tified and perpetuated by bourgeois religion and morality, and, by implication, the colonial logic that others and exploits non-normative bodies.[15] Like the fairground worker, whose arms are forced to continually turn the ride, Isabel's own body will be similarly subsumed into an economy that values only the decorative and sexual energies her body can expend. Egerton depicts a moment of feminine defiance; though ostensibly directing her rage against God, Isabel in fact turns it upon herself in self-injury. Significantly, as Isabel pounds her fists against the tree, she emphasises her words, calling attention to the expression that she is denied in her position as an adolescent and a woman. Isabel chooses to beat her fist against a tree, just as she chooses to imagine grinding her head into the bark of a tree in the first textual period, escalating from imagined to enacted self-wounding. The metaphor of the tree, with its deeply entrenched roots, suggests Victorian moral and social conventions, and hints at the object of Isabel's anger as much as does the reference to God.

Egerton subverts the process of mortification by directing not penance but anger towards the personification of patriarchal religious oppression, marking a distinct change to Isabel's identification with martyrdom, to a process akin to non-dissociative self-mutilation. The futility of Isabel's position is emphasised, not only by the damage done to her own body, but by the frustrated and ineffective gesture of shaking her injured fist at the sky. In the final part of the story, her impulse towards self-harm becomes more pronounced as, upon finding that she is to be forced into the position of mistress, Isabel considers suicide, wondering

> [i]f she could only steal away to some quiet wood and lie down and die! let the brown leaves, with their deep stains, blood stains cover her gently and hide her forever! Surely it would not be hard to die? She has often felt her heart beat, she knows exactly where it is, a good long hat pin would reach it. (Egerton 2006: 80)

Isabel not only contemplates suicide, regarded as a distinctly subversive and unwomanly act that contravened Christian and criminal law, but she aligns a bloody death by stabbing with comfort and release. The description of bloody leaves forming a gentle shroud instils a sense of calm, a distraction from emotional trauma and pain, through which Isabel might free herself from the confines of her position as both sexual slave and fallen woman.

Tellingly, Isabel's weapon of choice is a hat pin, an implement inherently domestic and decorative, but also suggestively medical. Egerton endows her heroine with a long metallic object capable of poking, prodding or piercing. In doing so, she references contemporary *fin-de-siècle* debates surrounding the 'hystericization' (Foucault 1990: 140) of women's bodies, the process by which the female body was pathologised and entered into medical discourse as an object to be observed and investigated. Egerton's staging of the pathologisation and penetration of the female body further signals her attempt to subvert the epistemophilic agenda, the desire to read, know and master the female body unconsciously underpinning the Victorian novelistic tradition. However, in doing so, her heroine's wounds are entered into narrative as signs; her body thus becomes part of the scopic drives it hopes to disrupt. Isabel's consideration of a hat pin as her self-harming modus operandi implies femininity through ornamentation, whilst its use to puncture the heart connotes an abortive act. Such an act is symbolic of the protagonist's enforced concubinage, and the potentially disastrous consequences of illegitimate motherhood that Egerton depicts elsewhere in *Keynotes*, *Discords* and *Symphonies*. In entertaining a hat pin as a suicide method, Isabel proposes a strategy by which to wear her damage as a 'fashion accessory'. Isabel emphasises the irony of female bodily spectacle, which threatens a disruption of male dominance over her body, yet plays directly into the hands of those who would seek to make her a commodity. Isabel proposes to release herself from bondage via death, using an instrument symbolic of the eroticised domesticity into which she has been forced for the purpose of self-mutilation and self-display. By giving her heroine a hypothetical weapon symbolic of phallic power, Egerton attacks Victorian patriarchy whilst simultaneously allowing her character to succumb to its pressures.

Whilst Egerton examines the potential for sensationalism inherent in displaying the wounded female body, acts of display are almost entirely absent from recorded accounts of self-mutilation as both a historic and a contemporary condition. Substantive data on levels of self-mutilation in Victorian Britain do not exist, possibly due to widespread misdiagnosis or ignorance of the condition outside of specialist hospitals or private mental health facilities. Although twentieth-century records are readily available, few cases of repeated self-mutilation include the overt display of wounds as a feature of the condition. The few that do so occur in cases where patients self-mutilate as a symptom of psychosis or other severe mental health problems unrelated to self-mutilation, or the mutilation forms part of culturally sanctioned behaviour such as tattooing or body modification (Hewitt 1997: 58). The only displays of wounded female bodies permissible by Victorian standards were for medical, pedagogical purposes, or for entertainment in specific contexts. Twenty-first-century case studies suggest that the experience of most self-mutilators is characterised by concealment of wounds rather than display. Egerton's work thus adopts the spectacle of self-wounding as a broad thematic motif that encapsulated *fin-de-siècle* anxieties about the Woman Question, rather than a medical condition with which she had had contact.

In 'A Psychological Moment' Isabel does not commit suicide but, instead, survives her ordeal. However, as she considers her sad position, Isabel 'meets her teeth in her arm, it is a sort of relief to counteract the agony of her soul by a pang of physical pain' (Egerton 2006: 82). Similarly, when she is freed at the end of the text by the return of incriminating documents, Isabel 'holds them to the flame [. . .] She sears her nails and there is a smell of singed horn; she rubs the last bit of ash between her fingers and bursts into a laughing sob of relief' (2006: 86). These two excerpts represent Egerton's most explicit dramatisation of the restorative psychological effects of bodily self-damage. Considered alongside contemporary psycho-analytic models, Isabel attempts to manage extreme psychological disturbance through physical pain, recasting mental anxiety on to the surface of her body by non-dissociative self-mutilation. Through the paradigm of *The Skin Ego* Isabel's actions can be understood as communication between the psyche and the dermis denied during the pre-Oedipal phase. Isabel's mother is very briefly mentioned, and although Isabel certainly has a family, the text notes her close relationship with her siblings and emphasises her mother's excessive Catholicism. Isabel's potential failure to develop or maintain a 'normal' maternal relationship could account for the destruction of her body as a site of unsatisfactory identification with the maternal body. Such a reading corresponds to Isabel's rejection of Catholicism and her sustained metaphorical attack on the self-renunciation advocated by her religious upbringing.

In dramatising the paradoxical gesture of self-harm and self-care adopted by her heroine as a strategic response to anxiety, Egerton displays the wounded female body as both tragic spectacle and site of heroic survival. Furthermore, by so dramatically depicting self-mutilation, Egerton's work orchestrates a distortion of what Anzieu has called the 'inner and outer surfaces' of the female psyche, and demarcates a temporary space between where the body ends and the outside world begins. In doing so, I would argue, like the Ripper murders before it, Egerton's work serves to address and destabilise 'our most basic sense of the body and society, identity and desire, violence and intimacy' (Seltzer 1998: 2) by bringing such issues to crisis through publication. The understanding of the body as indicative of the wider social body, and of desire and violence as compartmentalised and private entities, is undermined by Egerton's literary display of female self-mutilation in 'A Psychological Moment'.

Biting as Self-Wounding: Appropriating the Vampire Narrative

Egerton references self-mutilation again in another story from *Discords*. 'Her Share' narrates a chance meeting between a young girl, who has just become engaged, and an older woman of a decidedly modern character. The older woman returns to the scene of her sexual awakening as a vicar's daughter in a country village, where she meets the younger girl happily anticipating her marriage. The older woman describes a passionate but entirely unfulfilled cross-class infatuation with a foreign tradesman working at the vicarage during her youth. As in 'Gone Under', Egerton utilises a common plot device through which a naive girl is educated in life's cruelty by a more experienced female counterpart. Possessed of a bicycle, with frequent references to her work, and an interest in German and Scandinavian literature (Egerton 2006: 96), the older character is clearly a New Woman. She imparts her story of thwarted desire, describing how upon revisiting painful memories 'I set my teeth in my arm to relieve the pain it gave me' (2006: 100). The narrator's remark is incongruous in the rest of the story, and is the only example of violent imagery in a narrative that condemns the multigenerational cycle of culturally enforced sexual repression. This particular reference to self-mutilation appears just pages after the similarly worded incidence from 'A Psychological Moment' in which Isabel 'meets her teeth in her arm' to produce a 'sort of relief' (2006: 82).

In 'Her Share' the word 'meets' is replaced by 'set', yet the excerpts invoke the image through near-identical phrasing. This repetition, within pages of its first use in 'A Psychological Moment', exemplifies a recurrent preoccupation with self-mutilation in *Discords*. Egerton was to use this image again in *The Wheel of God*, in which Mary Desmond 'had bitten her wrist till her teeth drew blood' (1898b: 36), demonstrating a preoccupation with self-biting years after her first two collections of short stories had originally appeared. *The Wheel of God* replicates 'A Psychological Moment' in its tripartite structure, allowing Egerton to depict her heroine's development through the *Bildungsroman* format. The novel deploys certain features of Egerton's earlier short stories – textual gaps, introspective narration and fragmentary style – yet these are comparatively unsuccessful because the arrangement of the novel required the plot and character development that her short stories did not. The compulsory detail and coherent structure of the novel meant that Egerton could not so easily or overtly stage her heroine's self-harm, which is not foregrounded. The incidence of self-wounding is largely absorbed into the evolution of female character in *The Wheel of God*, and has evoked no critical comment in contemporary discussions of the novel; it also went unnoticed by favourable Victorian reviewers, who were generally less outraged by *The Wheel of God* than by Egerton's earlier stories (Nelson 2001: 7).

The act of biting human flesh and drawing blood had featured in a number of texts long before either *Discords* or Bram Stoker's definitive vampire novel *Dracula*. The publication of John Polidori's 'The Vampyre' (1819) had heralded the birth of a new form of Gothic fiction which continues to enjoy popularity in contemporary culture. The vampire myth had been a staple of traditional folklore in a variety of cultures, originating in Asia before finding fictional expression in Eastern European fairy tales, culminating in its cult status in the British fiction of the late nineteenth century and beyond.[16] The quest to corrupt female virtue that characterised the drives of Polidori's Lord Ruthven – whose victims are female – was complicated by subsequent literary representations, most notably by Sheridan Le Fanu's 'lesbian' vampire in 'Carmilla' (1872) and Stoker's child-eating Lucy Westenra in *Dracula*. In these texts, the female body is represented in 'distorted and monstrous form' (Williamson 2005: 11) demonstrating the dichotomy of fear and fetishisation at play in attempting to read it. Lucy Westenra's transformation from a pure and chaste girl into a 'voluptuous' and 'wanton' (Stoker 2011: 225–6) nocturnal predator is, as Gail Griffin points out, the 'worst nightmare and dearest fantasy of the Victorian male' (1988: 143). Lucy is depicted as a sexually aggressive vamp and – as certain critics have noted – a version of the New Woman, evoking the monstrous in her subversion of maternity.[17] Vampire narratives had explored and would continue to explore female sexuality and engage with the figure of the femme fatale, while at the same time consigning female characters to the function of mere sustenance for men – and, indeed, unwomanly or aggressively mannish women.

The trope of vampirism was widely adopted by women writers at the turn of the century – particularly following the publication of *Dracula* – yet it emerged largely in political writing rather than fiction. On both sides of the Atlantic, women's writing theorised female economic dependency by reworking the vampire trope to emblematise female 'parasitism' (Ford 2016). In her 1898 essay 'Women and Economics' Charlotte Perkins Gilman accused modern woman of being man's 'parasite mate' (2007: 70), expressing dissatisfaction at middle-class women who were comfortably dependent on their husbands and fathers. Gilman rendered women guilty of perpetuating a system of economic vampirism in which female independence remained impossible. Similarly, and more strikingly, Vernon Lee referenced parasitic feeding in her 1901 introduction to the Italian translation of Gilman's essay. She laments: 'man plays the part of the animal [. . .] and the woman the part of the parasitic creature who lives inside that animal's tissues' (Lee 1908: 265). Egerton's *Discords* appeared before both Gilman's and Lee's characterisations of women as parasitical or vampiric. However, I would suggest that *fin-de-siècle* debates surrounding female economic dependence are important in reading Egerton's use of biting in both 'Her Share' and 'A Psychological Moment'. Biting the flesh can be read as a fictional resistance to masculine forms of female representation evidenced in the vampire fiction of the nineteenth century – largely written in the novel format – that situated the female body as a narrative locus.[18] These texts, which saw the sexually liberated woman depicted as a horrifying other – either as powerless erotic spectacle or as New Woman threat – are subverted by the fictionalisation of women whose vampiric desires are enacted on their own bodies in acts of self-preservation.

Central to both of Egerton's stories of self-biting is the process of biting itself, as opposed to the consumption of blood. Egerton's self-biters enact violence, yet profit by distraction from pain, rather than the erotic or transformative product of that pain. In vampire fiction the typical victim experiences loss of blood, or finds that their energy is gradually drained from their body by an external force. However, Egerton's self-mutilating heroines feel no such sense of lifelessness; life is in fact briefly affirmed by communication between the inner and outer boundaries of the body. Egerton adopts the recognisably Gothic trope of biting into human flesh, yet de-sexualises and demystifies the act. By amassing the power of blood for themselves, self-mutilating heroines also metaphorically address the dangers of blood loss associated with the reproductive body. Characters whose bodies are subject to uncontrollable natural forces situating them as merely sexual slaves and mothers-in-waiting reclaim blood-letting as a form of self-control. By making her biters responsible for mastering their own pain, Egerton rewrites narratives that stereotyped women and punished sexual transgression with total bodily destruction. At the same time, however, she consigns her heroines' bodies to a fate that is, in many ways, as horrifying as vampiric consumption.

Art, Motherhood and the Fallen Body in Egerton's Short Stories

The trope of self-mutilation reappears in 'Gone Under', the third successive story in *Discords* discussed in Chapter 3 in relation to drunkenness. Edith Grey is haunted by maternal loss, expressing her psychological trauma through severe bouts of excessive drinking and suicidal thoughts. She describes how, after the death of her infant, 'I had no occupation, and the child haunted me! I drank to kill it!' (Egerton 2006: 109). Thus, Edith frames her physical response to trauma as dissociative self-harm, harming herself as a means of distraction from the hallucinatory visions that characterise her experience of maternal loss. Edith's inability to form a bond with her dead child suggests a reversal of the skin ego wherein the mother, rather than the child, is compelled to attack the skin to re-enforce a lost maternal connection. After Edith violently damages her body, the girl-narrator describes how 'a trickle of blood ran from one of her white wrists' (2006: 103). Egerton's narrator describes Edith's cutting as a trickle of blood rather than a gush, a cry for help but not a serious attempt at suicide, an act of which Edith is 'afraid' (2006: 109). In fact, Edith discusses suicide repeatedly; she describes wanting to 'kill [her]self straight away' (2006: 109) after a sexual transgression, and also threatens to throw herself overboard (2006: 111). These threats are considered childish by the girl-narrator, who reads Edith's threats of suicide as attention-seeking, in line with her impractical dress and immature manner of speech. Edith's act of self-mutilation exemplifies Egerton's direct engagement with a dialectic of bodily rebellion and submission in that her tragic heroine repeatedly defies social expectations, whilst succumbing to dramatic repetition of trauma through self-harm. In expressing and challenging her position as a sexually compromised commodity, Edith resists by displaying her body as an 'icon, or stigma, of the everyday openness of *every* body' in which she wears her 'damage like [a] badge [. . .] of identity, or fashion accessor[y]' (Seltzer 1998: 2). In this way, Edith's wounds become somatically significant, as a text to be read and known, in this case by the women who judge her and the men who discard her.

In both 'A Psychological Moment' and 'Gone Under', Egerton maintains a complex and somewhat dubious ambivalence towards the wounded female body as spectacle. Despite her implicit criticism of patriarchal constructions of femininity and her resistance to traditional masculine forms of writing the body, Egerton's short stories often display a recidivism into the very representations she rejects. In the self-mutilation scene from 'A Psychological Moment' Isabel imagines lying down amongst the brown leaves to die, and makes specific references to the reds and browns of her blood, and the leaves that might envelop her corpse. Evoking the Pre-Raphaelite art discussed in relation to 'Gone Under' in Chapter 3, 'A Psychological

Moment' also finds inspiration in the figure of the female corpse in Millais's *Ophelia*. As I have already discussed, the submerged female body is surrounded by dense brown foliage, highlighting and extending Ophelia's auburn hair as it evokes the image of weeds in water. Millais's picture inspired later representations of Ophelia, including Alexandre Cabanel's 1883 painting and John William Waterhouse's 1894 version, both of which feature strict attention to the detail of the female figure's natural surroundings in, or at the edge of, water thick with vegetation.[19] Sexually compromised, Egerton's Isabel desires to be hidden forever by brown leaves stained with her own blood. When she bites into her arm, she describes a distinctly rustic scene reminiscent of all three paintings. Egerton stages Isabel's self-wounding in the pastoral mode, satirising Romantic notions of the sublime through juxtaposition with the mundane, undermining the awesome power and beneficence of God in nature, as Isabel describes:

> mild evening breeze, the monotonous note of the sea, the shiver of leaf, scent of night-plants, all seem to accentuate her misery [. . .] And the leaves just rustle, rustle and the sea croons on, and the great blue canopy stretches away impenetrably. (Egerton 2006: 82)

The use of idyllic, rustic imagery, and references to the red and browns of the scene, gesture at Pre-Raphaelite renderings of Ophelia, all of which pay particular attention to the movement of the surrounding foliage. Egerton's protagonist evokes other tragic heroines, of whom Alfred, Lord Tennyson's 'The Lady of Shalott' (1833) is one example. The eponymous Lady of Tennyson's epic poem dares to venture beyond the boundaries of the domestic sphere to which she has been confined. After leaving her tower, she is punished for transgressing patriarchal order by drifting down-river to her death. Although not precisely 'fallen' women, both Ophelia and the Lady are the victims of desires that fall outside of the strict moral boundaries within which the Victorians sought to confine femininity.

In art, Tennyson's Lady has been depicted in a similar way to Shakespeare's Ophelia. Arthur Hughes, who painted several versions of Ophelia, depicts the Lady of Shalott, in his 1873 canvas, lying helplessly in a boat with her long auburn hair drifting behind her, half-immersed in the water. Her face is white, and she is disembodied below the waist by her floating white skirts, which appear to vanish at the end of the boat into smoke-like whirls. In the background, ruddy-faced men and women in colourful Puritan costume stand back aghast, creating a bodily and spiritual contrast to the ghostly, ethereal and otherworldly Lady. The voyeurs are unwilling to offer aid but instead gaze intently upon the spectacle, in a scene of female objectification characteristic of Pre-Raphaelitism. Similarly, John William Waterhouse's 1888 painting of the same subject shows the Lady sitting upright, with a look of expectation, in a boat that drifts through brown reeds, her long amber hair billowing in the breeze. In both Millais's *Ophelia* and the paintings inspired by Tennyson's poem, the heroine is infantilised and eroticised.[20] Her pallid complexion and helplessness as a woman alone and adrift work to denote childlike innocence and purity. Her unkempt red hair flowing without containment suggests wantonness and desire, and the irrepressibility of female sexuality 'invested with an over-determination of sexual meaning' (Ofek 2009: 3). The submersion, or partial submersion, of these women is also intrinsic to Victorian literary and artistic stereotypes that often featured the drowned woman as sexually compromised.[21] Egerton's critique of objectifications of transgressive women has been noted by Nicole Fluhr, who explains that the narrator in 'Gone Under' at first 'sees the woman as an object of analysis, reducing her to easily read symbols [. . .] as the girl comes to know Edith, however, [she] is neither virgin nor whore, but a grieving mother' (Fluhr 2001: 260).

The dichotomy of virgin and whore examined in Chapter 1 and explored in Egerton's work in Chapter 3 is complicated by these images, which, while suggesting the limitations of such binarisms, offer alternatives that drive women to self-destruction. The impulse to visualise her characters as the tragic heroines of art suggests an understanding that the ability of any writer in the period to imagine femininity is limited and defined by the language and the belief systems made available by the society they inhabit. Egerton vehemently rejected such belief systems in both her fiction and her personal correspondence, criticising conventional marriage and instead championing 'free unions' based on egalitarian values of sexual equality. Her reliance on established mid-Victorian stereotypes to construct her fictional 'fallen' women suggests an inability to break free of the male-dominant ideological representations of femininity diffused by the work of Pre-Raphaelite artists like Millais, Hughes and Waterhouse. By aligning her imagery of female sexual corruption with sensual Pre-Raphaelite objects of desire, Egerton attempts to reinscribe authoritative male discourse but adopts limiting feminine topoi tied implicitly to the very cultural mores against which she fought. While not complicit in the cultural objectification and eroticisation of women's bodies, Egerton's conflicted stance is a testament to her own complex and ambivalent position in the gender debates of the *fin de siècle*. Egerton championed sexual rather than legal or social equality for women, radically advocating unconventional relationships and fighting against the restrictive tyrannies of marriage. While she was an outspoken advocate of certain freedoms for women, her radicalism was at times undermined in her writing by her complicated and extremely restrictive attitude towards motherhood.

In Grant Allen's 'Plain Words on the Woman Question' (1889), Egerton included her own contribution to the debate surrounding Victorian motherhood, noting of the emancipated woman that

> I should like to see her a great deal more emancipated than she herself as yet at all desires. Only, her emancipation must not be of a sort that interferes in any way with this prime natural necessity. To the end of all time, it is mathematically demonstrable that most women must become the mothers of at least four children, or else the race must cease to exist. (Allen 1889b: 172)

The irony aside, Egerton's contribution gestures towards an essentialist view of women's reproductive duties that prioritised maternity over women's personal or professional achievements. The fictional characters who achieve the greatest happiness in *Keynotes* and *Discords* are those who reject conventional relationships and accept the joys of maternal enterprise. The mother characters in 'A Cross Line', 'The Spell of the White Elf', 'Under Northern Sky' and 'The Heart of the Apple' all benefit from motherhood, if not necessarily from other roles as wives or mistresses. Conversely, the most miserable of Egerton's heroines are those to whom motherhood (if not parturition) is denied; Mrs Jones in 'Wedlock' and Edith in 'Gone Under' both die as a consequence of failed motherhood, whilst the childless mistress of 'A Psychological Moment' is held captive by a man whose own wife has suffered several infant mortalities. Although maternal drives are championed, they are also posited as 'potentially dangerous to individuality and personal development' (Liggins 2000: 27). As Lyn Pykett has observed, 'in Egerton's work sexual and maternal feeling are both woman's glory and her curse' (2006: 174) and it is her tendency to valorise maternity while critiquing a range of other biologically determined duties into which women were forced that exemplifies Egerton's ambivalent position on the Woman Question. Egerton often depicted a world in which unmarried mothers prosper, compared to those who are contained within unproductive or unequal unions. However, she also portrayed the punitive economic and social realities faced by women who defy social expectations in favour of asserting maternal rather than matrimonial instincts. While Egerton's stories disavow the link between motherhood and oppression that had been established by contemporaries like Mona Caird, or complicated by male authors like Grant Allen, they work to strongly assert yet quietly undermine her advocacy of sexual freedom for women as a practical solution to the Woman Question.[22]

Egerton reluctantly, but repeatedly, altered the stories in her later collections, yet traces of her preoccupation with self-mutilation continued to appear. In *Symphonies* the process of self-mutilation is depicted as a strategic choice, crucial to one of Egerton's most disturbing stories. Set in the Basque region, at the border between France and Spain, 'Pan' is the story of Tienette, a young girl who is sexually assaulted by a man from her village. After having refused his proposal of marriage, Tienette is lured by Sebastian into a wood, where, despite her attempts to struggle, she is raped. After conceiving a child, Tienette is abandoned by Sebastian, who transfers his affections to a woman with a large dowry. Sebastian is eventually encouraged to marry his victim by her uncle, who offers a more substantial sum. Conspired against by her family, and the women of her village – who advise her attacker that 'some must be wooed and some must be taken' (Egerton 1897: 224) – Tienette is sacrificed to custom by a society that asserts male authority over the female body. Restricted by censorship laws, Egerton depicts the rape scene as a narrative blackout. Like her use of textual aporia in 'Wedlock', Egerton signposts her heroine's experience of trauma through the total narrative absence of the significant event, the 'avoidance of [. . .] stimuli recalling the event' (Caruth 1995: 4). In denying the textual expression of her heroine's violated body, Egerton herself creates a narrative body with a textual wound. This gap, through its very presence as absence, foregrounds the wounded female body as spectacle whilst complicating, and ultimately erasing, it as a site of epistemophilic appropriation.

As Tienette meets with Sebastian early in the story, the narrator describes how 'his nearness oppressed her, as it always did, half-frightened her, until she became a mere jangle of sensory nerves and almost desired to be hurt in some way as a relief' (Egerton 1897: 230). Egerton's heroine expresses the desire to avoid a dissociative state of depersonalisation, through painful distraction that asserts her reality as more than a 'jangle of sensory nerves'. The second part of the extract that describes the 'relief' of physical pain repeats the words first used in 'A Psychological Moment' from *Discords*. Through Tienette, Egerton articulates, in 1897, the psychological process by which dissociative self-mutilation would be defined a century later. Although the character communicates a desire to 'be hurt' rather than to self-harm, such pain is elicited as a means of release from mental anxiety via the enactment of such anxiety on the body. Tienette articulates the paradoxical process of self-harm and self-care inherent in self-mutilation, at a time during which the psychological and pathological framework for such behaviour had yet to be established.

In three of the four stories within which Egerton deploys the imagery of self-mutilation, the characters who harm or wish to harm themselves as a means of relief from their respective anxieties are fallen women. In 'A Psychological Moment' Isabel is black-mailed into becoming a mistress; Edith from 'Gone Under' is return-ing to her lover, only to reappear later in the story as a prostitute; whilst Tienette is pregnant and unmarried throughout much of the narrative in 'Pan'. All three characters are depicted as working class or lower-middle class, and all three have been sexually ruined and socially disgraced by their relationships with men. Although the New Woman character in 'Her Share' is not fallen, her sexual desire for a working-class man suggests a transgressive attitude towards class and sexuality that would have been shocking to Victorian readers, aligning her, to a certain extent, with the other female characters. Unlike Caird, Cross, Grand, Gissing and Mary Angela Dickens, Egerton's female self-harmers are not highly educated middle-class women forced into unhappy marriages or fallen on hard financial times. Instead they are poor, usually forced to sell or give away their bodies in one way or another to survive in a society that values them only in relation to their sexual labour. While the other writ-ers examined represent the struggle for middle-class women who resort to self-harm to both conceal and communicate their psycho-logical pain, Egerton insists on casting the fallen body as the canvas upon which self-harming signifiers emerge. Since the readership of New Woman short stories would have been limited to those able to buy the periodicals and collections in which they were published, Egerton's use of the discourse of self-mutilation in relation to the impoverished (but not always working-class) fallen body is perhaps understandable. A strategy by which to shock her readership and garner sympathy for these women, it also exploits the fallen body as a site of sexual corruption and dooms it through *fin-de-siècle* discourses that warned of the dangers of degeneration. Despite Egerton's disdain for conventional marriage and alleged support for sexual freedom, the fate of all four of these characters suggests the painful reality of such freedoms in all but exceptional, and largely well-funded, circumstances.

In 'A Psychological Moment' Isabel describes herself as 'a target for every woman to shoot at with arrows dipped in the venom the best of them have in their nature' (Egerton 2006: 92), whilst Edith's sufferings are met by women who 'purse their lips, look virtuous, and change the subject' (2006: 105), and Tienette 'dreads the gossip, the prying eyes, the tongues of women' (Egerton 1897: 235). In 'Her Share' it is the potential for social ruin that stops the heroine from pursuing her romantic feelings, leaving her miserable. Egerton's stories respond to George Eliot's insistence on the power of female community to rehabilitate the self-harmer, discussed in Chapter 3. Egerton's ambivalence surrounding the derision of women by their own kind, and their sexual exploitation by men, appears inextricably intertwined with the figure of the self-mutilating fallen woman. In deploying and displaying the sexually compromised body as a site for narrative exploration, Egerton gives credence to the very social anxieties about women's sexual freedoms against which she wrote. While her imagery is highly subversive, condemning severely both sexes by publicising women's traumatised psyches through the dramatisation of their wounded bodies, it also promotes self-mutilation as a possible form of self-defence.

Egerton's fallen women embark unsuccessfully upon unconventional relationships, and internalise their transgressions through physical pain. They repeatedly resort to self-wounding, and the fictional repetition of this process (in one instance three times in one collection) demonstrates Egerton's participation in wound culture in which self-harm, like serial murder, is 'bound up through and through with the drive to make sex and violence visible in public' (Seltzer 1998: 31). In the late-nineteenth-century wound culture that produced the New Woman short story, it is not the serial killer but the self-mutilator who is compelled towards repetitive bodily violence. The psychological scars of wounded feminine consciousness are exhibited as public atrocities by the fictionalisation and publication of stories situating self-mutilation as a means to survive. Rather than increasing the range of emancipatory models made available by her more maternally successful heroines, in the stories that feature self-harming women Egerton decries, yet fails to discount fully, the dynamic of self-harm and self-care deployed by these characters. In doing so, Egerton's work suggests the extent to which any woman writing against the grain of late-nineteenth-century propriety was forced to participate (perhaps even unconsciously) in a self-mutilative act of literary and political self-sabotage.

Notes

1. In 1846, a grieving widow was described as having practised self-enucleation, removing her own eyes. Reported by Bergman (cited in Favazza and Conterio 1989).
2. Richard von Krafft-Ebing's *Psychopathia Sexualis* (1886) documented 'perversions' and pathologised non-normative behaviour as sexually deviant.
3. Favazza's 1998 study found that childhood abuse was reported by 62 per cent of respondents, sexual abuse by almost 50 per cent, and 33 per cent had lost a family member. Although not all self-mutilation is the product of childhood abuse or neglect, virtually all recorded cases indicate a breakdown of 'normal' family relationships (Favazza 2011: 236).
4. See *Diagnostic and Statistical Manual of Mental Disorders Volume 5*, pp. 291–3.
5. See Turp 2002 for discussion of Winnicott's theory of the 'continuity of being' in relation to self-harm.
6. This theory was first proposed by Karl Menninger in *Man Against Himself* (1938) but failed to gain universal currency until the 1960s. The misconception still prevails in certain contexts.
7. See Bristow 2000 and Hetherington and Valman 2010.
8. Levy died a year after Grand published *Ideala* and Mona Caird's infamous essay 'Marriage' had become a national discussion point. Although the majority of Levy's work was published before Grand's and Caird's, it is likely she would have been aware of their respective public involvement in the Woman Question.
9. Levy's strategy can be aligned with lesbian appropriations of the 'boy' figure in Decadent poetry. See Vicinus 1994.
10. For example, in 'A Minor Poet' (1884) the speaker poisons himself, and in 'Magdalene' (1884) the speaker asserts 'a poison lies upon your kiss' (line 43).
11. See Matthew 26: 17–30, Mark 14: 12–26, Luke 22: 7–39 and John 3: 7–26, as well as Paul's First Epistle to the Corinthians 11: 23–6, for references to the Grail. See Chrétien de Troyes's *Perceval, le Conte du Graal* (c. 1180–90) for an account of the chivalric Grail quest.
12. Lucas Malet's *The Survivors* (1923), Virginia Woolf's *Mrs Dalloway* (1925) and Radclyffe Hall's *The Well of Loneliness* (1928) are all set in or around World War I.
13. From the Latin word *poena* meaning 'punishment'. One of the seven sacraments of the Catholic Church, it is also a non-sacramental process of confession and reconciliation within other denominations. Catholics usually perform penance in the form of confession, at which they are absolved of sin having completed a course of prayer. Physical pain functions as a penitential activity and usually involves fasting or

self-flagellation, but is now extremely rare even in monastic practice. See Hanson 1997 and O'Mally 2006.

14. References to mortification feature in the New Testament in Paul's Letters to the Romans 8: 13 and Colossians 3: 5.

15. Iveta Justová makes this point, arguing that Egerton's disruption of class and gender expectations also disrupted the hegemony of colonialism (2000: 28).

16. See Gelder 1994, Holte 2002 and Gordon and Hollinger 1997.

17. Both Elaine Showalter (1991) and Sally Ledger (1997) describe Lucy Westenra as an 'oversexed' New Woman.

18. A similar subversion of *fin-de-siècle* men's Gothic fiction can be seen in Egerton's *Symphonies*. Egerton's 'Pan' draws on and rewrites Arthur Machen's *The Great God Pan* (1890), which was also reprinted by John Lane as part of his Keynotes series in 1894. Machen's Helen Vaughan is a terrifying and demonic femme fatale, and Egerton disrupts this reading of female sexual desire with her own version of the Pan myth in 'Pan'.

19. Waterhouse also painted Ophelia in 1889, noted in Chapter 3.

20. Notably, the Pre-Raphaelite artist William Holman Hunt depicted a version of the Lady (1905) which neither infantilises nor eroticises her.

21. See Bronfen 1992 and Gates 1989, who discuss the image of the drowned woman as sexually compromised in Victorian culture.

22. In Allen's *The Woman Who Did*, Herminia Barton chooses to live in a free union with the father of her child. However, this strategy is rendered dangerous when her partner dies, leaving her alone and penniless. The child grows up to despise Herminia because she is illegitimate, thus Allen's novel laments the practical problems of free unions and free maternity.

Conclusion

In New Woman writing, self-harm emerges as a central concern in narratives about female experience within a restrictive society that values women's bodies in complicated ways, and limits their capacity for achievement. Self-harm is also a way of reading the process of New Woman writing – a disruptive literary strategy through which the damaged body was dramatised, by writers who rebelled against Victorian patriarchy but also wrote within its cultural, political and religious frameworks. In the wound culture of the *fin-de-siècle* publishing environment, women writers exploited new opportunities to represent the female body 'as spectacle or representation – and, most insistently, as spectacle or representation of crisis, disaster, or atrocity' (Seltzer 1998: 40). Damaging the self, a seemingly futile act encoding frustrations at women's subordinate position in Victorian society, thus becomes 'one of the most powerful ways of keeping visible the possibility of the shared social spaces of the public sphere itself' (Seltzer 1998: 35), challenging separate sphere ideology yet surrendering to insurmountable social, legal and political obstacles. In keeping with the dichotomy of rebellion and defeat inherent in the acts of self-harm I discuss, women writers drew upon the only language for representing women's self-harm that they had – a symbolic and dialogic nexus through which female suffering was often sensationalised, valorised or eroticised. Such language was both highly disruptive – highlighting the injustices of Victorian sexual double standards, and arguing for a collapse of separate sphere ideology – and, in some ways, also part of the very problem it challenged. Despite this, the range of texts examined in *Self-Harm in New Woman Writing* attests to the complexity of the double bind faced by the New Woman author, whose work had to remain commercially viable despite her progressive views.

Women's position in the late-nineteenth-century literary marketplace was precarious. Often, women's survival was dependent on the publication of literary work, a fact sometimes reflected in the depreciation of these authors' texts and their exclusion from the canon. The omission of some of these authors from cultural and literary history is the consequence of both their gender – which made the subject of self-harm an unsuitable one – and their ambiguous, and thus potentially threatening, identities. Almost all the women whose writing I have examined operated at the margins of the British Empire, and presented a challenge to the notion of a single, male, heteronormative and middle-class literary identity. They wrote from positions of racial, cultural, sexual and social liminality, of hybridity, modernity and even transgressivity. As the nineteenth century came to a close, these women wrote back to the centre of a writerly canon that would exclude them based on their gender. Equally, it sought to devalue their contributions and resist its own expansion, since these women questioned the assumption of superiority implicit in masculine narrative authority. It is telling that, in the search for examples of self-harm in women's writing, the most explicit of such disturbing subject matter emerges from those who were doubly outside the boundaries of tradition, and who were derided as threateningly modern and 'new'. Although Mary Angela Dickens was an Englishwoman with a prestigious literary lineage, her refusal to consistently embrace the conservatism and sentimentalism of the Dickensian tradition marks her out as bold and modern with a penchant for revolt. Such revolt is evidenced in all the New Woman texts I have explored, which, despite the clear divergence of thought and policy espoused by their respective authors, share an interest in self-harm by women writers that cannot be ignored.

It is possible to demarcate a roughly chronological arc of textual production, in which the novels of the 1880s and early 1890s gradually gave way to shorter narrative forms. This was, in part, a consequence of the increased accessibility of print media, at a time in which serial publishing was endlessly reproducing new bodies of text. These texts featured the images and rhetoric of female self-harm as 'a way of imagining the relations of private bodies and private persons to public spaces' (Seltzer 1998: 21), as inhabitants of a pathological public sphere in which the suffering female form was a synecdoche for the social and political upheavals of the period. Suffering female bodies had hitherto been contained within traditional narrative forms like the novel and – in both social and diegetic worlds – within the private, domestic sphere. Some of the writers I have considered – Sarah Grand, for example – continued to produce novels throughout the period. However, by 1894, when George Egerton's *Discords* appeared, New Woman writers had largely abandoned the form, and the novels they did produce were far closer to the Modernism of the early twentieth century than the Realism of the nineteenth.[1]

Key to my conceptualisation of self-harm in New Woman writing is the assertion of a correspondence between depictions of violent self-harm and the increasingly short forms in which they appeared. In the novel, New Woman writers both foregrounded and elided the damaged body from the plot; its corporeal absence and symbolic presence are the paradox at the heart of the New Woman social purity romance. In my readings of Amy Levy's lyric poetry, I posit her use of male speakers as a strategy through which to express that which would have offended her readership had it originated from a female voice. Levy appropriates the notion of the Romantic genius poet to manifest the passion and emotional excess that transgressed Victorian ideals of womanhood. She goes as far as to imitate Swinburne's subversion of poetic convention, his undermining of religious tropes through bodily self-wounding, to express dissatisfaction at a range of issues, including the exclusion of women from public life. I have argued that Levy's poems exemplify a transitional point between New Woman writers' use of the unwieldy and restrictive realist novel, and the more permissive space of the short story. Levy is an example of the pioneer work of New Woman poets, which opened rhetorical spaces where concerns about the female body could be broached without fear of censorship.[2]

George Egerton's collection *Discords* marks the apotheosis of the formal and thematic development in New Woman writing. It was the high point, disrupted by the trial and conviction of Oscar Wilde in 1895, after which all forms of writing became subject to closer scrutiny, particularly those written by New Women.[3] Egerton was unable to achieve commercial or critical success with the novel; her attempts to reproduce the psychological interiority of her female characters largely failed, and her protagonists are written back into the hegemonic order she so often satirised. Similarly, Mary Angela Dickens, who was better able to weather the post-1895 publishing environment, was nevertheless unable to make a cohesive critique of patriarchy in her novelistic offerings. In her short stories, however, Dickens mercilessly parodies the clerical establishment and, by implication, Victorian patriarchy. If the development of the New Woman oeuvre was interrupted by its perceived association with the moral corruption of literary Decadence, the onset of the First World War in 1914 brought the genre to a premature end.

Where self-harm emerges as a trope in late-Victorian women's writing, it metaphorises the female body's response to patriarchal injustice, resisting the epistemophilic control exerted by the apparatus of Victorian social, economic, medical and religious power. However, self-harm in women's writing also manifests a disruptive dialectic of subversion and compliance, by which the masculine gaze is undermined but also reinforced by the display of wounded female bodies in texts by and about the New Woman. These displays were numerous, various and concerned with different forms of self-harm, each of which encoded specific challenges faced by women who failed to adhere to the expectations of their gender as well as other markers of identity. Strikingly, these dramatisations of self-harm corresponded less to any sustained scientific investigation into self-starvation, excessive drinking or self-mutilation, and more to the lived experience of women in the period. Thus, the New Woman writer tapped into concerns about the female body as a repository of ideology, long before any coherent psychiatric explanation for the practice of self-harm was to emerge.

Underpinning, in different ways, most of the texts I have discussed was the cultural ubiquity of self-sacrifice as a gesture of saintliness. Such acts drew on both the potency of self-denial as a form of religiosity, and the subversive component of martyrdom. New Woman writers often expressed their frustrations at an unjust Victorian social system through hyperbolic images of sacrifice, aligning female experience with Christian mysticism. In doing so, they challenged religious authority yet also imbued their heroines' sufferings with spiritual qualities that corresponded to the middle-class domestic ideal. Mona Caird's dramatisations of martyrdom confronted women's meek acceptance of sacrifice yet offered no escape for her female victims, emphasising the tyranny of marriage in sensational fashion. Using similar imagery to different effect, Victoria Cross's shorter texts reversed the gendering of female sacrifice, depicting a quasi-masochistic relationship in which martyrdom is a form of divine, erotic submission. Cross's shocking depiction in *Anna Lombard* of a woman whose sexuality takes precedence over both her domestic duties and her maternal responsibilities was, of course, tempered by the same gender reversal, in which the feminised male body supersedes that of the typical heroine. Neither Caird nor Cross could imagine a narrative trajectory in which their female characters might harness the healing power of faith, or identify with a less immobilised example of Christian goodness. All the women writers whose work I have discussed address the paradox of rebellion and submission embedded in martyrdom in some way, and all explore models of sacrifice legitimated by the crucifixion of Jesus Christ.

In the social purity novels of Sarah Grand the anorexic body embodies the constraints placed on intellectual women. As New

Woman characters exercise their minds, they become correspondingly corporeally diminished, and they are depicted as so entrenched
in Cartesian dualism that their bodies are of no use to them.
Tellingly, the bodies of her female characters are of little narrative
importance in Grand's discursive scheme. Heroines are described
only in terms of their thinness and bodily lack, despite the fact that
the novel form provides as many as nine hundred pages in which to
elaborate. Although emphasising the dire lengths to which women
must go to compete on a level footing with their male counterparts,
Grand fails to fully escape celebrating bodily self-sacrifice through
self-starvation. Whereas her short stories and political writings often
critique both women who are artificially thin and those without the
necessary health for improving the species, such rhetoric does not
fully emerge in her novels.

In George Gissing's *The Odd Women*, the self-harming female
body is largely absent, referred to only in the language of conduct,
mood and manners. Conversely, in the short stories of George
Egerton and Mary Angela Dickens, the visceral minutia of female
drinkers is directly described; their 'alcoholism' forms the primary
plot concern around which the narratives revolve, and their bodies
are the focus of significant textual detail. In an opposite manoeuvre
to that undertaken by the starving heroines in Grand's novels, the
drunken female body demands to be heard, and asserts its corporeality in a world that requires its erasure. Self-mutilation in New
Woman writing is, like heavy drinking, a strategy that requires the
fictional body to be deployed as a communicative surface on which
traumas are inscribed. However, self-mutilation, much more so than
alcoholism, violently ruptures the boundaries between the inner and
outer surfaces of the body and society, exploiting a 'public fascination with torn and open bodies and torn and open persons, a collective gathering around shock, trauma and the wound' (Seltzer 1998:
1). While the female drinker swallows her pain in the New Woman
fiction I have examined, reproducing Christian conceptual frameworks, self-mutilation is furthered by New Woman writers as a tactic to both disrupt patriarchal control of the body and survive the
internalisation of religious codes.

By deploying the topoi of corporeal self-destruction, New Woman
writers ruptured the boundaries between private and public, and
undermined the power of the gaze by taking control of women's
bodies and their bodies of text. However, they did so in ways that
at times placed the female body as an object of fascination at the
heart of their texts, inviting, and thus ultimately strengthening, the
masculine field of vision. In attempting to redistribute the gendered

power dynamics of the nineteenth-century sexual economy, the New Woman asserted women's right to transcend their roles as commodities within a male-oriented and male-produced literary and social marketplace. However, in doing so she adopted traditional, and often disappointingly conventional, representations of the female body in pain that reproduced internalised masculine religious, moral and literary codes, and situated the damaged body as a melodramatic spectacle – corrupted by patriarchy, but corrupt all the same. The New Woman thus both resists and partakes in the epistemophilic project of the Western literary tradition, even when deploying experimental forms that rejected the realist imperative for conclusions reinforcing cultural hierarchies.

In addition to the literary and theoretical understandings of New Woman writing provided by this study, this research also contributes to cultural and historical accounts of the period. Virtually no substantive evidence of the rates of self-harming amongst Victorian women has ever been recorded. It is impossible to know the rates at which women starved, consumed excessive quantities of alcohol, or wounded themselves, because only the most sensational cases of these acts were reported. However, fictional texts produced by the New Woman represent one source of evidence that these practices were adopted by women to cope with a range of pressures at the *fin de siècle*. Self-harm in New Woman writing functions as a metaphor for women's powerlessness and lack of bodily control, as well as for a range of socio-historical and political debates that were cast on to the female body as a source of masculine anxiety. Much work remains to be done in bringing to light the historical silences about women's self-harm I have explored. Given that so little documentary evidence exists today, literary accounts may represent our best hope in giving voice to experiences otherwise elided from our cultural history.

Notes

1. For example, Egerton's *The Wheel of God*, Lucas Malet's *The History of Sir Richard Calmady* (1901) and, later, Ada Leverson's *The Limit* (1911).
2. See also the work of Olive Custance, Charlotte Mew, 'Michael Field' and Constance Naden.
3. After Wilde's conviction for gross indecency in 1895 all forms of transgressive literature were subject to increased scrutiny, but particularly those by 'subversive' New Woman authors like Egerton.

Works Cited

Acland, Theodore Dyke (ed.) (1894), *A Collection of the Published Writings of William Withey Gull*, London: New Sydenham Society.

Adam, James (1883), 'Cases of Self-Mutilation by the Insane', *The Journal of Mental Science* 29.126: 213–19.

Adshead, Gwen (1997), 'Written on the Body: Deliberate Self-Harm and Violence', in E. V. Welldon, E. Waters and S. Wall (eds), *A Practical Guide to Forensic Psychotherapy*, London: Kingsley, pp. 110–14.

— (2010), 'Written on the Body: Deliberate Self-Harm as Communication', *Psychoanalytic Psychotherapy* 24.2: 69–80.

Aldridge, Judith, Fiona Measham and Lisa Williams (2011), *Illegal Leisure Revisited: Changing Patterns of Alcohol and Drug Use in Adolescents and Young Adults*, London: Routledge.

Allen, Grant (1889a), 'Plain Words on the Woman Question', *Fortnightly Review* 46: 448–58.

— (1889b), 'Plain Words on the Woman Question', *Popular Science Monthly* 36: 170–81.

— (2006), *The Woman Who Did*, Teddington: The Echo Library.

Anderson, Amanda (1993), *Tainted Souls and Painted Faces: The Rhetoric of Fallenness in Victorian Culture*, London: Cornell University Press.

Anderson, Olive (1987), *Suicide in Victorian and Edwardian England*, Oxford: Clarendon.

Andres, Sophia (2005), *The Pre-Raphaelite Art of the Victorian Novel: Narrative Challenges to Visual Gendered Boundaries*, Columbus: Ohio State University Press.

'Another Shocking East-End Murder' (1888), *The Penny Illustrated Paper and Illustrated Times*, 25 August, p. 126.

Anzieu, Didier (1989), *The Skin Ego*, London: Yale University Press.

Arnold, Lois (1994), *Women and Self Injury: Understanding Self Injury*, Bristol: Bristol Crisis Service for Women.

Arnold, Lois, and Gloria Babiker (1997), *The Language of Injury: Comprehending Self-Mutilation*, Leicester: BPS Books Ltd.

The Art of Beautifying and Improving the Face and Figure (1858), London: G. Vickers.

Ashcroft, Bill, Gail Griffin and Helen Tiffin (2002), *The Empire Strikes Back: Theory and Practice in Postcolonial Literature*, 2nd edn, London: Routledge.

Auerbach, Nina (1980), 'The Rise of the Fallen Woman', *Nineteenth-Century Fiction* 35.1: 29–52.

— (1982), *Woman and the Demon: The Life of a Victorian Myth*, Cambridge, MA: Harvard University Press.

Austen, Jane (2008), *Mansfield Park*, Oxford: Oxford University Press.

Ausubel, Nathan (1964), *The Book of Jewish Knowledge*, New York: Crown Publishers.

Bailin, Miriam (1994), *The Sickroom in Victorian Fiction: The Art of Being Ill*, Cambridge: Cambridge University Press.

Bakhtin, Mikhail (1984), *Rabelais and His World*, Bloomington: Indiana University Press.

Banting, William (2005), *Letter on Corpulence*, New York: Cosimo.

Barthes, Roland (1990), *S/Z*, trans. Richard Miller, Oxford: Blackwell.

Bartley, Paula (2012), *Emmeline Pankhurst*, London: Routledge.

Barton, Carlin (1994), 'Savage Miracles: The Redemption of Lost Honour in Roman Society and the Sacrament of the Gladiator and the Martyr', *Representations* 45: 41–7.

— (2002), 'Honour and Sacredness in the Roman and Christian Worlds', in Margaret Cormack (ed.), *Sacrificing the Self: Perspectives in Martyrdom and Religion*, Oxford: Oxford University Press, pp. 23–38.

'Battle of the Alma' (1854), *The Huddersfield Chronicle and West Yorkshire Advertiser*, 4 October, p. 8.

Baudelaire, Charles (2008), *The Flowers of Evil*, Oxford: Oxford University Press.

Beckman, Linda Hunt (1999), 'Leaving the "Tribal Duckpond": Amy Levy, Jewish Self-Hatred, and Jewish Identity', *Victorian Literature and Culture* 27.1: 185–201.

— (2000), *Amy Levy: Her Life and Letters*, Athens: Ohio University Press.

— (2005), 'Amy Levy: Urban Poetry, Poetic Innovation, and the Fin-de-Siècle Woman Poet', in Joseph Bristow (ed.), *The Fin-de-Siècle Poem: English Literary Culture and the 1890s*, Athens: Ohio University Press, pp. 207–30.

Beckwith, Sarah (1993), *Christ's Body: Identity, Culture and Society in Late Medieval Writings*, London: Routledge.

Beetham, Margaret, and Kay Boardman (eds) (2001), *Victorian Women's Magazines: An Anthology*, Manchester: Manchester University Press.

Beisel, Nicola (1993), 'Morals versus Art: Censorship, the Politics of Interpretation, and the Victorian Nude', *American Sociological Review* 58.2: 145–62.

Bending, Lucy (2000), *The Representation of Bodily Pain in Late Nineteenth-Century English Culture*, Oxford: Clarendon Press.

Beresford, David (1994), *Ten Men Dead*, London: HarperCollins.

Bernstein, Susan David (2010), '"Mongrel Words": Amy Levy's Jewish Vulgarity', in Naomi Hetherington and Nadia Valman (eds), *Amy Levy: Critical Essays*, Athens: Ohio University Press, pp. 135–56.

Berridge, Virginia (1978), 'Victorian Opium Eating: Responses to Opiate Use in Nineteenth-Century England', *Victorian Studies* 21.4: 437–62.

Berrios, German E. (1996), *The History of Mental Symptoms: Descriptive Psychopathology since the Nineteenth Century*, Cambridge: Cambridge University Press.

Bethlem Royal Hospital Casebooks 1860–1884, London: Wellcome Library.

The Bible: Authorised King James Version (2008), Oxford: Oxford University Press.

Bonnell, Marilyn (1995), 'Sarah Grand and the Critical Establishment: Art for [Wo]Man's Sake', *Tulsa Studies in Women's Literature* 14.1: 123–48.

Booth, Charles (1886–1903), 'Life and Labour of the People in London', <https://archive.org/stream/lifeandlabourpe02bootgoog/lifeandlabourpe-02bootgoog_djvu.txt> (last accessed 28 April 2017).

Booth, William (2000), 'In Darkest England and the Way Out', in Sally Ledger and Roger Luckhurst (eds), *The Fin de Siècle: A Reader in Cultural History c. 1880–1900*, Oxford: Oxford University Press, pp. 45–9.

Bordieu, Pierre (1991), *Language and Symbolic Power*, Cambridge: Polity Press.

Bordo, Susan (2003), *Unbearable Weight: Feminism, Western Culture, and the Body*, Berkeley: University of California Press.

Braddon, Mary Elizabeth (2003), *Lady Audley's Secret*, London: Broadview.

Braziel, Jana E., and Kathleen Le Besco (2001), *Bodies out of Bounds: Fatness and Transgression*, Berkeley: University of California Press.

Breton, Rob (2013), 'Diverting the Drunkard's Path: Chartist Temperance Narratives', *Victorian Literature and Culture* 41.1: 139–52.

Bristow, Joseph (2000), '"All out of Tune in this World's Instrument": The "Minor" Poetry of Amy Levy', *Journal of Victorian Culture* 4.1: 76–103.

— (ed.) (2005), *The Fin-de-Siècle Poem: English Literary Culture and the 1890s*, Athens: Ohio University Press.

Brittain, Melissa (2001), 'Erasing Race in the New Woman Review: Victoria Cross's *Anna Lombard*', *Nineteenth-Century Feminisms* 4: 75–95.

Bronfen, Elisabeth (1992), *Over Her Dead Body: Death, Femininity and the Aesthetic*, Manchester: Manchester University Press.

— (1998), *The Knotted Subject: Hysteria and Its Discontents*, Princeton: Princeton University Press.

Bronstein, Jamie L. (2008), *Caught in the Machinery: Workplace Accidents and Injured Workers in Nineteenth-Century Britain*, Stanford: Stanford University Press.

Brontë, Charlotte (2007), *Shirley*, Oxford: Oxford University Press.

Brooks, Peter (1992), *Reading for the Plot: Design and Intention in Narrative*, London: Harvard University Press.

— (1993), *Body Work: Objects of Desire in Modern Narrative*, London: Harvard University Press.

Brown, Laura S. (1995), 'Not Outside the Range: One Feminist Perspective on Psychic Trauma', in Cathy Caruth (ed.), *Trauma: Explorations in Memory*, London: Johns Hopkins University Press, pp. 100–12.

Brownstein, Michael J. (1993), 'A Brief History of Opiates, Opoid Peptides, and Opoid Receptors', *Proceedings of the National Academy of Sciences* 90.15: 5391–3.

Bruch, Hilde (1979), *The Golden Cage: The Enigma of Anorexia Nervosa*, New York: Vintage.

Bruhm, Steven (1994), *Gothic Bodies: The Politics of Pain in Romantic Fiction*, Philadelphia: University of Pennsylvania Press.

Brumberg, Joan J. (2000), *Fasting Girls: The History of Anorexia Nervosa*, London: Random House.

Bullen, J. B. (1998), *The Pre-Raphaelite Body: Fear and Desire in Painting, Poetry, and Criticism*, Oxford: Oxford University Press.

Burne-Jones, Edward (1863–7), *St. Theophilus and the Angel*, Private Collection.

Burrus, Virginia (2007), *Sex Lives of the Saints: An Erotics of Ancient Hagiography*, Philadelphia: University of Pennsylvania Press.

Burstyn, Joan N. (1980), *Victorian Education and the Ideal of Womanhood*, London: Croom Helm.

Busst, A. J. L. (1967), 'The Image of the Androgyne in the Nineteenth Century', in Ian Fletcher (ed.), *Romantic Mythologies*, London: Routledge, pp. 1–87.

Butler, Judith (2006), *Gender Trouble: Feminism and the Subversion of Identity*, London: Routledge.

Butler, Rex (2006), *The New Prophecy and 'New Visions': Evidence of Montanism in the Passion of Saints Perpetua and Felicitas*, Washington, DC: Catholic University of America Press.

Byrne, Katherine (2010), *Tuberculosis and the Victorian Literary Imagination*, Cambridge: Cambridge University Press.

Cabanel, Alexandre (1883), *Ophelia*, Private Collection.

Caird, Mona (1888), 'Marriage', *Westminster Review*, 186–201.

— (1894), *The Daughters of Danaus*, Minneapolis: Filiquarian.

— (1897), *Beyond the Pale: An Appeal on Behalf of the Victims of Vivisection*, London: W. Reeves.

— (1898), *The Pathway of the Gods*, London: George Bell and Sons.

— (1987), 'Letter to Lady Wilde, 27 June 1889', in Richard Ellman (ed.), *Oscar Wilde*, Harmondsworth: Penguin, p. 556.

— (2010a), 'A Defence of the "Wild Women"', in M. Caird (ed.), *The Morality of Marriage and Other Essays on the Status and Destiny of Women*, Cambridge: Cambridge University Press, pp. 157–91.

— (2010b), *The Wing of Azrael*, Kansas City: Valancourt.

Calderon, Philip H. (1891), *St Elizabeth of Hungary's Great Act of Renunciation*, Tate, London.

Capellanus, Andreas (1982), *On Love*, trans. P. G. Walsh, London: Bloomsbury.

Carpenter, Mary Wilson (2003), *Imperial Bibles, Domestic Bodies: Women, Sexuality, and Religion in the Victorian Market*, Athens: Ohio University Press.

Carr, David M. (2003), *The Erotic Word: Sexuality, Spirituality, and the Bible*, Oxford: Oxford University Press.

Caruth, Cathy (ed.) (1995), *Trauma: Explorations in Memory*, London: Johns Hopkins University Press.

Castelli, Elizabeth (1996), *Visions and Voyeurism: The Politics of Sight in Early Christianity*, Berkeley: University of California Press.

Cavanagh, Sheila, Angela Failler and Rachel A. J. Hurst (eds) (2013), *Skin, Culture and Psychoanalysis*, Basingstoke: Palgrave Macmillan.

Caviness, Madeline H. (2001), *Visualizing Women in the Middle Ages: Sight, Spectacle, and Scopic Economy*, Philadelphia: University of Pennsylvania Press.

Chaney, Sarah (2011a), '"A Hideous Torture on Himself": Madness and Self-Mutilation in Victorian Literature', *The Journal of Medical Humanities* 32.4: 279–89.

— (2011b), 'Self-Control, Selfishness and Mutilation: How "Medical" Is Self-Injury Anyway?', *Journal of Medical History* 55.3: 375–82.

— (2017), *Psyche on the Skin: A History of Self-Harm*, Chicago: Reaktion Books.

Channing, Walter (1878), 'The Case of Helen Miller', *American Journal of Psychiatry* 34: 368–78.

Chapman, Alexander L., and Kim Gratz (2009), *Freedom from Self-Harm: Overcoming Self-Injury with Skills from DBT and Other Treatments*, Oakland: New Harbinger.

Chernin, Kim (1986), *The Hungry Self*, New York: Harper & Row.

Cholmondeley, Mary (1900), *Red Pottage*, New York: Harper & Brothers.

Chopin, Kate (2007), 'The Story of an Hour', in Elaine Showalter (ed.), *Scribbling Women: Short Stories by Nineteenth-Century American Women*, London: J. M. Dent, pp. 377–9.

Christ, Carol T., and John O. Jordan (1995), *Victorian Literature and the Victorian Visual Imagination*, Berkeley: University of California Press.

Clouston, Thomas S. (1887), *Mental Diseases*, London: Churchill.

Connors, Steven (2004), *The Book of Skin*, London: Reaktion Books.

Cothran, Casey A. (2009), 'Mona Caird and the Spectacle of Suffering', in Melissa Purdue and Stacey Floyd (eds), *New Woman Writers, Authority and the Body*, Newcastle: Cambridge Scholars, pp. 63–88.

Cozzi, Annette (2010), *The Discourses of Food in Nineteenth-Century British Fiction*, Basingstoke: Palgrave Macmillan.

Cranton, Lillian (2009), *The Victorian Freak Show: The Significance of Disability and Physical Differences in 19th-Century Fiction*, New York: Cambria Press.

Cronwright-Schreiner, S. C. (1924), *The Life of Olive Schreiner*, London: T. Fisher Unwin.

Cross, Victoria (1895), *The Woman Who Didn't*, London: Dodo Press.

— (1993), 'Theodora: A Fragment', in Elaine Showalter (ed.), *Daughters of Decadence: Women Writers of the Fin-de-Siècle*, London: Virago, pp. 6–37.

— (2006), *Anna Lombard*, London: Continuum.

Cunningham, Gail (2006), 'Introduction', in Victoria Cross, *Anna Lombard*, London: Continuum.

Custance, Olive (1897), *Opals; With Rainbows*, New York: Woodstock Books.

— (1911), *The Inn of Dreams*, London: John Lane.

D'Arcy, Ella (1895), 'The Pleasure Pilgrim', in *Monochromes*, London: Garland, pp. 111–75.

Da Vinci, Leonardo (1513–16), *St. John the Baptist*, The Louvre, Paris.

Daly, Nicholas (2004), *Literature, Technology, and Modernity, 1860–2000*, Cambridge: Cambridge University Press.

David, Deirdre (1984), 'Ideologies of Patriarchy, Feminism, and Fiction in *The Odd Women*', *Feminist Studies* 10.1: 117–39.

De Beauvoir, Simone (2010), *The Second Sex*, London: Vintage.

De La Sizeranne, Robert (2008), *The Pre-Raphaelites*, New York: Parkstone.

De Troyes, Chétrien (2012), *Perceval, le Conte du Graal*, Paris: Flammarion.

De Vere White, Terence (ed.) (1958), *A Leaf from the Yellow Book: The Correspondence of George Egerton*, London: Richards Press.

Deleuze, Giles (1991), *Masochism: Coldness and Cruelty and Venus in Furs*, New York: Zone Publishing.

Delyfer, Catherine (2011), *Art and Womanhood in Fin-de-Siècle Writing: The Fiction of Lucas Malet, 1880–1931*, London: Pickering & Chatto.

Dennis, Abigail (2007), '"A Study in Starvation": The New Girl and the Gendered Socialisation of Appetite in Sarah Grand's *The Beth Book*', *Australasian Journal of Victorian Studies* 12.1: 19–34.

Descartes, René (2008), *Meditations on First Philosophy*, Oxford: Oxford University Press.

Diagnostic and Statistical Manual of Mental Disorders Volume 5 (2013), Washington, DC: American Psychiatric Association.

Dickens, Charles (2002), *Dombey and Son*, London: Wordsworth.

— (2006), *Hard Times*, Oxford: Oxford University Press.

— (2008a), *Bleak House*, Oxford: Oxford University Press.

— (2008b), *David Copperfield*, Oxford: Oxford University Press.

— (2008c), *Our Mutual Friend*, Oxford: Oxford University Press.

— (2008d), *A Tale of Two Cities*, Oxford: Oxford University Press.

— (2012), *Little Dorrit*, Oxford: Oxford University Press.

Dickens, Mary (1885), *Charles Dickens by His Eldest Daughter*, London: Cassell.

Dickens, Mary Angela (1894), *A Valiant Ignorance*, London: Macmillan and Co.

— (1896), *Some Women's Ways*, 2nd edn, London: Jarrold and Sons.

— (1897a), 'The Catch of the Season', *The Strand Magazine* 14: 66–74.

— (1897b), 'A Child's Memories of Gad's Hill', *The Strand Magazine* 13: 69–74.

— (1898), *Against the Tide*, London: Hutchinson and Co.

— (1916), *Sanctuary*, London: R&T Washbourne.

Dierkes-Thrun, Petra (2016), 'Victoria Cross's *Six Chapters of a Man's Life*: Queering Middlebrow Feminism', in Christoph Ehland and Cornelia Wachter (eds), *Middlebrow and Gender*, Boston: Brill Rodopi, pp. 202–27.

Directors of Convict Prisons: Millbank (1853), London: Wellcome Library.

Divine, Luke (2011), '"The Ghetto at Florence": Reading Jewish Identity in Amy Levy's Early Poetry, 1880–86', *Prooftexts* 31.1–2: 1–30.

Dixon, Ella Hepworth (2004), *The Story of a Modern Woman*, New York: Broadview Press.

Donoghue, Emma (ed.) (1997), *What Would Sappho Have Said? Four Centuries of Love Poems between Women*, London: Hamish Hamilton.

Dowie, Ménie Muriel (1995), *Gallia*, London: Everyman.

Durbach, Nadja (2010), *Spectacle of Deformity: Freak Shows and Modern British Culture*, Berkeley: University of California Press.

Edwards, Griffith (1990), 'Withdrawal Symptoms and Alcohol Dependence: Fruitful Mysteries', *British Journal of Addiction* 85: 447–61.

Egerton, George (1897), *Symphonies*, London: The Bodley Head.

— (1898), *The Wheel of God*, London: G. P. Putnam's Sons.

— (2006), *Keynotes and Discords*, ed. Sally Ledger, London: Continuum.

Eliot, George (2008a), *Middlemarch*, Oxford: Oxford University Press.

— (2008b), *The Mill on the Floss*, Oxford: Oxford University Press.

— (2009a), *Daniel Deronda*, Oxford: Oxford University Press.

— (2009b), 'Janet's Repentance', in *Scenes of Clerical Life*, Oxford: Oxford University Press.

Ellis, Sarah Stickney (1842), *The Daughters of England: Their Position in Society, Character, and Responsibilities*, New York: Appleton.

Ellmann, Maud (1993), *The Hunger Artists: Starving, Writing, and Imprisonment*, Cambridge, MA: Harvard University Press.

An Enquiry into Destitution, Prostitution and Crime in Edinburgh, by a Medical Gentleman (1851), Edinburgh: J. Bertram & Co.

Evans, Heather (2000), 'Power-Eating and the Power-Starved: The New Woman's New Appetite in Sarah Grand's *Babs the Impossible*', in Julia Hallam and Nickianne Moody (eds), *Consuming for Pleasure: Selected Essays on Popular Culture*, Liverpool: John Moores University and the Association for Research in Popular Fictions, pp. 121–39.

— (2001), '"Nor Shall I Shirk My Food": The New Woman's Balanced Diet and Sarah Grand's *Babs the Impossible*', *Nineteenth-Century Feminisms* 4: 136–47.

'Extraordinary Case of Self-Mutilation', *The York Herald*, 17 January 1880, p. 2.

Farmer, David H. (ed.) (2011), *The Oxford Dictionary of Saints*, Oxford: Oxford University Press.

Favazza, Armando (1996), *Bodies under Siege: Self-Mutilation and Body Modification in Culture and Psychiatry*, London: Johns Hopkins University Press.

— (2011), *Bodies under Siege: Self-Mutilation, Nonsuicidal Self-Injury, and Body Modification in Culture and Psychiatry*, London: Johns Hopkins University Press.

— and Kim Conterio (1989), 'Female Habitual Self-Mutilators', *Acta Psychiatria Scandinavia* 79.3: 283–9.

— and Daphne Simeon (2001), 'Self-Injurious Behaviors: Phenomenology and Assessment', in Daphne Simeon and Eric Hollander (eds), *Self-Injurious Behaviors: Assessment and Treatment*, Washington, DC: American Psychiatric Association, pp. 1–28.

Fleming, George (1993), 'By Accident', in Elaine Showalter (ed.), *Daughters of Decadence: Women Writers of the Fin-de-Siècle*, London: Virago, pp. 74–83.

Fluhr, Nicole (2001), 'Figuring the New Woman: Writers and Mothers in George Egerton's Early Stories', *Texas Studies in Literature and Language* 43.3: 243–66.

Foote, Jeremy (2013), 'Speed that Kills: The Role of Technology in Kate Chopin's "The Story of an Hour"', *The Explicator* 71.2: 85–9.

Ford, Jane (2016), 'Greek Gift and "Given Being": The Libidinal Economies of Vernon Lee's Supernatural Tales', in Jane Ford, Kim Edwards Keats and Patricia Pulham (eds), *Economies of Desire at the Victorian Fin de Siècle: Libidinal Lives*, London: Routledge, pp. 106–21.

Forward, Stephanie, and Ann Heilmann (eds) (2000a), *Sex, Social Purity and Sarah Grand Volume I: Journalistic Writings and Contemporary Reception*, London: Routledge.

— (eds) (2000b), *Sex, Social Purity and Sarah Grand Volume II: Selected Letters 1889–1943*, London: Routledge.

Foucault, Michel (1990), *The History of Sexuality Volume 1*, London: Vintage.

— (1995), *Discipline and Punish: The Birth of the Prison*, 2nd edn, New York: Random House.

— (2001), *Madness and Civilization: A History of the Age of Reason*, London: Routledge.

Foxe, John (2009), *Foxe's Book of Martyrs*, Oxford: Oxford University Press.

Francis, Emma (1990), 'Amy Levy: Contradictions? – Feminism and Semitic Discourse', in Isobel Armstrong and Virginia Blain (eds), *Women's Poetry,*

Late Romantic to Late Victorian: Gender and Genre, 1830–1900, London: Macmillan, pp. 183–204.

Freud, Sigmund (2001a), *The Standard Edition of the Complete Psychological Works of Sigmund Freud, Volume 7*, London: Vintage.

— (2001b), *The Standard Edition of the Complete Psychological Works of Sigmund Freud, Volume 17*, London: Vintage.

— (2001c), *The Standard Edition of the Complete Psychological Works of Sigmund Freud, Volume 18*, London: Vintage.

Furey, Constance M. (2012), 'Sexuality', in Amy Hollywood and Patricia Z. Beckman (eds), *The Cambridge Companion to Christian Mysticism*, Cambridge: Cambridge University Press, pp. 328–40.

Gagnier, Regenia (2010), *Individualism, Decadence and Globalization: On the Relationship of Part to Whole, 1859–1920*, Aldershot: Palgrave Macmillan.

Gannon, Charles E. (2003), *Rumours of War and Infernal Machines: Technomilitary Agenda Setting in American and British Fiction*, Lanham, MD: Rowman & Littlefield.

Gardner, Fiona (2001), *Self-Harm: A Psychotherapeutic Approach*, London: Routledge.

Gardner, Viv, and Susan Rutherford (eds) (1992), *The New Woman and Her Sisters: Feminism and Theatre, 1850–1914*, London: Harvester Wheatsheaf.

Gaskell, Elizabeth (2008), *Mary Barton*, Oxford: Oxford University Press.

— (2011), *Ruth*, Oxford: Oxford University Press.

Gates, Barbara T. (1989), *Victorian Suicide: Mad Crimes and Sad Histories*, Princeton: Princeton University Press.

Gawsworth, John (1932), *Ten Contemporaries: Notes Toward Their Definitive Bibliography*, London: Joiner & Steele Ltd.

Gelder, Ken (1994), *Reading the Vampire*, London: Routledge.

Gilbert, Pamela K. (2005), *Disease, Desire and the Body in Victorian Women's Popular Novels*, Cambridge: Cambridge University Press.

— (2008), *Cholera and Nation: Doctoring the Social Body in Victorian England*, Albany: State University of New York Press.

Gilbert, Sandra, and Susan Gubar (1984), *The Madwoman in the Attic: The Woman Writer and the Nineteenth-Century Literary Imagination*, London: Yale University Press.

Gilman, Charlotte Perkins (1993), 'The Yellow Wallpaper', in Elaine Showalter (ed.), *Daughters of Decadence: Women Writers of the Fin-de-Siècle*, London: Virago, pp. 98–117.

— (2007), *Women and Economics*, New York: Cosimo.

Gilman, Sander (1986), *Jewish Self-Hatred: The Hidden Language of the Jews*, London: Johns Hopkins University Press.

— (2008), *Fat: A Cultural History of Obesity*, Cambridge: Polity Press.

Gissing, George (2007), *The Unclassed*, Teddington: The Echo Library.

— (2008a), *The Netherworld*, Oxford: Oxford University Press.

— (2008b), *The Odd Women*, Oxford: Oxford University Press.

Glick, Robert A., and Donald J. Meyers (eds) (1993), *Masochism: Current Psychoanalytic Perspectives*, Hove: Psychology Press.

Gomez, Jennifer M., Kathryn Becker-Blease and Jennifer J. Freyd (2015), 'A Brief Report on Predicting Self-Harm: Is It Gender or Abuse that Matters?', *Journal of Aggression, Maltreatment & Trauma* 24.2: 203–14.

Goody, A. (2006), 'Murder in Mile End: Amy Levy, Jewishness, and the City', *Victorian Literature and Culture* 34.2: 461–79.

Gordon, Joan, and Veronica Hollinger (eds) (1997), *Blood Read: The Vampire as Metaphor in Contemporary Culture*, Philadelphia: University of Pennsylvania Press.

Gould, G. M., and W. L. Pyle (1956), *Anomalies and Curiosities of Medicine 1896*, New York: Julian Press.

Graham-Dixon, Andrew (2009), *Caravaggio: A Life Sacred and Profane*, New York: Norton.

Grand, Sarah (1894), 'The New Aspect of the Woman Question', *North American Review* 158.44: 270–6.

— (1901), *Babs the Impossible*, London: Harper & Brothers.

— (1980), *The Beth Book*, London: Virago.

— (1993), 'The Undefinable: A Fantasia', in Elaine Showalter (ed.), *Daughters of Decadence: Women Writers of the Fin-de-Siècle*, London: Virago, pp. 262–87.

— (2000), 'The Baby's Tragedy', in Stephanie Forward and Ann Heilmann (eds), *Sex, Social Purity and Sarah Grand Volume III: Shorter Writings*, London: Routledge, pp. 100–10.

— (2007), *The Heavenly Twins*, 3 vols, London: Bibliobazaar.

— (2008), *Ideala: A Study from Life*, Kansas City: Valancourt Books.

Gray, Elizabeth F. (2010), *Christian Lyric Tradition in Victorian Women's Poetry*, London: Routledge.

Griffin, Gail (1988), '"Your Girls That You All Love Are Mine": Dracula and the Victorian Male Sexual Imagination', in Margaret Carter (ed.), *Dracula: The Vampire and the Critics*, Ann Arbor: University of Michigan Press, pp. 137–48.

Groschwitz, Rebecca C., and Paul L. Plener (2012), 'The Neurobiology of Non-Suicidal Self-Injury (NSSI): A Review', *Suicidology* 3: 24–32.

Gutierrez, Nancy (2003), *Shall She Famish Then? Female Food Refusal in Early Modern England*, Farnham: Ashgate.

Hager, Lisa (2006), 'A Community of Women: Women's Agency and Sexuality in George Egerton's *Keynotes and Discords*', *Nineteenth-Century Gender Studies* 2.2.

Haley, Bruce (1978), *The Healthy Body and Victorian Culture*, Cambridge, MA: Harvard University Press.

Hall, Radclyffe (2006), *The Well of Loneliness*, London: Wordsworth.

Hamilton, Susan (ed.) (2007), *Nineteenth-Century British Women's Education 1840–1900: Higher Education for Women*, London: Routledge.

Hammond, William A. (2010), *Fasting Girls: Their Physiology and Pathology*, London: Kessinger.

Hanson, Ellis (1997), *Decadence and Catholicism*, London: Harvard University Press.

Hardy, Thomas (2002), *Tess of the D'Urbervilles*, Oxford: Oxford University Press.

— (2009), *Jude the Obscure*, Oxford: Oxford University Press.

Harrington, Ralph (1999), 'The Railway Accident: Trains, Trauma and Technological Crisis in Nineteenth-Century Britain', *Institute of Railway Studies*, pp. 31–56.

Harrison, Brian (1994), *Drink and the Victorians: The Temperance Question in England 1815–1872*, Keele: Keele University Press.

Haw, Camilla, Keith Hawton, Deborah Casey, Elizabeth Bale and Anna Shepherd (2005), 'Alcohol Dependence, Excessive Drinking and Deliberate Self-Harm Trends and Patterns in Oxford, 1989–2002', *Social Psychiatry and Psychiatric Epidemiology* 40.12: 964–71.

Heilmann, Ann (1999), 'Mona Caird (1854–1932): Wild Woman, New Woman, and Early Radical Feminist Critic of Marriage and Motherhood', *Women's History Review* 5.1: 67–95.

— (2002), 'Narrating the Hysteric: Fin-de-Siècle Medical Discourse and Sarah Grand's *The Heavenly Twins*', in A. Richardson and C. Willis (eds), *The New Woman in Fiction and Fact: Fin-de-Siècle Feminisms*, Basingstoke: Palgrave Macmillan, pp. 123–35.

— (2004), *New Woman Strategies: Sarah Grand, Olive Schreiner, Mona Caird*, Manchester: Manchester University Press.

Heimann, Nora M. (2005), *Joan of Arc in French Art and Culture 1700–1855: From Satire to Sanctity*, Farnham: Ashgate.

Helsinger, Elizabeth K., Robin L. Sheets and William Veeder (eds) (1983), *The Woman Question: Society and Literature in Britain and America 1837–1883*, vol. 2, London: University of Chicago Press.

Hempel, Sandra (2007), *The Medical Detective: John Snow, Cholera and the Mystery of the Broad Street Pump*, 2nd edn, London: Granta Books.

Henderson, Kate Krueger (2001), 'Mobility and Modern Consciousness in George Egerton's and Charlotte Mew's *Yellow Book* Stories', *ELT* 54.2: 185–211.

Hennegan, Alison (2000), *The Lesbian Pillow Book*, London: Fourth Estate.

Herringer, Carol Engelhardt (2008), *Victorians and the Virgin Mary: Religion and Gender in England, 1830–1885*, Manchester: Manchester University Press.

Hetherington, Naomi (2012), 'The Seventh Wave of Humanity: Hysteria and Moral Evolution in Sarah Grand's *The Heavenly Twins*', in Adrienne E. Gavin and Carolyn W. Oulton (eds), *Writing Women of the Fin de Siècle*, Basingstoke: Palgrave Macmillan, pp. 153–65.

Hetherington, Naomi, and Nadia Valman (eds) (2010), *Amy Levy: Critical Essays*, Athens: Ohio University Press.

Hewitt, Kim (1997), *Mutilating the Body: Identity in Blood and Ink*, Bowling Green: Bowling Green State University Popular Press.

Heywood, Leslie (1996), *Dedication to Hunger: The Anorexic Aesthetic in Modern Culture*, London: University of California Press.

Higgs, Michelle (2007), *Prison Life in Victorian England*, Stroud: History Press.

Higonnet, Margaret R. (2015), '"This Winged Nature Fraught": Suicide and Agency in Women's Poetry', *Literature Compass* 12.12: 683–9.

Hilton, Timothy (2002), *John Ruskin*, London: Yale University Press.

Hogarth, William (1751), *Beer Street*, The British Museum, London.

— (1751), *Gin Lane*, The British Museum, London.

Hollander, Michael (2008), *Helping Teens Who Cut: Understanding and Ending Self-Injury*, New York: Guilford Press.

Hollywood, Amy (2004), 'That Glorious Slit: Irigaray and the Medieval Devotion to Christ's Side Wound', in Elizabeth D. Harvey and Theresa Krier (eds), *Luce Irigaray and Premodern Culture: Thresholds of History*, London: Routledge, pp. 105–25.

Holte, James (ed.) (2002), *The Fantastic Vampire: Studies in the Children of the Night*, London: Greenwood Press.

Houston, Gail Turley (1994), *Consuming Fictions: Gender, Class and Hunger in Dickens's Novels*, Edwardsville: Southern Illinois University Press.

— (2013), *Victorian Women Writers, Radical Grandmothers, and the Gendering of God*, Columbus: Ohio State University Press.

Huggins, Mike (2015), *Vice and the Victorians*, London: Bloomsbury.

Hughes, Arthur (1871), *Ophelia (And He Will Not Come Again)*, University of Oxford, Oxford.

— (1873), *The Lady of Shalott*, Private Collection.

Hughes, Derek (2007), *Culture and Sacrifice*, Cambridge: Cambridge University Press.

Hughes, Kathryn (2001), *The Victorian Governess*, London: Hambledon and London.

Hughes, Linda K. (2007), 'A Club of Their Own: The "Literary Ladies", New Women Writers, and Fin-de-Siècle Authorship', *Victorian Literature and Culture* 35.1: 233–60.

Huguet, Christine, and Simon J. James (eds) (2013), *George Gissing and the Woman Question: Convention and Dissent*, Farnham: Ashgate.

Humble, Nicola (ed.) (2000), *Mrs Beeton's Book of Household Management*, Oxford: Oxford University Press.

Hunt, William Holman (1853), *The Awakening Conscience*, Tate, London.

— (1854), *The Light of the World*, St Paul's Cathedral, London.

— (1876–9), *The Triumph of the Innocents*, Walker Art Gallery, Liverpool.

— (1883–4), *The Triumph of the Innocents*, Tate, London.

Hurley, Kelly (1996), *The Gothic Body: Sexuality, Materialism, and Degeneration at the Fin de Siècle*, Cambridge: Cambridge University Press.

Huysmans, Joris-Karl (2003), *À Rebours*, London: Penguin.

Ibsen, Henrick (2008), *A Doll's House*, in *Four Major Plays*, Oxford: Oxford University Press, pp. 1–88.

'Imputations against the British Army in Cabul' (1880), *The Pall Mall Gazette*, 12 January, pp. 145–6.

Irigaray, Luce (1985), *Speculum of the Other Woman*, New York: Cornell University Press.

'Is Marriage a Failure?' (1888), *The Daily Telegraph*, 27 August, p. 2.

Jenkins, Ruth Y. (1995), *Reclaiming Myths of Power: Women Writers and the Victorian Spiritual Crisis*, Lewisburg: Bucknell University Press.

Jones, Ann (2009), *Women Who Kill*, New York: Feminist Press.

Jones, Anna Maria (2007), 'A Track to the Water's Edge: Learning to Suffer in Sarah Grand's *The Heavenly Twins*', *Tulsa Studies in Women's Literature* 26.2: 217–41.

Justová, Iveta (2000), 'George Egerton and the Project of British Colonialism', *Tulsa Studies in Women's Literature* 19.1: 27–55.

Killick, Tim (2008), *British Short Fiction in the Early Nineteenth Century: The Rise of the Tale*, Farnham: Ashgate.

Kleinot, Pamela (2009), 'Speaking with the Body', in Anna Motz (ed.), *Managing Self-Harm: Psychological Perspectives*, London: Routledge, pp. 119–41.

Klonsky, E. D., A. M. May and C. R. Glenn (eds) (2013), 'The Relationship between Nonsuicidal Self-Injury and Attempted Suicide: Converging Evidence from Four Samples', *Journal of Abnormal Psychology* 122: 231–7.

Krafft-Ebing, Richard von (1909), *Psychopathia Sexualis: With Special Reference to Antipathic Sexual Instinct*, New York: Rebman Company.

Kucich, John (2002), 'Olive Schreiner, Masochism and Omnipotence: Strategies of Pre-Oedipal Politics', *Novel: A Forum on Fiction* 36.1: 79–109.

Lacan, Jacques (1998), *The Four Fundamental Concepts of Psychoanalysis*, London: Vintage.

Langley, Jenny (2006), *Boys Get Anorexia Too: Coping with Male Eating Disorders in the Family*, London: Sage Publications.

Lanser, Susan (2009), 'Novel (Sapphic) Subjects: The Sexual History of Form', *Novel: A Forum on Fiction* 42.3: 497–503.

Lasner, Mark Samuels, and Margaret Stetz (1990), *England in the 1890s: Literary Publishing at the Bodley Head*, Washington, DC: Georgetown University Press.

Le Fanu, Sheridan (2008), 'Carmilla', in *In a Glass Darkly and Other Tales*, Oxford: Oxford University Press.

Ledger, Sally (1997), *The New Woman: Fiction and Feminism at the Fin de Siècle*, Manchester: Manchester University Press.

— (2006), 'Introduction', in George Egerton, *Keynotes and Discords*, ed. Sally Ledger, London: Continuum, pp. ix–xxiv.

Lee, K. H., et al. (2015), 'Self-Harm in Schizophrenia Is Associated with Dorsolateral Prefrontal and Posterior Cingulate Activity', *Progress in Neuro-Psychopharmacology and Biological Psychiatry* 61: 18–23.

Lee, Vernon (1908), *The Gospels of Anarchy and Other Contemporary Studies*, London: T. Fisher Unwin.

— (1993), 'Lady Tal', in Elaine Showalter (ed.), *Daughters of Decadence: Women Writers of the Fin-de-Siècle*, London: Virago, pp. 192–261.

'A Letter' (1867), *The Englishwoman's Domestic Magazine*, p. 502.

Levenkron, Steven (2006), *Cutting: Understanding and Overcoming Self-Mutilation*, London: Norton.

Levine, Harry Gene (1978), 'The Discovery of Addiction: Concepts of Habitual Drunkenness in America', *Journal of Alcohol Studies* 15: 493–506.

Lewis, Matthew (2008), *The Monk*, Oxford: Oxford University Press.

Leys, Ruth (2000), *Trauma: A Genealogy*, Chicago: University of Chicago Press.

Liggins, Emma (2000), '"With a Dead Child in Her Lap": Bad Mothers and Infant Mortality in George Egerton's *Discords*', *Literature & History* 9.2: 17–36.

— (2006), *George Gissing, the Working Woman, and Urban Culture*, Farnham: Ashgate.

Lloyd, Ann (1995), *Doubly Deviant, Doubly Damned: Society's Treatment of Violent Women*, London: Penguin.

Logan, Deborah A. (1998), *Fallenness in Victorian Women's Writing: Marry, Stitch, Die, or Do Worse*, London: University of Missouri Press.

Louis, Margot (1990), *Swinburne and His Gods: The Roots and Growth of Agnostic Poetry*, Montreal: Queen's University Press.

Luckhurst, Roger (2008), *The Trauma Question*, London: Routledge.

Lundberg, Patricia Lorrimer (2003), *An Inward Necessity: The Writer's Life of Lucas Malet*, London: Peter Lang.

McAllister, Margaret (2003), 'Multiple Meanings of Self-Harm: A Critical Review', *International Journal of Mental Health Nursing* 12.3: 177–85.

MacSween, Morag (1993), *Anorexic Bodies: A Feminist Sociological Perspective on Anorexia Nervosa*, London: Routledge.

Malet, Lucas (1891), *The Wages of Sin*, 2nd edn, London: S. Sonnenschein & Co.

— (1896), *The Carissima: A Modern Grotesque*, London: Methuen & Co.

— (1923), *The Survivors*, New York: Dodd, Mead & Co.

Mangum, Teresa (2001), *Married, Middlebrow, and Militant: Sarah Grand and the New Woman Novel*, Ann Arbor: University of Michigan Press.

Margolis, Stacey (2002), 'Addiction and the Ends of Desire', in Janet Farrell and Marc Redfield (eds), *High Anxieties: Cultural Studies in Addiction*, Berkeley: University of California Press, pp. 19–37.

Marsh, Richard (2004), *The Beetle*, London: Broadview.

Masson, Jeffrey (ed.) (1985), *The Complete Letters of Sigmund Freud to Wilhelm Fliess, 1887–1904*, Cambridge, MA: Harvard University Press.

Maxwell, Catherine (1997), *Swinburne: Writers and Their Work*, London: Orion.

May, Trevor (2006), *Victorian and Edwardian Prisons*, Colchester: Osprey.

Mearns, Andrew (2002), 'The Bitter Cry of Outcast London: An Inquiry into the Condition of the Abject Poor', in Sally Ledger and Roger Luckhurst (eds), *The Fin de Siècle: A Reader in Cultural History c. 1880–1900*, Oxford: Oxford University Press, pp. 27–31.

Mee, Jon (2010), *The Cambridge Introduction to Charles Dickens*, Cambridge: Cambridge University Press.

Melnyk, Julie (2003), 'Mighty Victims: Women Writers and the Feminization of Christ', *Victorian Literature and Culture* 31.1: 131–57.

Menninger, Karl (1972), *Man Against Himself*, San Diego: Harvest.

Michie, Helena (1987), *The Flesh Made Word: Female Figures and Women's Bodies*, Oxford: Oxford University Press.

Millais, John Everett (1852), *Ophelia*, Tate, London.

— (1871), *The Martyr of Soloway*, National Museums Liverpool.

Millard, Chris (2015), *A History of Self-Harm in Britain: A Genealogy of Cutting and Overdosing*, Basingstoke: Palgrave Macmillan.

Mitchell, Charles William (1885), *Hypatia*, Laing Art Gallery, Newcastle.

Mitchell, Charlotte (2002), *Victoria Cross: A Bibliography*, Brisbane: Victorian Fiction Research Unit, University of Queensland.

Moore, George (1885), 'Literature at Nurse, or Circulating Morals', London: Vizetelly & Co., pp. 3–22.

— (1893), *A Mummer's Wife*, New York: Liveright Publishing.

— (2012), *Esther Waters*, Oxford: Oxford University Press.

Moran, Maureen (2004), 'The Art of Looking Dangerously: Victorian Images of Martyrdom', *Victorian Literature and Culture* 32.2: 475–93.

— (2007), *Catholic Sensationalism and Victorian Literature*, Liverpool: Liverpool University Press.

Morgan, Jon (2008), *The Invisible Man: A Self-Help Guide for Men with Eating Disorders, Compulsive Exercise and Bigorexia*, London: Routledge.

Morrison, Arthur (1997), *Tales of Mean Streets*, Chicago: Academy Victorian Classics.

— (2012), *A Child of the Jago*, Oxford: Oxford University Press.

Mosse, George L. (1993), 'Introduction', in Max Nordau, *Degeneration*, London: University of Nebraska Press, pp. xiii–xxxvi.

Motz, Anna (2008), *The Psychology of Female Violence: Crimes against the Body*, 2nd edn, London: Routledge.

— (ed.) (2009), *Managing Self-Harm: Psychological Perspectives*, London: Routledge.

Mulvey, Laura (2010), 'Visual Pleasure and Narrative Cinema', in Amelia Jones (ed.), *The Feminism and Visual Culture Reader*, 2nd edn, London: Routledge, pp. 57–65.

Musurillo, Herbert (1972), *The Acts of the Christian Martyrs*, Oxford: Clarendon Press.

Nead, Lynda (1992), *The Female Nude: Art, Obscenity and Sexuality*, London: Routledge.

Nelson, Carolyn (ed.) (2001), *A New Woman Reader: Fiction, Articles, and Drama of the 1890s*, Letchworth: Broadview.

Nelson, Claudia (2007), *Family Ties in Victorian England*, London: Praeger.

New, Melvyn (ed.) (1993), *The Complete Novels and Selected Writings of Amy Levy 1861–1889*, Gainesville: University of Florida Press.

Newman, Beth (2004), *Subjects on Display: Psychoanalysis, Social Expectation, and Victorian Femininity*, Athens: Ohio University Press.

'NHS Choices: Your Health, Your Choices', 1 March 2014, <http://www.nhs.uk/conditions/Self-injury/Pages/Introduction.aspx> (last accessed 28 April 2017).

Nicholls, James (2009), *The Politics of Alcohol: A History of the Drink Question in England*, Manchester: Manchester University Press.

Nock, Matthew K. (2008), 'Actions Speak Louder than Words: An Elaborated Theoretical Model of the Social Functions of Self-Injury and Other Harmful Behaviours', *Applied and Preventive Psychology* 12.4: 159–68.

— (2012), 'Future Directions for the Study of Suicide and Self-Injury', *Journal of Clinical Child and Adolescent Psychology* 41: 255–9.

Nord, Debra Epstein (1990), '"Neither Pairs Nor Odd": Female Community in Late Nineteenth-Century London', *Signs* 15.4: 733–54.

Nordau, Max (1993), *Degeneration*, 2nd edn, London: Heinemann.

Nott, Samuel (1831), *Temperance and Religion: Or, the Best Means and Highest End of the Temperance Reformation*, Boston: Peirce & Parker.

Odell, Robin (2006), *Ripperology: A Study of the World's First Serial Killer and a Literary Phenomenon*, Kent, OH: Kent State University Press.

Ofek, Galia (2009), *Representations of Hair in Late-Victorian Literature and Culture*, Farnham: Ashgate.

Olverson, Tracy D. (2009), 'Libidinous Laureates and Lyrical Maenads: Michael Field, Swinburne and Erotic Hellenism', *Victorian Poetry* 47.4: 759–76.

— (2010), '"Such Are Not Woman's Thoughts": Amy Levy's "Xantippe" and "Medea"', in Naomi Hetherington and Nadia Valman (eds), *Amy Levy: Critical Essays*, Athens: Ohio University Press, pp. 110–32.

O'Mally, Patrick (2006), *Catholicism, Sexual Deviance, and Victorian Gothic Culture*, Cambridge: Cambridge University Press.

O'Toole, Tina (2013), *The Irish New Woman*, London: Palgrave Macmillan.

Ouida (1894), 'The New Woman', *North American Review* 158: 610–19.

Parish of Hampstead Register of Patients in the Workhouse Infirmary 1854–1896, London: Metropolitan Archives.

Parker, Sarah (2015), *The Lesbian Muse and Poetic Identity, 1889–1930*, London: Routledge.

Parsons, Joanne Ella (2014), 'Eating Englishness and Causing Chaos: Food and the Body of the Fat Man in R. S. Surtees' *Jorrocks's Jaunts and Jollities, Handley Cross*, and *Hillingdon Hall*', *Nineteenth-Century Contexts* 36.4: 335–46.

Patai, Raphael (1983), *Encyclopaedia of Jewish Folklore and Tradition*, London: Routledge.

Patmore, Coventry (2013), *The Angel in the House and Other Poems*, London: Bibliobazaar.

Patterson, Anthony (2013), 'Making Mrs Grundy's Flesh Creep: George Egerton's Assault on Late-Victorian Censorship', *Victoriographies* 3.2: 64–77.

Pearl, Sharrona (2010), *About Faces: Physiognomy in Nineteenth-Century Britain*, Cambridge, MA: Harvard University Press.

Pick, Daniel (1993), *War Machine: The Rationalisation of Slaughter in the Modern Age*, Bath: Bath Press.

Polidori, John (2008), *The Vampyre and Other Tales of the Macabre*, Oxford: Oxford University Press.

Priestly, Philip (1999), *Victorian Prison Lives*, New York: Random House.

Pulham, Patricia (2007), 'Tinted and Tainted Love: The Sculptural Body in Olive Custance's Poetry', *The Yearbook of English Studies* 37.1: 161–76.

Pullen, Christine (2010), *The Woman Who Dared: A Biography of Amy Levy*, Kingston: Kingston University Press.

Purdue, Melissa (2012), '"I Have Expiated My Sins to You at Last": Motherhood in Victoria Cross's Colonial Fiction', in Adrienne E. Gavin and Carolyn W. Oulton (eds), *Writing Women of the Fin de Siècle: Authors of Change*, Basingstoke: Palgrave Macmillan, pp. 124–36.

Pykett, Lyn (2006), *The Improper Feminine: The Woman's Sensation Novel and the New Woman Writing*, 6th edn, London: Routledge.

R. W. (1860), 'Railway Accidents', *The Morning Post*, 18 January, p. 3.

Randolph, Lyssa (2010), 'Verse or Vitality? Biological Economies and the New Woman Poet', in Naomi Hetherington and Nadia Valman (eds), *Amy Levy: Critical Essays*, Athens: Ohio University Press, pp. 198–218.

Reed, Thomas L. (2006), *The Transforming Draught: Jekyll and Hyde, Robert Louis Stevenson and the Victorian Alcohol Debate*, London: McFarland & Co.

Register of Admissions to Bethlem Royal Hospital 1859–1881, London: Wellcome Library.

Register of Admissions to Hampstead Workhouse 1893–1896, London: Metropolitan Archives.

Register of Admissions to Royal Holloway Asylum at Virginia Waters 1825–1900, London: Wellcome Library.

Register of Deaths at Hampstead Workhouse 1893–1896, London: Wellcome Library.

Renzetti, Claire M., Susan L. Miller and Angela R. Gover (eds) (2013), *Routledge International Handbook of Crime and Gender Studies*, London: Routledge.

'Review of *Discords* by George Egerton' (1895), *Athenaeum*, 23 March, p. 375.

'Review of Sarah Grand's *Ideala*' (1888), *Saturday Review*, 1 September, p. 277.

Reynolds, Margaret (2000), *The Sappho Companion*, London: Chatto & Windus.

Richardson, Angelique (2008), *Love and Eugenics in the Late Nineteenth Century: Rational Reproduction and the New Woman*, 2nd edn, Oxford: Oxford University Press.

— (2016), 'Who *Was* the New Woman?', in Laura Marcus, Michèle Mendelssohn and Kristen E. Shepherd-Barr (eds), *Late Victorian into Modern*, Oxford: Oxford University Press, pp. 150–67.

Richardson, James (1988), *Vanishing Lives: Style and Self in Tennyson, D. G. Rossetti, Swinburne, and Yeats*, Charlottesville: University Press of Virginia.

Richter, Simon (1992), *Laocoön's Body and the Aesthetics of Pain: Winckelmann, Lessing, Herder, Moritz, Goethe*, Michigan: Wayne State University Press.

— (2006), *Missing the Breast: Gender, Fantasy and the Body in the German Enlightenment*, London: University of Washington Press.

Rosenberg, Tracey S. (2010), 'Introduction', in Tracey S. Rosenberg (ed.), *The Wing of Azrael*, Kansas City: Valencourt, pp. viii–xxii.

Rossetti, Christina (2008), *Christina Rossetti: Poems and Prose*, Oxford: Oxford University Press.

Rossetti, Dante Gabriel (1858), *Mary Magdalene at the Door of Simon the Pharisee*, Fitzwilliam Museum, Cambridge.

— (1864), *Joan of Arc*, Tate, London.

— (1874), *Proserpine*, Tate, London.

— (1877), *Mary Magdalene*, Delaware Art Museum, Wilmington.

— (1882), *Joan of Arc*, Fitzwilliam Museum, Cambridge.

Ruskin, John (1854), 'To the Editor of *The Times*', *The London Times*, 5 May, p. 9.

— (1902), *Of Queens' Gardens*, London: G. Allen.

Russell, James B. (1888), *Life in One Room or, Some Serious Considerations for the Citizens of Glasgow*, Glasgow: Maclehose.

Sacher-Masoch, Leopold von (2006), *Venus in Furs*, Teddington: Echo Library.

St Pancras Workhouse Infirmary Log 1890, London: Metropolitan Archives.

Sandys, Frederick (1862), *Mary Magdalene*, Delaware Art Museum, Wilmington.

— (1862), *The Boy Martyr*, Birmingham Museum and Art Gallery.

Scarry, Elaine (1985), *The Body in Pain: The Making and Unmaking of the World*, Oxford: Oxford University Press.

Scheffer, Ary (1850), *The Heavenly and Earthly Love*, Dordrecht Museum.

Scheinberg, Cynthia (2002), *Women's Poetry and Religion in Victorian England: Jewish Identity and Christian Culture*, Cambridge: Cambridge University Press.

Scholz, Piotr O. (2001), *Eunuchs and Castrati: A Cultural History*, Princeton: Markus Weiner Publishers.

Schramm, Jan-Melissa (2012), *Atonement and Self-Sacrifice in Nineteenth-Century Narrative*, Cambridge: Cambridge University Press.

Seal, Lizzie (2010), *Women, Murder and Femininity: Gender Representations of Women Who Kill*, London: Palgrave Macmillan.

Sedgwick, Eve Kosofsky (1990), *Epistemology of the Closet*, London: Penguin.

— (1994), *Tendencies*, London: Routledge.

'Self-Mutilation by a Soldier' (1887), *The Huddersfield Daily Chronicle*, 28 February, p. 3.

Seltzer, Mark (1998), *Serial Killers: Death and Life in America's Wound Culture*, London: Routledge.

Shakespeare, William (2008), *Hamlet*, Oxford: Oxford University Press.

Shapiro, Susan C. (1991), 'The Mannish New Woman: *Punch* and Its Precursors', *Review of English Studies* 42.168: 510–22.

Shiman, Lilian Lewis (1988), *Crusade against Drink in Victorian England*, London: Palgrave Macmillan.

Shoreditch Workhouse Register of Deaths 1871–1889, London: Metropolitan Archives.

Showalter, Elaine (1991), *Sexual Anarchy: Gender and Culture at the Fin de Siècle*, London: Bloomsbury.

— (1993), *The Female Malady: Women, Madness, and English Culture 1830–1980*, London: Virago.

— (2007), *A Literature of Their Own: From Charlotte Brontë to Doris Lessing*, 11th edn, London: Virago.

Silver, Anna Krugovoy (2002), *Victorian Literature and the Anorexic Body*, Cambridge: Cambridge University Press.

Smith, Alison (1996), *The Victorian Nude: Sexuality, Morality and Art*, Manchester: Manchester University Press.

Smith, Andrew (2004), *Victorian Demons: Medicine, Masculinity and the Gothic at the Fin de Siècle*, Manchester: Manchester University Press.

Smith, Gerrilyn, Dee Cox and Jacqui Saradjian (eds) (1998), *Women and Self-Harm*, London: Women's Press.

Smith, Harold L. (2010), *The British Women's Suffrage Campaign 1866–1928*, 2nd edn, London: Longman.

Stacey, Michelle (2002), *The Fasting Girl: A True Victorian Medical Mystery*, Los Angeles: Tarcher Putnam.

Stanbury, Sarah (1991), 'The Virgin's Gaze: Spectacle and Transgression in Middle English Lyrics of the Passion', *PMLA* 106.5: 1083–93.

Standlee, Whitney (2010), 'George Egerton, James Joyce and the Irish *Künstlerroman*', *Irish Studies Review* 18.4: 439–52.

Stead, William Thomas (1885), *The Maiden Tribute of Modern Babylon*, London: Lowood Press.

— (1894), 'The Book of the Month: The Novel of the Modern Woman', *Review of Reviews* 10: 64–78.

Stevenson, Robert Louis (2008), *The Strange Case of Dr Jekyll and Mr Hyde and Other Tales*, Oxford: Oxford University Press.

Stewart, Dana E. (2003), *The Arrow of Love: Optics, Gender, and Subjectivity in Medieval Love Poetry*, London: Rosemont.

Stiles, Anne (2007), *Neurology and Literature 1860–1920*, Basingstoke: Palgrave Macmillan.

Stoker, Bram (2011), *Dracula*, Oxford: Oxford University Press.

Strong, Marilee (2000), *A Bright Red Scream: Self-Mutilation and the Language of Pain*, London: Virago.

Stutfield, Hugh E. M. (2001), 'Tommyrotics', in Carolyn Nelson (ed.), *A New Woman Reader: Fiction, Articles, and Drama of the 1890s*, Letchworth: Broadview, pp. 234–43.

Sussman, Herbert (2009), *Victorian Technology: Invention, Innovation, and the Rise of the Machine*, Santa Barbara: Greenwood.

Sutherland, Gillian (2015), *In Search of the New Woman: Middle-Class Women and Work in Britain 1870–1914*, Cambridge: Cambridge University Press.

Sutton, Jan (2007), *Healing the Hurt Within*, 3rd edn, Oxford: Pathways.

Swafford, Kevin (2007), *Class in Victorian Britain: The Narrative Concerns with Social Hierarchy and Its Representation*, New York: Cambria Press.

Swinburne, Algernon Charles (2000), *Poems and Ballads and Atalanta in Calydon*, London: Penguin.

Talairach-Vielmas, Laurence (2013), *Moulding the Female Body in Victorian Fairy Tales and Sensation Novels*, 2nd edn, Farnham: Ashgate.

Tennyson, Alfred Lord (2000a), 'In Memoriam A.H.H.', in *Tennyson: The Major Works*, Oxford: Oxford University Press, pp. 203–92.

— (2000b), 'The Lady of Shalott', in *Tennyson: The Major Works*, Oxford: Oxford University Press, pp. 21–5.

Thackeray, William Makepeace (2008), *Vanity Fair*, Oxford: Oxford University Press.

Tromp, Marlene (ed.) (2008), *Victorian Freaks: The Social Context of Freakery in Britain*, Columbus: Ohio State University Press.

Tuke, D. H. (ed.) (1976), *A Dictionary of Psychological Medicine*, vol. 2, New York: Arno Press.

Turner, V. J. (2002), *Secret Scars: Uncovering and Understanding the Addiction of Self-Injury*, Centre City, MN: Hazelden.

Turp, Maggie (2002), *Hidden Self-Harm: Narratives from Psychotherapy*, Philadelphia: Jessica Kingsley Publishers.

Vadillo, Ann Parejo (2005), *Women and Urban Aestheticism*, Basingstoke: Palgrave Macmillan.

Valman, Nadia (2010), 'Amy Levy and the Literary Representation of the Jewess', in Naomi Hetherington and Nadia Valman (eds), *Amy Levy: Critical Essays*, Athens: Ohio University Press, pp. 90–109.

Valverde, Mariana (1998), *Diseases of the Will: Alcohol and the Dilemmas of Freedom*, Cambridge: Cambridge University Press.

Vandereycken, Walter, and Ron Van Deth (1990), 'A Tribute to Lasègue's Description of Anorexia Nervosa (1873) with Completion of Its English Translation', *The British Journal of Psychiatry*, pp. 902–8.

— (1994), *Fasting Saints and Anorexic Girls: The History of Self-Starvation*, London: Athlone Press.

Vanita, Ruth (1996), *Sappho and the Virgin Mary: Same-Sex Love and the English Literary Imagination*, New York: Columbia University Press.

Vernon, James (2009), *Hunger: A Modern History*, Cambridge, MA: Harvard University Press.

Vicinus, Martha (1994), 'The Adolescent Boy: *Fin de Siècle* Femme Fatale?', *Journal of the History of Sexuality* 5.1: 90–114.

'Victory of the Alma' (1854), *The Morning Chronicle*, 4 October, p. 4.

Vigarello, Georges (2013), *Metamorphoses of Fat: A History of Obesity*, New York: Columbia University Press.

Vincent, John (1997), 'Flogging Is Fundamental: Applications of Birch in Swinburne's *Lesbia Brandon*', in Eve Kosofsky-Sedgwick (ed.), *Novel Gazing: Queer Readings in Fiction*, London: Duke University Press, pp. 269–99.

Waldman, Suzanne M. (2008), *The Demon and the Damozel: Dynamics of Desire in the Works of Christina Rossetti and Dante Gabriel Rossetti*, Athens: Ohio University Press.

Walkowitz, Judith (1992), *City of Dreadful Delight: Narratives of Sexual Danger in Late-Victorian London*, London: Virago.

Wallis, Elizabeth Macleod (2002), '"A Little Afraid of the Women Today": The Victorian New Woman and the Rhetoric of Modernism', *Rhetoric Review* 21.3: 229–46.

Walpole, Horace (2008), *The Castle of Otranto*, Oxford: Oxford University Press.

Walter, William (ed.) (1987), *The Plays of Euripides, Aeschylus, Aristophanes*, London: Simon & Schuster.

Warner, Maria (2013), *Joan of Arc: The Image of Female Heroism*, Oxford: Oxford University Press.

Warrington, F. W. (1882), 'The Strange Confession in Staffordshire', *The Times*, 13 January, pp. 81–2.

Warwick, Alexandra (2007), 'Blood and Ink: Narrating the Whitechapel Murders', in Alexandra Warwick and Martin Willis (eds), *Jack the Ripper: Media, Culture, History*, Manchester: Manchester University Press, pp. 71–87.

— and Martin Willis (eds) (2007), *Jack the Ripper: Media, Culture, History*, Manchester: Manchester University Press.

Waterhouse, John William (1872), *Saint Joan*, Private Collection.

— (1885), *Saint Eulalia*, Tate Britain, London.

— (1888), *The Lady of Shalott*, Tate, London.

— (1889), *Ophelia*, Private Collection.

— (1894), *Ophelia*, Private Collection.

— (1894), *The Lady of Shalott*, Leeds Art Gallery.

— (1910), *Ophelia*, Private Collection.

Watt, George (1984), *The Fallen Woman in the Nineteenth-Century English Novel*, London: Croom Helm.

Weedon, Alexis (2003), *Victorian Publishing: The Economics of Book Production for a Mass Market*, Farnham: Ashgate.

Welldon, Estella (2000), *Mother, Madonna, Whore: The Idealization and Denigration of Motherhood*, London: Carnac.

Whelan, Lara Baker (2009), *Class, Culture and Suburban Anxieties in the Victorian Era*, London: Routledge.

Wilde, Oscar (2008), *The Picture of Dorian Gray*, Oxford: Oxford University Press.

Williams, Raymond (1975), *The Country and the City*, Oxford: Oxford University Press.

Williamson, Milly (2005), *The Lure of the Vampire: Gender, Fiction and Fandom from Bram Stoker to Buffy*, London: Wallflower Press.

Wilson, Thomas M. (ed.) (2005), *Drinking Cultures: Alcohol and Identity*, Oxford: Berg.

Wingerden, Sophia A. van (1999), *The Woman's Suffrage Movement in Britain 1866–1928*, Basingstoke: Palgrave.

Winnicott, Donald (1989), *Holding and Interpretation: Fragment of an Analysis*, London: Hogarth Press.

'Women and Votes' (1908), *Gloucester Journal*, 12 December.

Woolf, Virginia (2008), *Mrs Dalloway*, Oxford: Oxford University Press.

Woolwich Union Workhouse Register of Lunatics in the Asylum 1890–1895, London: Metropolitan Archives.

Woolwich Union Workhouse Register of Lunatics in the Asylum 1897–1899, London: Metropolitan Archives.

Wright, Thomas (1867), *Some Habits and Customs of the Working Classes*, London: Tinsley Brothers.

'The Year in Review' (1894), *Athenaeum*, 6 January, p. 118.

Yonge, Charlotte (2001), *The Clever Woman of the Family*, London: Broadview.

Youngkin, Molly (ed.) (2008), *Ideala*, Kansas City: Valancourt Books.

Zieger, Susan (2008), *Inventing the Addict: Drugs, Race, and Sexuality in Nineteenth-Century British and American Literature*, Amherst: University of Massachusetts Press.

Zola, Émile (2009a), *L'Assommoir*, Oxford: Oxford University Press.

— (2009b), *La Bête Humaine*, Oxford: Oxford University Press.

Index